Federal Law Enforcement Agencies in America

Aspen College Series

Federal Law Enforcement Agencies in America

Nancy E. Marion

Professor and Ray C. Bliss Institute of Applied Politics Fellow
The University of Akron

Willard M. Oliver

Professor of Criminal Justice
Sam Houston State University

Wolters Kluwer

Printed in the United States of America.

1 2 3 4 5 6 7 8 9 0

ISBN 978-1-4548-5833-1

Marion, Nancy E.
  Federal law enforcement agencies in America / Nancy Marion, Willard M. Oliver.
       pages cm. — (Aspen college series)
  Includes bibliographical references and index.
  ISBN 978-1-4548-5833-1 (alk. paper)
  1. Law enforcement — United States. I. Oliver, Willard M. II. Title.
  HV8139.M37 2015
  363.20973 — dc23
                                      2014045528

About Wolters Kluwer Law & Business

Wolters Kluwer Law & Business is a leading global provider of intelligent information and digital solutions for legal and business professionals in key specialty areas, and respected educational resources for professors and law students. Wolters Kluwer Law & Business connects legal and business professionals as well as those in the education market with timely, specialized authoritative content and information-enabled solutions to support success through productivity, accuracy and mobility.

Serving customers worldwide, Wolters Kluwer Law & Business products include those under the Aspen Publishers, CCH, Kluwer Law International, Loislaw, ftwilliam.com and MediRegs family of products.

CCH products have been a trusted resource since 1913, and are highly regarded resources for legal, securities, antitrust and trade regulation, government contracting, banking, pension, payroll, employment and labor, and healthcare reimbursement and compliance professionals.

Aspen Publishers products provide essential information to attorneys, business professionals and law students. Written by preeminent authorities, the product line offers analytical and practical information in a range of specialty practice areas from securities law and intellectual property to mergers and acquisitions and pension/benefits. Aspen's trusted legal education resources provide professors and students with high-quality, up-to-date and effective resources for successful instruction and study in all areas of the law.

Kluwer Law International products provide the global business community with reliable international legal information in English. Legal practitioners, corporate counsel and business executives around the world rely on Kluwer Law journals, looseleafs, books, and electronic products for comprehensive information in many areas of international legal practice.

Loislaw is a comprehensive online legal research product providing legal content to law firm practitioners of various specializations. Loislaw provides attorneys with the ability to quickly and efficiently find the necessary legal information they need, when and where they need it, by facilitating access to primary law as well as state-specific law, records, forms and treatises.

ftwilliam.com offers employee benefits professionals the highest quality plan documents (retirement, welfare and non-qualified) and government forms (5500/PBGC, 1099 and IRS) software at highly competitive prices.

MediRegs products provide integrated health care compliance content and software solutions for professionals in healthcare, higher education and life sciences, including professionals in accounting, law and consulting.

Wolters Kluwer Law & Business, a division of Wolters Kluwer, is headquartered in New York. Wolters Kluwer is a market-leading global information services company focused on professionals.

This book is dedicated to the memory of
U.S. Customs and Border Protection Agent Javier Vega, Jr.,
who was killed in the line of duty.
End of Watch: August 4, 2014.

Summary of Contents

Contents

9.   U.S. Immigration and Customs Enforcement 159

There are many law enforcement bureaucracies on the federal level, and each one plays an important role in maintaining public order. Although they each have a different jurisdiction and goal, every agency enforces federal laws and statutes that are passed by Congress. In doing so, they help to ensure that society is safe and crime is held to a minimum.

Federal law enforcement bureaucracies have evolved over time. Some have been enacted by Congress, such as the U.S. Marshals Service, which was created through the Judiciary Act of 1789, or the Bureau of Alcohol, Tobacco, Firearms, and Explosives, which was originally created by Congress in the 1860s. Other bureaucracies were created as a result of reorganization efforts or by the consolidation of the responsibilities of agencies previously housed in multiple places, such as when Nixon transferred portions of many agencies into one new agency, called the Drug Enforcement Administration. Similarly, Immigration and Customs Enforcement was created when President Bush reorganized different agencies after the terrorist attacks on the United States in September 2001, consolidating agencies responsible for different aspects of homeland security into one bureaucracy. Both of these agencies were reformulated so they would be more efficient in addressing the problems at hand.

Some federal law enforcement bureaucracies have been assigned new tasks over time as new problems have been identified or become more prevalent. For example, the U.S. Marshals Service, originally created to protect the safety of federal judges and other court personnel, was given the additional task of protecting top governmental officials and hunting down escaped federal prisoners. Likewise, the Bureau of Alcohol, Tobacco, and Firearms, or BATF, was given the additional responsibility of overseeing explosives, expanding it to BATFE.

The many federal law enforcement agencies cover a wide breadth of roles and responsibilities. The Marshals oversee the safety of the courts, while the Postal Inspection Service helps ensure that the postal system is free of fraud and abuse. The Drug Enforcement Administration oversees the enforcement of drug laws in the country, while the Park Police watch over the safety of the national parks. Although there may be slight overlap and cooperation during times of emergency, the agencies each have different jurisdictions.

The agencies also differ as to how long they have been in existence. Some of the agencies have existed for many years, whereas others were created relatively recently. The oldest agency, the Postal Inspection Service, dates back to the colonial era and Benjamin Franklin. The FBI, also one of the oldest federal law enforcement agencies, dates back to the early 1900s. But one of the newest federal law enforcement agencies, Immigration and Customs Enforcement, was created in 2003. Despite the age differences, these agencies are all pertinent and necessary in today's world.

One more difference between the agencies lies with where they are found within the hierarchy of the federal government. As Table I-1 shows, the organizations are spread throughout the administration. Five of the agencies are housed within the Department of Justice. Those include the Federal Bureau of Investigation, the Drug Enforcement Administration, the U.S. Marshals, and the Bureau of Alcohol, Tobacco, Firearms, and Explosives. Six agencies are found within the Department of Homeland Security. These include the U.S. Secret Service, Customs and Border Protection, Immigration and Customs Enforcement (ICE), the Federal Law Enforcement Training Center (FLETC), the Transportation Security Administration (TSA), and the Coast Guard Investigative Service. The Federal Air Marshals and Federal Protective Service are found within ICE.

The Department of the Interior is home to four federal law enforcement agencies. They are the U.S. Park Police, the U.S. Fish and Wildlife Service Office of Law Enforcement, the Hoover Dam Police, and the Bureau of Indian Affairs. The Department of State houses only one law enforcement group, the Bureau of Diplomatic Security. One agency is also housed in the U.S. Post Office: the U.S. Postal Inspectors. Many of the law enforcement agencies described in later chapters of this book are found in other locations, as noted in Table I-1.

When needed, federal law enforcement bureaucracies cooperate with state and local law enforcement agencies to provide assistance or guidance. When a major crime occurs, or when local agencies may be unable to investigate a crime because of insufficient manpower or other resources (including technology or equipment), or if they are overwhelmed by a serious crime, they can call on federal agents for advice or support. Federal bureaucracies also interact with agencies in other countries when there is a problem of international scope or interest.

Because the agencies have different responsibilities and jurisdictions, they hire individuals who have a wide variety of backgrounds. They hire people from all social and economic classes, of all ages (with some age restrictions), and with different upbringings. They also seek to hire people with different experiences and educational backgrounds. This means that it is not necessary for students and others who seek to pursue a career to have earned a degree in criminal justice. While many believe that this type of degree is necessary to be hired in a federal agency, it is not the case. Most federal agencies seek to hire a diverse group of individuals with degrees such as accounting, criminal justice, a language (English, Spanish, Chinese, Arabic, etc.), political science, or even business. What may be more important to an agency is a person's background (they must have no criminal record or evidence of drug use) and previous experience in a law enforcement or a related field.

The basic training for all federal agents, regardless of the agency, is very similar. Many federal agencies have their newly hired agents attend the Federal Law Enforcement Training Center (FLETC) in Glynco, Georgia, an interagency training facility for law enforcement personnel. FLETC provides training in basic law

Table I-1: Federal Law Enforcement Agencies

Department of Justice	Department of Homeland Security	Department of Interior	Department of State	U.S. Post Office	Other Agencies
FBI	U.S. Secret Service	U.S. Park Police	Bureau of Diplomatic Security	US Postal Inspectors	U.S. Supreme Court Police
FBI Police	Customs & Border Protection	U.S. Fish & Wildlife Service Office of Law Enforcement			U.S. Capitol Police
DEA	ICE	Police Hoover Dam			Amtrak Police
U.S Marshals	Federal Air Marshals	Bureau of Indian Affairs			NOAA Office of Law Enforcement
BATFE	Federal Protective Service				Pentagon Force Protection Agency
U.S. Marshals	Federal Law Enforcement Training Center				Smithsonian National Zoological Park Police
	TSA				U.S. Mint Police
	Coast Guard Investigative Service				Tennessee Valley Authority Police
					U.S. Forest Service Law Enforcement and Investigations
					Bureau of Land Management Office of Law Enforcement and Security
					Federal Reserve Police
					Library of Congress Police
					National Security Agency Police
					Internal Revenue Service, Criminal Investigation Division
					Veterans Affairs Police
					CIA Security Protective Service
					NASA Security Services
					National Institute of Standards and Technology Police
					Department of Defense Police
					Defense Logistics Agency Police
					Defense Intelligence Agency Police
					National Geospatial-Intelligence Agency Police
					Housing & Urban Development Protective Service Division

enforcement techniques. More detailed training for each agency is then provided by the agency itself.[1]

Federal Law Enforcement Training Center (FLETC)

Agencies use FLETC primarily because in the years before 1970, the quality of training received by federal law enforcement officers and agents varied greatly from agency to agency. Standardized training did not exist. Moreover, many facilities were inadequate, and training was often duplicated as each agency independently trained its own personnel.

Some studies of law enforcement training during the late 1960s showed a need for high-quality, cost-efficient training in law enforcement techniques for federal agents by professional instructors with modern training facilities and standardized course content. Congress responded by authorizing funds for planning and constructing the Consolidated Federal Law Enforcement Training Center (CFLETC). In 1970, the CFLETC was established as a bureau of the Department of the Treasury (Treasury Order #217) and began training personnel in temporary facilities in Washington, D.C.

The permanent location of the training center was originally planned for a site in the Washington, D.C. area. However, when there was a three-year construction delay, Congress asked if there were any surplus federal facilities that could be used as the permanent training site. In May 1975, after an extensive review of existing facilities, Congress chose the former Glynco Naval Air Station near Brunswick, Georgia as the new site for the training program. In the fall of 1975, the new Federal Law Enforcement Training Center (FLETC) began training new agents at the Glynco site. Currently, Glynco is the headquarters and main campus for the FLETC. There are also facilities in Artesia, N.M., Charleston, S.C., Cheltenham, M.D., and Gabarone, Boswana.[2]

On March 1, 2003, FLETC was formally transferred from the Treasury Department to the Department of Homeland Security. This reflected the government's mission of a unified homeland security effort that became essential after the terrorist attacks of September 11, 2001.

Coverage of Textbook

This book gives an overview of federal law enforcement agencies that currently exist. Each of the following chapters focuses on a particular agency, describing its history, leadership, organization, and responsibilities. The focus of Chapter 1 is on the U.S. Marshals Service, which was given the task of protecting federal judges and other personnel who work in the federal court system as well as visitors to the courts. The Bureau of Alcohol, Tobacco, Firearms, and Explosives, which enforces federal laws related to those items, is the focus of chapter 2. In chapter 3, the roles and responsibilities of the Postal Inspection Service are discussed, and the jurisdiction of the Park Police is described in Chapter 4.

The organization and tasks of the U.S. Secret Service are detailed in Chapter 5. Another more widely recognized agency, the Federal Bureau of Investigation, is the topic of chapter 6. The agency that oversees enforcement of laws concerning illicit drugs and narcotics is the DEA, and is the topic of Chapter 7. Many federal agents work at Customs and Border Protection, and their roles are the topic of Chapter 8. The newest federal law enforcement agency, the Immigration and Customs Enforcement (ICE) agency, is the topic of chapter 9. Chapter 10 provides an examination of the Federal Protective Services (GSA Police), and Chapter 11 describes the Federal Air Marshals Service, which helps to guarantee the safety of air travel in the U.S. and abroad.

The final chapter of the book, Chapter 12, focuses on some of the more well-known, smaller federal agencies: the Supreme Court Police, the U.S. Capitol Police, Amtrak Police, the National Oceanic and Atmospheric Administration Office for Law Enforcement, the Bureau of Indian Affairs Police, the U.S. Fish and Wildlife Service Office of Law Enforcement, the Pentagon Force Protection Agency, the Smithsonian National Zoological Park Police, and the Bureau of Diplomatic Security.

Endnotes

1. Federal Law Enforcement Training Center. (2012). "FLETC History." Available online at http://www.fletc.gov/about-fletc/fletc-history.
2. Federal Law Enforcement Training Center, "FLETC History."

1

U.S. Marshals Service

The mission of the U.S. Marshals Service is multi-faceted. One primary goal of the agency is to protect the federal judiciary and the judicial process by shielding judges, attorneys, witnesses, jurors, other courtroom personnel, and administrative staff from potential harm. This entails ensuring a safe and secure courtroom environment before, during, and after criminal proceedings take place. Each inappropriate or potentially threatening communication with any court personnel is analyzed by the Marshals to determine if further legal action is warranted.

The protection role of the Marshals extends to safeguarding any government witnesses to ensure their security, health, and safety through the Witness Security Program. Moreover, agents in the Marshals protect the director of the Office of National Drug Control Policy, the deputy attorney general, and the Supreme Court justices when they must travel as part of their duties. During sessions of the UN General Assembly, the Marshals also protect foreign officials.[1] Finally, the Marshals protect the judges presiding over the 13 U.S. Courts of Appeals (the Circuit Courts). These judges are protected by the particular Marshals office in whose district that court is located.

The second part of the Marshals' mission is to pursue and apprehend federal fugitives. As directed through the Adam Walsh Child Protection and Safety Act of 2006, the Marshals are now also required to assist local police in locating and apprehending sex offenders. To that end, Marshals may be required to execute relevant court orders and arrest warrants. Once captured, the Marshals must transport any federal prisoner who is in custody to court proceedings. Federal inmates may also need to be transferred from one housing facility to another if they are being relocated to a new facility or one closer to a courthouse. The Marshals oversee housing of federal inmates who are either charged with a federal offense and are awaiting trial or who have already been convicted of criminal offenses. Medical care is provided to those inmates as needed.

Marshals are also responsible for seizing any property that was acquired by criminals if it is determined that the property was acquired through illegal means. Then they must store and track that material for processing and possible selling.[2]

Today, the Marshals are part of the fight against terrorism as they investigate any threats made against members of the judiciary. It is often the case that trials involving violent criminals and terrorist-related offenders require provisions for high-level security from the Marshals. Deputy marshals have been assigned to FBI Joint Terrorism Task Forces to track terrorism cases.

The statutory authority of the U.S. Marshals is found in the Federal Code, Title 28, which describes Judiciary and Judicial Procedure, Part II (the Department of Justice), Chapter 37 §566, as shown in Figure 1.1.

Figure 1.1: Statutory Authority of U.S. Marshals

(a) It is the primary role and mission of the United States Marshals Service to provide for the security and to obey, execute, and enforce all orders of the United States District Courts, the United States Courts of Appeals, the Court of International Trade, and the United States Tax Court, as provided by law.

(b) The United States marshal of each district is the marshal of the district court and of the court of appeals when sitting in that district, and of the Court of International Trade holding sessions in that district, and may, in the discretion of the respective courts, be required to attend any session of court.

(c) Except as otherwise provided by law or Rule of Procedure, the United States Marshals Service shall execute all lawful writs, process, and orders issued under the authority of the United States, and shall command all necessary assistance to execute its duties.

(d) Each United States marshal, deputy marshal, and any other official of the Service as may be designated by the Director may carry firearms and make arrests without warrant for any offense against the United States committed in his or her presence, or for any felony cognizable under the laws of the United States if he or she has reasonable grounds to believe that the person to be arrested has committed or is committing such felony.

(e)

   (1) The United States Marshals Service is authorized to—

      (A) provide for the personal protection of Federal jurists, court officers, witnesses, and other threatened persons in the interests of justice where criminal intimidation impedes on the functioning of the judicial process or any other official proceeding;

      (B) investigate such fugitive matters, both within and outside the United States, as directed by the Attorney General; and

(C) issue administrative subpoenas in accordance with section 3486 of title 18, solely for the purpose of investigating unregistered sex offenders (as defined in such section 3486).

(2) Nothing in paragraph (1)(B) shall be construed to interfere with or supersede the authority of other Federal agencies or bureaus.

(f) In accordance with procedures established by the Director, and except for public money deposited under section 2041 of this title, each United States marshal shall deposit public moneys that the marshal collects into the Treasury, subject to disbursement by the marshal. At the end of each accounting period, the earned part of public moneys accruing to the United States shall be deposited in the Treasury to the credit of the appropriate receipt accounts.

(g) Prior to resignation, retirement, or removal from office—

(1) a United States marshal shall deliver to the marshal's successor all prisoners in his custody and all unserved process; and

(2) a deputy marshal shall deliver to the marshal all process in the custody of the deputy marshal.

(h) The United States marshals shall pay such office expenses of United States Attorneys as may be directed by the Attorney General.

(i) The Director of the United States Marshals Service shall consult with the Judicial Conference of the United States on a continuing basis regarding the security requirements for the judicial branch of the United States Government, to ensure that the views of the Judicial Conference regarding the security requirements for the judicial branch of the Federal Government are taken into account when determining staffing levels, setting priorities for programs regarding judicial security, and allocating judicial security resources. In this paragraph, the term "judicial security" includes the security of buildings housing the judiciary, the personal security of judicial officers, the assessment of threats made to judicial officers, and the protection of all other judicial personnel. The United States Marshals Service retains final authority regarding security requirements for the judicial branch of the Federal Government.

History

The United States Marshals Service is generally considered to be one of the first federal law enforcement agencies established, if not actually the first. Once the U.S. Constitution was ratified in 1787, the U.S. Congress began the process of establishing a new federal government. In order to set the judiciary into motion, Congress passed the Judiciary Act of 1789. This act, establishing the original 13 federal court districts, called for the appointment of a United States marshal for each district.[3] These marshals were nominated by President George Washington on September 24, 1789, and two days later they were confirmed by the United States Senate. This date is generally considered to be the birthday of the U.S. Marshals Service.

The U.S. Marshals were appointed to a four-year term and were eligible for renewal. While serving those four years, however, they served at the will and pleasure of the president. They received no salary but, rather, took their pay from the fees collected by the court. The primary duties of these early marshals consisted of serving, supporting, and protecting the federal courts. They served subpoenas, court summonses, writs, and warrants; transported and guarded prisoners; and protected the courtrooms. Interestingly, when it came to collecting fees, it was the U.S. Marshals that would do so, while at the same time paying the expenses that were necessary to run the courtroom. These fees included paying for the rented courtrooms (there were not federal court buildings as of yet), jails (there were no federal jails or prisons either), and those necessary to run the federal courts such as bailiffs, criers, and even people to clean the courtrooms. They also, of course, paid themselves.

The duty was generally not considered very hazardous, but it quickly became clear that there was an element of danger to the job when U.S. Marshal Robert Forsyth became the first federal law enforcement officer killed in the line of duty.[4] Forsyth, a native of Scotland, moved to America and settled in New England before moving to Virginia. He enlisted in the Continental Army and served the duration of the Revolutionary War. Forsyth was one of the first 13 U.S. marshals appointed by George Washington and he was asked to serve the Georgia court, the same state to which he had moved after the war.[5] On January 11, 1794, U.S. Marshal Forsyth had civil process papers to deliver to one Beverly Allen. Rather than going alone, Forsyth brought along two deputies. When they arrived, they found Beverly and his brother talking with some friends. In order not to embarrass Beverly, the agents asked to speak to Beverly outside. They proceeded outside, but Beverly and his brother ran up the stairs and locked themselves in a room. Forsyth and the deputies followed and, upon arriving at the door, a gunshot resounded inside the room, a bullet smashed through the door, and Forsyth was struck in the head. He was killed instantly. Although the two brothers were arrested by the deputies, they later escaped and were never seen again.

While in the first several years the U.S. Marshals primarily served as court administrators, it did not take long for these duties to expand. As the new government passed new laws, there was no entity other than the U.S. Marshals available to enforce those laws. Hence, the Marshals began to take on additional duties such as being responsible for carrying out the decennial census demanded by the U.S. Constitution, a duty they continued through the 1870 census.[6] They also served as customs and revenue collectors, and they were responsible for levying the tariffs and taxes on trade goods. It was this collection of taxes that would lead one U.S. marshal to be at the center of the famous Whiskey Rebellion.[7]

When the American Revolution ended, both the national and state governments were greatly in debt from the war. The Secretary of the Treasury encouraged the federal government to absorb the states' debt, but he needed a way to pay off the accumulated debt. Through his advocacy, Congress passed the Tariff Act of 1789, which included an excise tax on imported spirits. This did not raise enough funds, so in 1792 Congress imposed a tax on domestic distilled spirits. For many farmers who depended on the sale of whiskey to subsidize their farms and had served in the American Revolution to rid America of onerous taxation by the government, this was too much. The western Pennsylvanian farmers began to openly rebel and refused to pay the taxes. They began targeting tax collectors to demonstrate their dissatisfaction with the law. U.S. Marshal David Lenox was sent to serve writs summoning the delinquent distillers to court, and while in most cases this went peacefully, on one occasion in July of 1794, he was fired upon and ultimately captured and held prisoner by the Rebels. Although he would escape, assistance from the federal government was already requested by Pennsylvania, and President George Washington himself led the United States Military to quell the Rebellion. The Whiskey Rebels, as they were known, disbanded before he ever arrived.[8]

Another duty added to the U.S. Marshals came in 1798, when the second president of the United States, John Adams, signed into law the Sedition Act, which made it illegal for anyone to say or write anything negative about the U.S. government.[9] This was largely a political law meant to weaken the opposition party (Republican-Democrats) and to prevent America from fomenting another revolution, such as was occurring in France at the time. Once again, with the passage of a new law, there needed to be an enforcement agency, and the U.S. Marshals were called upon. U.S. Marshals would be involved in a number of the famous cases arising out of the Sedition Act, including the arrest of Thomas Cooper for openly criticizing the Sedition Act and Congressman Matthew Lyon for criticizing the Federalist Party and its figurehead, President John Adams. Interestingly, Lyon ran his reelection campaign from his jail cell and managed to win by a landslide. When Jefferson became president, the law was repealed; but while it was in effect, the U.S. Marshals enforced the constitutionally shaky law.

As the U.S. Marshals reported directly to the secretary of state in these early years, the secretary of state often employed the Marshals to enforce federal law as it was exercised over the states. In 1809, the Commonwealth of Pennsylvania openly defied federal law mandating they pay money to the federal government. U.S. Marshal John Smith was forced to take up arms against Pennsylvania state officials in order to deliver his court order. Another example came when the U.S. Congress passed the Fugitive Slave Law Act of 1850, which mandated that escaped slaves who fled to northern (free) states had to be returned to their owners. It was the U.S. Marshals who were ordered to enforce this draconian law all the way up to the Civil War.

After Lincoln won the election and just prior to his inauguration, he rode the train from his home in Illinois to Washington, D.C. There were numerous threats against Lincoln's life at this time, and a rumor began to circulate that there was a plot to assassinate him when he reached Baltimore.[10] Because there was no U.S. Secret Service to guard the president, U.S. Marshal Ward Hill Lamon was called upon to accompany Lincoln to Washington, D.C. and to keep him from harm. Marshal Lamon would continue performing this duty until the end of the war. He was sent to Union-occupied Richmond, by Lincoln, the day before he was assassinated.[11]

During the Civil War, the U.S. Marshals had been recalled from the South as they were federal agents no longer able to operate in their districts. The Marshals were put to use though, for it was their job to investigate reports of Confederate spies and to confiscate property that was intended for transport into the southern states. In addition, because President Lincoln had suspended the writ of habeas corpus and southern sympathizers were being jailed for the duration of the war, threats against the courts and jails increased as the war progressed. In the meantime, the Marshals also continued to serve at the will and pleasure of the secretary of state, and so they were responsible for carrying out any additional duties assigned to them during and immediately following the Civil War. All of that would change in 1870.

On July 1, 1870, the U.S. Congress created a new department in the president's cabinet, the U.S. Department of Justice. They named the U.S. attorney general to serve as the department's director, the only federal bureaucracy not headed by a secretary. The position of attorney general had been around since George Washington's administration, and it was Washington, himself, who incorporated the attorney general into the cabinet meetings, but he had no staff or agency working for him and he served more as the lawyer for the United States government. By late 1870, the U.S. Department of Justice obtained supervisory control over the U.S. Marshals Service, where the agency remains today. At approximately the same time, the U.S. Congress passed two laws, the Force Act of 1870 and the Civil Rights Act of 1871.[12]

In the post-Civil War South, many of the citizens did not take kindly to the changes in the U.S. Constitution that ended slavery and gave blacks equal rights as citizens. Protests against these laws were driven somewhat underground and caused the Ku Klux Klan (KKK), a white supremacist group, to rise in power and membership. The KKK began terrorizing blacks in the South and targeted any black that attempted to assert their new-found rights. These new laws were aimed at protecting the rights of black citizens, and it was the U.S. Marshals who were sent to the South to enforce these new laws. It has been noted that between the very end of the 1860s and 1877, which marked the end of Reconstruction, "over 7,000 Klan members in the South had been arrested by U.S. Marshals and their deputies."[13] Greatly outnumbered, they still strived to carry out their duties, often at the expense of their lives.

The U.S. Marshals would soon face more challenges as many of their duties in the post-Civil War era would move to the American West. It was there that the U.S. Marshals assumed the role of being the mediating authority between Native Americans and white settlers moving west. While the U.S. Marshals were more often able to maintain the peace, there were circumstances that erupted into violence. One such violent episode that has come to be known as the Going Snake Massacre, occurred on April 15, 1872. It was the worst loss of deputy marshals in the agency's history.[14] A Cherokee Indian known as Proctor shot a white settler in Indian Territory (later the Oklahoma Territory) and then killed his wife. A warrant was secured for Proctor's arrest and Deputy Marshals Jacob Owens and Joseph Peavy, along with a posse of ten men, tracked Proctor to an Indian schoolhouse. As they approached the building, armed Cherokees came pouring out and a gunfight ensued. Seven members of the posse were killed outright and Deputy Marshal Owens died from his wounds several hours later. According to U.S. Marshals historian, Ted Calhoun, "It was the worst slaughter of Marshals in history."[15]

The late 1800s would see a number of interesting characters serve as U.S. Marshals. One of the most famous was Wyatt Earp of the legendary gunfight at the OK Corral, who served as a deputy U.S. marshal in Arizona for less than six months in 1882. In addition, Wyatt's brothers, Morgan and Virgil Earp, also served as U.S. deputy marshals. William "Bat" Masterson, the famous lawman, served as a U.S. deputy marshal in Kansas from 1879 to 1881 and, in his later years in New York City, he served from 1905 to 1909. Even a man as famous as Frederick Douglas, more renowned for his work as an abolitionist, served as a U.S. deputy marshal in Washington, D.C. after being appointed by President Rutherford B. Hayes, making Douglas the first African American deputy marshal to hold that position.[16]

As the close of the nineteenth century drew near, many changes were made to the duties of the U.S. Marshals. In the 1880s, they were given more responsibility for the custody of federal prisoners, and in 1889 a specific incident highlighted the importance of protecting federal judges. On August 14, 1889, a man by the name of David S. Terry assaulted U.S. Supreme Court Justice Stephen J. Field, and Deputy U.S. Marshal David Neagle shot and killed Terry to stop the assault.[17] The U.S. Marshals Service was also given further protection duties during the Pullman Strike of 1894, when they were tasked to keep the trains moving and to prevent the strikers from stopping and assaulting the trains. Then, at the end of the century, in 1896, a profound change occurred within the way in which U.S. Marshals were paid. The old fee system was abolished and on July 1 of that year, U.S. Marshals began to receive an annual salary. They were moving toward becoming members of the U.S. government's civil service.

The twentieth century brought new challenges to the U.S. Marshals Service. Beginning in 1910, the Border Wars (1910-1919) between the United States and Mexico would see numerous deputy marshals being sent to the border to protect American interests.[18] During World War I (1917-1919), the U.S. Marshals took on numerous additional duties, including the investigation of selective service laws, registering German enemy aliens, arresting enemy aliens under presidential arrest warrants, interviewing enemy aliens being held in military camps, and guarding various government locations.[19] Then, in 1920, after the passage of the Volstead Act and ratification of the Eighteenth Amendment, Prohibition went into effect and the U.S. Marshals Service was called upon to enforce the new federal laws. While there were other agencies responsible for prohibition enforcement, the U.S. Marshals were there from the beginning until such agencies as the Bureau of Prohibition and the Federal Bureau of Investigation were able to assist.[20]

Interestingly, it was the rise of these other agencies that would change the role of the U.S. Marshals Service during the twentieth century.[21] Although the Bureau of Prohibition would cease to exist, absorbed into the Federal Bureau of Narcotics at the end of Prohibition, these agencies took away a minor aspect of the duties the U.S. Marshals had performed up to this point in history. More obviously, with the rise of J. Edgar Hoover's Federal Bureau of Investigation, many of the core duties that the U.S. Marshals Service had been responsible for were removed and the new Bureau of Investigation took those over. As the decades began to pass and new federal law enforcement agencies were created, the duties of the U.S. Marshals Service were beginning to be more specialized and focused, eventually ending with the three core functions: the service of federal court papers and warrants, court security, and the transport and custody of federal prisoners.

This did not mean a complete end to these additional duties, but they were becoming more limited. As changes in the federal law and court orders arose with the civil rights movement of the 1960s, the U.S. Marshals Service was often called upon to enforce desegregation and to once again, as it did in the 1870s, uphold the new Civil Rights Act passed by the U.S. Congress. Several famous examples of this include the protection of James Meredith, who had enrolled at the University of Mississippi in 1962, where 127 Deputy marshals were called in to provide him protection against threats on his life, and in 1964, when deputy marshals protected Ruby Bridges on her way to the desegregated schools of New Orleans (made famous in the painting by Norman Rockwell).[22] In addition, other unrest during this time period called for the deployment of the U.S. Marshals Service, from the Pentagon Riot in 1969, resulting from protests of the Vietnam War to the occupation of Wounded Knee, South Dakota in 1973 by the American Indian Movement (AIM). U.S. Marshals were called in to both of these situations to assist in restoring order.

In the 1970s, the U.S. Marshals Service would pick up some additional duties that they remain responsible for to this day. The first was the 1971 establishment of the Witness Security Program (witness protection) that came as a result of passage of the Organized Crime Control Act of 1970.[23] In the event that individuals involved in organized crime organizations were willing to present evidence in court that would lead to the conviction of the organized crime leadership, the U.S. government would provide these witnesses protection by giving them new identities and ensuring their protection for the remainder of their lives or until the threat no longer existed. A Special Operations Group (SOG) was established to be able to respond to an activation order ordering a witness to be protected and a new identity to be created.

The second new duty is one in which they are most well-known because of Hollywood: apprehending federal fugitives. As of 1973, when a federal prisoner escapes from federal custody, it is now the duty of the U.S. Marshals Service to capture the escapee.[24] In 1981, the U.S. Marshals Service was praised for its capture of escaped federal prisoner and Soviet spy, Christopher Boyce, who was most known from the book and movie *The Falcon and the Snowman* (1985). In fact, it was probably the Hollywood movie *The Fugitive* (1993), starring Tommy Lee Jones as a deputy marshal, which made this duty of the U.S. Marshals Service most renown. Learning from the difficulties faced in the Boyce investigation, the U.S. Marshals Service established the Fugitive Investigation Strike Team (FIST) as a means of coordinating the operations of hunting down fugitives through a multi-agency operational structure.

As the twentieth century drew to a close, the U.S. Marshals Service added more specialized duties, were involved in some highly visible cases, and celebrated a unique anniversary. As the federal government's war on drugs rose to prominence in the 1980s, one of the new laws passed by the U.S. Congress was the Asset Forfeiture Law, which mandated that any assets seized by federal law enforcement that are were associated with these crimes would become the property of the U.S. government.[25] The amount of items that the government began to obtain in these forfeitures was enormous, and it became necessary for someone to be responsible for managing and disposing of these goods; that task was given to the U.S. Marshals Service. A highly visible case was the Oklahoma City Bombing in 1995, when after the arrest of Timothy McVeigh and Terry Nichols, the U.S. Marshals Service was responsible for their protection. Finally, the unique anniversary came in 1989, when the U.S. Marshals Service celebrated its 200th anniversary.

As the U.S. Marshals Service entered the twenty-first century, its main duties and responsibilities remained the same: serving papers and warrants and providing court security and the transport of prisoners. In addition, the U.S. Marshals continue to be responsible for escaped fugitives, the witness protection program, and the managing and disposal of assets seized through asset forfeiture. Although perhaps a less visible and prominent federal law enforcement agency today than it was in its first one-hundred years, the U.S. Marshals Service remains an important part of the federal law enforcement structure of the U.S. government.

Who Gets Hired

To become an agent in the U.S. Marshals Service, a candidate must be a U.S. citizen between 21-36 years old and be in good physical condition. He or she must have earned a bachelor's degree or have three years' experience in law enforcement or some other qualifying job experience. A candidate should have a valid driver's license with a good driving record and must meet specified medical qualifications. All successful candidates must pass a structured interview and other assessments including a complete background investigation.

The most qualified candidates are chosen from a Deputy U.S. Marshal Competitive Exam. Other qualified candidates are identified through the Centralized Student Career Experience Program. This is a cooperative education program that prepares undergraduate students for positions in the Marshals Service as deputy marshals.

After candidates are chosen, they are trained in a seventeen-week long training and development program held at the U.S. Marshals Service Training Academy in Glynco, Georgia. There, the new agents are instructed by the Federal Law Enforcement Training Center (FLETC) and U.S. Marshal Service (USMS) instructors. The training includes legal instruction, defensive tactics, driver training, courtroom evidence and procedure, court security, officer survival, search and seizure, protective service training, firearms training, physical conditioning, first aid, prisoner search and restraint, computer training, building entry and search, high threat trials, and surveillance techniques.[26]

Some of those hired to work for the Marshals Service become detention enforcement officers. These men and women are responsible for transporting prisoners, conducting searches of prisoners/detainees, applying and/or removing restraints (handcuffs, leg irons, and waist chains), cellblock management, and processing prisoners.[27] To become a detention enforcement officer, an applicant must have one year of experience, which demonstrates the ability to transport prisoners, conduct searches of prisoners/detainees, and apply and/or remove restraints from detainees.[28]

Others are hired as aviation enforcement officers. These officers are responsible for transporting prisoners safely from one location to another by means of air transportation. They also conduct searches of prisoners/detainees, apply and/or remove restraints, manage prisoners (administer necessary medication, respond to individual or group disturbances, and ensure that all documents and official records are in order), and process prisoners in the custody of the Marshals.

The Marshals also hire administrative positions. Found in all 94 judicial districts, these positions include administrative officers, human resource specialist/assistants; management and program analysts, budget analysts, investigative research specialists, and administrative support assistants.[29]

Budgets

The Marshals' budget is divided into five categories. The first covers judicial and courthouse security. These funds in this category are used to ensure the protection of members of the federal judiciary including judges, jurors, and others. The second category of funding is set aside for fugitive apprehension. The funds in this category are used to carry out investigations involving federal prisoners who have escaped from custody as well as former detainees who violate probation, parole, and bonds. They also seek to find fugitives who have outstanding warrants from cases revolving around drug investigations.

Prisoner security and transportation is the third category for funds in the Marshals. Agents use this money to pay for the transportation of prisoners between judicial districts, correctional facilities, and foreign countries. The protection of witnesses is the fourth category of funding. This fund allows the Marshals to provide for the security, health, and safety of prosecution witnesses and their families whose lives may be at risk as a result of their testimony against offenders, especially drug traffickers, terrorists, and organized crime groups. The final funding group is for tactical operations support. These funds are used to allow the Marshals to conduct special assignments and security missions in those situations that involve crisis response, homeland security, or other national emergencies.[30]

Table 1.1 details the annual budget for the U.S. Marshals. It shows that the U.S. Congress has allocated this agency somewhere between one- and two-billion dollars each year to carry out its required functions.

Table 1.1	Budget Authority (In Billions of Dollars)
2011 enacted	$1.140
2012 enacted	$1.189
2013 request	$2.882
2013 request	$2.850

Source: United States Department of Justice, Fiscal Year 2013 Budget of the U.S. Government, available at http://www.whitehouse.gov/sites/default/files/omb/budget/fy2013/assets/budget.pdf.

Organization

The U.S. Marshals Service is located within the Department of Justice. It is headed by a director, who is appointed by the president. The deputy director provides assistance to the director. Both officials are under the authority of the attorney general of the United States. The Marshals Service is headquartered in Arlington, Virginia, but there are also four foreign field offices.

The Marshals Office is organized around the court system in the United States. The court system is divided into 94 federal districts, and the Marshals Service is organized along the same district boundaries. There is one marshal in each of the 94 court districts, with 218 sub-offices around the nation. In larger districts, an assistant chief deputy U.S. marshal has been appointed. There is also a supervisory deputy U.S. marshal and as many deputy U.S. marshals as required.

There are also special deputy U.S. marshals. These men and women are deputized as needed during special occasions to carry out the powers and duties of the Marshals. This could happen, for example, in high-profile cases which require extra security in the courthouse because of the threat of terrorist attacks, intense media attention, the public's interest, and even global interest.[31] The special deputies are typically employees from the Department of Justice; federal, state, or local law enforcement officers; private security personnel, and other people as determined by the associate attorney general.

Criminal investigators and inspectors are also hired as agents. These men and women assist senior deputy U.S. marshals who are assigned to the Witness Protection Program. Detention enforcement officers and administrative staff also assist the marshals. Currently, there are 3,953 deputy U.S. marshals and criminal investigators located around the country.[32] Senior deputy U.S. marshals are also assigned to Regional Fugitive Task Forces or are assigned to special assignments that require highly skilled criminal investigators.

Leader

The current director of the U.S. Marshals Service is Stacia A. Hylton. Director Hylton has 30 years of law enforcement experience. She began her career as a deputy U.S. marshal, serving in the District of Columbia, Southern District of Florida, and the Eastern District of Virginia. She has held numerous positions during her career with the United States Marshals Service, including ten years in the USMS Elite Special Operations Group. Director Hylton was also an instructor at the training academy, teaching firearms, physical fitness, and kinesic interrogation interviewing techniques; a witness security inspector; and the agency's emergency response incident commander for such assignments as Ground Zero after 9/11, before eventually becoming the chief for the Judicial Security Programs at Headquarters.

In 1998, Director Hylton was promoted to chief deputy U.S. marshal in South Carolina and in 2003 to assistant director for prisoner operations. In 2004, she was appointed as the attorney general's federal detention trustee, and then in 2010 she was appointed director of the United States Marshals Service. As director, Ms. Hylton leads a key Department of Justice (DOJ) law enforcement agency responsible for federal judicial security; fugitive apprehension; witness security; asset forfeiture; and prisoner transportation, custody, and safety.

What They Do

The Marshals are responsible for carrying out many tasks. They include those described below.

Judicial and Courthouse Security

One of the core responsibilities of the Marshals has been the safe and secure operation of the federal courts. As such, they provide security for judges, magistrates, attorneys, jurors, witnesses, defendants, other personnel, and the public in courthouses, federal buildings, and facilities that are occupied by members of the federal judiciary. To protect the courthouses, the Marshals use electronic security systems, cameras, alarms, and other security devices. They protect all parts of the courthouse, including any inmate holding cells that are adjacent to courtrooms, interview rooms, cellblocks, elevators, and office space.[33]

The Office of Protective Intelligence (OPI) is responsible for reviewing and analyzing relevant intelligence and information that concerns the safety and security of any members of the judiciary.[34] Today, the Marshals assess approximately 1,400 threats or other inappropriate communications received by or made toward members of the judiciary each year. They are able to respond quickly and effectively to the threats through the National Threat Management Center. The Marshals help to determine if the suspect intends to harm the individual.[35] They must also try to limit any opportunities that criminals have to tamper with potential evidence or to intimidate, extort, or bribe anyone involved in the judicial proceedings.[36]

In some cases, former law enforcement officers help the Marshals with court security through the Court Security Officer (CSO) program. Law enforcement officers may be deputized and can help the Marshals with monitoring security systems or screening visitors to the buildings, responding to alarms, screening mail that is delivered to the courthouse, or patrolling the perimeter of the buildings.[37]

Prisoner Medical Care

The Marshals provide medical care to all federal inmates who are housed in facilities while awaiting a trial or throughout the duration of a trial. Some inmates can be treated within the facility, while others require more serious treatment outside of the facility. Marshals must ensure those treated outside a facility do not escape or harm guards or other bystanders. Additionally, the risk of exposing the public to an infectious disease also exists in these situations.

Apprehension of Fugitives

The Marshals Service is the primary agency responsible for locating federal fugitives, anyone who has escaped from federal custody, or those who have outstanding warrants issued against them. Marshals hold all federal arrest warrants on those who are wanted by officials until it is executed or dismissed. Marshals often work with other federal, state, or local law enforcement officials, or even international law enforcement, to apprehend fugitives. To help with this task, the Marshals have four foreign field offices, one each in Jamaica, Mexico, the Dominican Republic, and Colombia.

As a way to locate fugitives, the Marshals participate in Regional Fugitive Task Forces (RFTFs) and local District Fugitive Task Forces (DFTFs). Moreover, the Marshals are part of 82 multi-agency task forces located throughout the country that investigate fugitives who are wanted for violent federal, state, and local crimes such as sex offenses, gang violence, and drug trafficking.[38] Sometimes the Marshals take part in the Sex Offender Apprehension Program that assists law enforcement agencies apprehend sex offenders.[39]

The Marshals distinguish federal fugitives as being wanted for either a felony or non-felony offense (i.e., a misdemeanor and a bench warrant). The Marshals identify violent fugitives on their 15 Most Wanted List and their Major Case List. The 15 Most Wanted List Program was established in 1983 and prioritizes the investigations of the most wanted violent fugitives. These men and women tend to be career criminals with a pattern of committing violent acts or whose current crimes may pose a threat to the safety of others. Their offenses tend to be murder, sex offenses, drug trafficking, or organized crime. The Major Case Fugitive Program was established in 1985 by the Marshals as an attempt to broaden the

15 Most Wanted Fugitive Program. The Major Case Fugitive Program is also a way to prioritize the investigation of some of the most dangerous cases of career criminals with a history of violence who may be a threat to public safety.[40]

The Fugitive Apprehension Unit of the Marshals carries out investigations both domestically and internationally. They also carry out technical operations, criminal information analysis, and at times can deputize other law enforcement officers as a way to support fugitive investigations. They can investigate the possible extradition or deportation of fugitives. They investigate sex offenders and can be involved in seizing of assets.[41]

In Fiscal Year 2012, the Marshals apprehended or cleared 53,888 violent state and local felony fugitives. They also apprehended or cleared 17,431 violent federal fugitives.[42] Table 1.2 provides information on the number of fugitives apprehended for the past years.

Asset Forfeiture

The Asset Forfeiture Program of the Marshals is an essential component of the federal government's attempts to combat major criminal activity. Through this program, the Marshals attempt to strip offenders of any profits and property resulting from the criminal activity. The Marshals manage and sometimes sell the seized assets by federal law enforcement agents across the nation, including the DEA, FBI, ATF, and others. Any proceeds from the sale of the items are used to help fund victim compensation programs, law enforcement initiatives, and community programs.[43] In 2013, the forfeited assets had a value of about $2.4 billion, including property, cash and financial instruments, and vehicles.[44] Of

Table 1.2 **Number of Fugitives Cleared**

Fiscal Year	Number of Fugitives
2004	29,140
2005	30,434
2006	30,192
2007	33,437
2008	34,393
2009	32,860
2010	33,000
2011	33,500

Source: United States Marshals Service FY 2011 Performance Budget, Congressional Submission, January 2010.

that money, $1.5 billion was distributed to victims of crime, and $616 million was shared with state and local law enforcement agencies.[45]

Fugitive Safe Surrender

In August 2005, the Marshals carried out their Fugitive Safe Surrender Program in which fugitives were allowed to surrender and receive initial court appearances in a non-threatening environment. The initial program was carried out in Cleveland, Ohio, during which 850 fugitives were taken into custody. After that, other Fugitive Safe Surrenders were carried out in other major cities including Phoenix, Indianapolis, Akron, Nashville, Memphis, and Washington, D.C.[46] Since the program was initially implemented, almost 6,500 fugitives have surrendered to the Marshals.[47]

Gang Resistance Education and Training (GREAT) Program

The Marshals supports Gang Resistance Education and Training, an educational program taught by law enforcement officers to teach school-age children to stay away from gangs and crime. Components of the program contain ways to improve the relationship between young people, their families, and law enforcement in their community.[48]

Prisoner Security and Transportation

Regardless of what agency arrests a federal offender, the Marshals are responsible for the safety of every prisoner who is charged with a federal offense. From the time an offender is arrested until they leave the system either through acquittal or conviction, the Marshals must house and transport all federal inmates in the custody of the federal government.

The Marshals must transport federal inmates from one place to another. The agents use a network of airplanes, automobiles, vans, and busses to take prisoners to the places they need to be, whether a court appearance or a new detention facility. The Marshals move prisoners between judicial districts for court appearances or for meetings with attorneys, to medical facilities, correctional institutions, and even to and from foreign countries. Their transportation system, called the Justice Prisoner and Alien Transportation System (JPATS) (otherwise referred to as "Con Air"), was expanded in 1995 when the Marshals and Immigration and Customs Enforcement (ICE) merged their fleets. Currently, JPATS handles almost 1,400 requests for transportation each day. During FY 2011 it transported inmates on 156,794 occasions (62,132 movements by air and 94,662 on the ground), at a cost of about $45 million.[49]

Many inmates must be taken to a Bureau of Prisons facility where the Marshals take on the responsibility to house the inmates. On average, the Marshals have more than 63,000 detainees in custody each day who are housed in either federal, state, local, or private jails.[50] In those places where there is little room to keep federal offenders, the Marshals have agreements with local jails to house inmates. In those situations, funds have been used to improve the conditions in the local jails in exchange for guaranteed space for federal inmates.[51]

Protection of Witnesses/Witness Security

The Witness Security Program (WSP) was originally established in the Organized Crime Control Act of 1970 and later amended in the Comprehensive Crime Control Act of 1984. Through WSP, the Marshals provide protection for witnesses who choose to testify against dangerous offenders and whose lives have been threatened or may be in danger as a result of their testimony. The Marshals provide a potential witness with physical security needed throughout any pretrial conferences, trial, or other appearances, as well as a new identity after the trial ends. Assistance with housing, medical care, job training, and even employment may be provided.[52] In Fiscal Year 2012, there were 18,437 participants in WSP.[53] As of that time, there have been over 8,300 witnesses in the program, with more than 18,000 participants needing protection, including both the witnesses and their immediate family members.[54]

Special Operations Group (SOG)

The Special Operations Group of the Marshals was originally created in 1971 to be a highly trained tactical force of about 80-100 volunteers who could be deployed quickly in high-risk situations such as protective details, national emergencies, civil disorders, and natural disasters. When needed, SOG participants are deployed in teams to the emergency site. Each team contains agents with training to be highly effective snipers/observers, explosives breachers, evasive drivers, scuba-trained waterborne personnel, high-risk entry personnel, and personnel trained in less lethal techniques and equipment.[55] They could be called upon to apprehend dangerous fugitives, protect visiting dignitaries, provide court security, transport high-profile and dangerous prisoners, or seize assets.

Conclusion

The U.S. Marshals Service has developed a multi-dimensional role in federal law enforcement. They are responsible for protecting the federal court system and its personnel, as well as other top officials. The Marshals also have the duty to apprehend federal fugitives and seize their assets, if obtained illegally. By carrying out these roles, the Marshals protect a vital part of the federal government and criminal justice system.

Key Terms

Witness Security Program
Robert Forsyth
Whiskey Rebellion
Tariff Act of 1789
Sedition Act
attorney general
Going Snake Massacre
Border Wars (1910-1919)
U.S. Marshals Competitive
    Exam
detention enforcement officers

aviation enforcement fficers
Stacia A. Hylton
Office of Protective Intelligence
Court Security Officer Program
Most Wanted Program
Fugitive Apprehension Unit
Asset Forfeiture
Fugitive Safe Surrender
Gang Resistance Education and
    Training Program
Special Operations Group

Review Questions

1. What are the roles and responsibilities of the U.S. Marshals Service?

2. Describe the history of the Marshals Service.

3. Why was the Tariff Act of 1789 important to the history of the Marshals?

4. What are the qualifications to be hired as a Marshals agent?

5. What is the budget of the Marshals Service?

6. Describe the organization of the Marshals.

Endnotes

1. U.S. Marshals Service, Fact Sheets, December 2009, available at http://www.usmarshals.gov/duties/factsheets/facts-1209.html; U.S. Marshals Service, Fact Sheets, April 2011, available at http://www.usmarshals.gov/duties/factsheets/facts-2011.html.

2. U.S. Department of Justice, Office of the Inspector General, Evaluation and Inspections Division July 2005, Review of the United States Marshals Service's Apprehension of Violent Fugitives; United States Marshals Service FY 2009 Performance Budget, Congressional Submission, February 2008; United States Marshals Service FY 2011 Performance Budget, Congressional Submission, January 2010; Statement of the United States Marshals Service Before the Senate Committee on Environment and Public Works, Subcommittee on Transportation and Infrastructure Regarding HR 809, the "Federal Protective Service Reform Act of 2000" September 28, 2000, available at http://epw.senate.gov/107th/mar_1003.htm; Debra M. Jenkins, "The U.S. Marshals Service's Threat Analysis Program for the Protection of the Federal Judiciary" (Annals, AAPSS, July 2001), pp. 69-77.

3. Calhoun, Frederick S. (1990). *The Lawmen: United States Marshals and Their Deputies, 1789 – 1989.* Washington, D.C.: Smithsonian Institution Press; U.S. Marshals Service. (2012). *U.S. Marshals Homepage.* Retrieved online at http://www.usmarshals.gov/.

4. U.S. Marshals Service. (2012). *U.S. Marshals Homepage.* Retrieved online at http://www.usmarshals.gov/.

5. Victor, Rae Anna. (2004). *George Washington's Revolutionary Marshals.* Concord, MA: Infinity Publishing.

6. Calhoun, *The Lawmen.*

7. Hogeland, William. (2010). *The Whiskey Rebellion.* New York: Simon & Schuster.

8. Hogeland, *The Whiskey Rebellion*; U.S. Marshals Museum. (2012). "Not Just for the Love of Whiskey: The Whiskey Rebellion of 1794." Retrieved online at http://www.usmarshalsmuseum.com/node/160.

9. U.S. Marshals Museum. (2012). "U.S. Marshals v. the First Amendment: The Sedition Act of 1798. Retrieved online at http://www.usmarshalsmuseum.com/node/161.

10. Kline, Michael J. (2009). *The Baltimore Plot: The First Conspiracy to Assassinate Lincoln.* Yardley, PA: Westholme Publishing.

11. U.S. Marshals Service. *U.S. Marshals Homepage.*

12. Bumgarner Jeffrey B. (2006). *Federal Agents: The Growth of Federal Law Enforcement in America.* Westport, CT: Praeger.

13. Bumgarner, *Federal Agents*, p. 40.

14. U.S. Marshals Service, *U.S. Marshals Homepage.*

15. U.S. Marshals Service, *U.S. Marshals Homepage.*

16. Goldstein, Norm. (1991). *Marshal: A History of the U.S. Marshals Service.* New York: Dialogue Systems Inc.; Sabbag, Robert. (1992). *Too Tough to Die: Down and Dangerous with the U.S. Marshals.* New York: Simon & Schuster; Sommer, Robin Langley. (1993). *The History of the U.S. Marshals: The Proud Story of America's Lawmen.* New York: Courage Books.

17. U.S. Marshals Service, *U.S. Marshals Homepage.*

18. Goldstein, *Marshal*; Sabbag, *Too Tough to Die*; Sommer, *The History of the U.S. Marshals*; U.S. Marshals Service, *U.S. Marshals Homepage.*

19. U.S. Marshals Service, *U.S. Marshals Homepage.*

20. Goldstein, *Marshal*; Sabbag, *Too Tough to Die*; Sommer, *The History of the U.S. Marshals*; U.S. Marshals Service, *U.S. Marshals Homepage.*

21. Goldstein, *Marshal*; Sabbag, *Too Tough to Die.*

22. U.S. Marshals Service, *U.S. Marshals Homepage.*

23. Goldstein, *Marshal*; Sabbag, *Too Tough to Die.*

24. Calhoun, *The Lawmen*; U.S. Marshals Service, *U.S. Marshals Homepage.*

25. U.S. Marshals Service, *U.S. Marshals Homepage.*

26. U.S. Marshals Service, "Basic training Academy," available at http://www.usmarshals.gov/careers/trainingacademy.html.

27. U.S. Marshals Service, Detention Enforcement Officer, available at http://www.usmarshals.gov/careers/deo.html.

28. U.S. Marshals Service, Detention Enforcement Officer, available at http://www.usmarshals.gov/careers/deo.html.

29. U.S. Marshals Service, Administrative Positions, available at http://www.usmarshals.gov/careers/admin_positions.html.

30. United States Marshals Service FY 2009 Performance Budget, Congressional Submission, February 2008; United States Marshals Service FY 2011 Performance Budget, Congressional Submission, January 2010.

31. United States Marshals Service FY 2009 Performance Budget.

32. U.S. Marshals Service, Fact Sheets, December 2009; U.S. Marshals Service, Fact Sheets.

33. United States Marshals Service FY 2009 Performance Budget.

34. United States Marshals Service FY 2009 Performance Budget; United States Marshals Service FY 2011 Performance Budget.

35. United States Marshals Service FY 2009 Performance Budget; United States Marshals Service FY 2011 Performance Budget; United States Marshals Service FY 2014 Performance Budget, President's Budget, April 2013, available at http://www.justice.gov/jmd/2014justification/pdf/usms-justification.pdf.

36. United States Marshals Service FY 2009 Performance Budget.

37. United States Marshals Service FY 2009 Performance Budget; Statement of the United States Marshals Service Before the Senate Committee on Environment and Public Works, Subcommittee on Transportation and Infrastructure Regarding HR 809, the "Federal Protective Service Reform Act of 2000" September 28, 2000, available at http://epw.senate.gov/107th/mar_1003.htm.

38. United States Marshals Service FY 2011 Performance Budget.

39. U.S. Marshals Service: Apprehension of Fugitives (U.S. Department of Justice), 2007, available at http://georgewbush-whitehouse.archives.gov/omb/expectmore/detail/10001173.2007.html.

40. U.S. Department of Justice, Office of the Inspector General, Evaluation and Inspections Division, July 2005, Review of the United States Marshals Service's Apprehension of Violent Fugitives; United States Marshals Service FY 2009 Performance Budget; United States Marshals Service FY 2011 Performance Budget.

41. United States Marshals Service FY 2009 Performance Budget.

42. United States Marshals Service FY 2014 Performance Budget.

43. U.S. Marshals Service, Overview of the U.S. Marshals Service, available at http://www.usmarshals.gov/duties/factsheets/general-2011.html; United States Marshals Service FY 2011 Performance Budget; U.S. Marshals Service, Fact Sheets, December 2009.

44. U.S. Marshals Service, Fact Sheets, December 2009.

45. United States Marshals Service, Fact Sheet, Judicial Security, 2013, available at http://www.usmarshals.gov/duties/factsheets/jsd-2013.pdf.

46. United States Marshals Service FY 2009 Performance Budget.

47. United States Marshals Service FY 2009 Performance Budget.

48. United States Marshals Service FY 2009 Performance Budget

49. U.S. Marshals Service, Fiscal 2013 Performance Budget, President's Budget: Federal Prisoner Detention Appropriation, February 2012, available at http://www.justice.gov/jmd/2013justification/pdf/fy13-fpd-justification.pdf; U.S. Marshals Service; available at http://www.usmarshals.gov/jpats/.

50. US. Marshals Service, Overview of the U.S. Marshals Service, available at http://www.usmarshals.gov/duties/factsheets/general-2011.html.

51. U.S. Marshals Service, Fact Sheets, December 2009.

52. United States Marshals Service FY 2009 Performance Budget; United States Marshals Service FY 2011 Performance Budget.

53. United States Marshals Service FY 2014 Performance Budget.

54. U.S. Marshals Service, Fact Sheets, December 2009; U.S. Marshals Service, "Fact Sheet: Witness Security," available at http://www.usmarshals.gov/witsec/index.html.

55. United States Marshals Service FY 2009 Performance Budget; U.S. Marshals Service, Fact Sheets, December 2009; United States Marshals Service FY 2011 Performance Budget.

2

Bureau of Alcohol, Tobacco, Firearms, and Explosives

The Bureau of Alcohol, Tobacco, Firearms, and Explosives (BATFE) is a well-established federal law enforcement agency whose multi-dimensional mission has evolved over many years. They provide a comprehensive approach to reducing violent crime across the country in an effort to protect the public and enhance national security.[1]

After the terrorist attacks of September 11, 2001, the key role that the BATFE played in investigating violations of the federal firearms and explosives laws became readily apparent. Their investigative responsibility was an integral part of the federal government's attempts to interrupt supply chains, disrupt the gray and black markets, and prevent potential terrorists from using weapons and explosives against Americans.

One of the primary duties of the BATFE is to investigate any criminal violations of federal laws related to the illegal manufacture, importation, and distribution of alcohol and tobacco products.[2] BATFE enforces all federal criminal statutes that revolve around the diversion of alcohol and tobacco products as a way to avoid federal, state, local, and/or foreign taxes. One law in particular is the Contraband Cigarette Trafficking Act, which makes it illegal for people to ship, transport, receive, possess, sell, distribute, or purchase contraband cigarettes.

The BATFE is also responsible for the investigation and prevention of federal offenses involving the unlawful use, sale, manufacture, possession, and trafficking of firearms and ammunition. Agents seek to identify those who violate firearms laws and investigate them to determine if those individuals should be recommended for prosecution. This could include criminals who use firearms as part of a criminal act, individuals who are actively involved in armed violent drug trafficking activities, or those people who may be prohibited from owning firearms, such as convicted felons, fugitives from justice, or those convicted of domestic violence offenses. The BATFE is the only federal agency with the statutory authority to license and inspect firearms dealers and approve import permits.

One way that BATFE agents oversee the importation of firearms and ammunition is through issuing and regulating import permits. The Bureau works closely with the U.S. Department of State and U.S. Customs and Border Protection to ensure that any permits issued do not conflict with U.S. national security interests and that those who have been granted licenses are operating legally. The BATFE also works closely with those in the firearms industry who are able to update others about the statutory and policy changes that may affect their operations. BATFE frequently publishes and distributes information to those who import firearms and ammunition as a way to inform them of new policy developments.

Another dimension of the BATFE mission is to oversee the use, sale, possession, storage, and transportation of explosives. The BATFE is the federal agency that has the ability to enforce both the regulatory and criminal provisions of the federal laws related to explosives, primarily the Safe Explosives Act of 2002. This law put additional controls on the intrastate transfer of explosives and required background checks on those with explosives licenses or those who acquire explosives. This law was passed as a way to prevent prohibited persons from having access to explosive materials. Related to that is the BATFE's responsibility to investigate acts of arson and bombings that have a federal nexus.

While some BATFE agents work independently to investigate offenses, many work in partnerships to investigate and reduce crimes. Some agents work as part of task forces that are comprised of state and local law enforcement officers, such as Project Safe Neighborhoods, and some special agents are also partners on the Joint Terrorism Task Forces within the Department of Justice[3] and the Law Enforcement Information Sharing Program (LEISP) network.

BATFE agents work with industry groups, international and domestic law enforcement agencies (i.e., state, local, and tribal governments), and other federal agencies as a way to keep neighborhoods safe. Agents also cooperate with the Federal Emergency Management Agency (FEMA) and state and local emergency preparedness agencies to identify law enforcement issues that may arise during a significant incident such as a natural disaster or terrorist event.[4]

The focus on preventing crimes related to alcohol, tobacco, weapons, and explosives is all part of the BATFE's mission of fighting terrorism. This is because organized crime groups and individuals with possible ties to terrorist organizations often traffic in illegal tobacco and alcohol products. Preventing this illegal trafficking can be a way to disrupt the potential funding for terrorist groups and their activities. Illegal firearms and explosives can be stolen and acquired by those involved in terrorism and used for criminal or terrorist purposes.

The statutory authority for the BATFE is found in two places. In the U.S. Code, it is found in 28 USC §599A. This is shown in Figure 2.1. Additionally, the general functions of the agency are found in 28 Code of Federal Regulations (CFR), 0.130, shown in Figure 2.2. Further information about the specific functions of the agency is found in 28 CFR 0.131, which is presented in Figure 2.3.

Figure 2.1: Statutory Authority for the Bureau of Alcohol, Tobacco, Firearms, and Explosives

---

(a) Establishment.—
    (1) In general.—There is established within the Department of Justice under the general authority of the Attorney General the Bureau of Alcohol, Tobacco, Firearms, and Explosives (in this section referred to as the "Bureau").
    (2) Director.—There shall be at the head of the Bureau a Director, Bureau of Alcohol, Tobacco, Firearms, and Explosives (in this subtitle referred to as the "Director"). The Director shall be appointed by the President, by and with the advice and consent of the Senate and shall perform such functions as the Attorney General shall direct. The Director shall receive compensation at the rate prescribed by law under section 5314 of title V, United States Code, for positions at level III of the Executive Schedule.
    (3) Coordination.—The Attorney General, acting through the Director and such other officials of the Department of Justice as the Attorney General may designate, shall provide for the coordination of all firearms, explosives, tobacco enforcement, and arson enforcement functions vested in the Attorney General so as to assure maximum cooperation between and among any officer, employee, or agency of the Department of Justice involved in the performance of these and related functions.
    (4) Performance of transferred functions.—The Attorney General may make such provisions as the Attorney General determines appropriate to authorize the performance by any officer, employee, or agency of the Department of Justice of any function transferred to the Attorney General under this section.
    (b) Responsibilities.—Subject to the direction of the Attorney General, the Bureau shall be responsible for investigating—
    (1) criminal and regulatory violations of the Federal firearms, explosives, arson, alcohol, and tobacco smuggling laws;
    (2) the functions transferred by subsection (c) of section 1111 of the Homeland Security Act of 2002 (as enacted on the date of the enactment of such Act); and
    (3) any other function related to the investigation of violent crime or domestic terrorism that is delegated to the Bureau by the Attorney General.

(c) Transfer of authorities, functions, personnel, and assets to the Department of Justice.—

(1) In general.—Subject to paragraph (2), but notwithstanding any other provision of law, there are transferred to the Department of Justice the authorities, functions, personnel, and assets of the Bureau of Alcohol, Tobacco and Firearms, which shall be maintained as a distinct entity within the Department of Justice, including the related functions of the Secretary of the Treasury.

(3) Building prospectus.—Prospectus PDC-98W10, giving the General Services Administration the authority for site acquisition, design, and construction of a new headquarters building for the Bureau of Alcohol, Tobacco and Firearms, is transferred, and deemed to apply, to the Bureau of Alcohol, Tobacco, Firearms, and Explosives established in the Department of Justice under subsection (a).

Figure 2.2: General Functions of the BATFE

Subject to the direction of the Attorney General and the Deputy Attorney General, the Director of the Bureau of Alcohol, Tobacco, Firearms, and Explosives shall:

(a) Investigate, administer, and enforce the laws related to alcohol, tobacco, firearms, explosives, and arson, and perform other duties as assigned by the Attorney General, including exercising the functions and powers of the Attorney General under the following provisions of law:

(1) 18 U.S.C. chapters 40 (related to explosives), 44 (related to firearms), 59 (related to liquor trafficking), and 114 (related to trafficking in contraband cigarettes);

(2) Chapter 53 of the Internal Revenue Code of 1986, 26 U.S.C. chapter 53 (related to certain firearms and destructive devices);

(3) Chapters 61 through 80, inclusive, of the Internal Revenue Code of 1986, 26 U.S.C. chapters 61-80, insofar as they relate to activities administered and enforced with respect to chapter 53 of the Internal Revenue Code of 1986, 26 U.S.C. chapter 53;

(4) 18 U.S.C. 1952 and 3667, insofar as they relate to liquor trafficking;

(5) 49 U.S.C. 80303 and 80304, insofar as they relate to contraband described in section 80302(a)(2) or 80302(a)(5); and

(6) 18 U.S.C. 1956 and 1957, insofar as they involve violations of:

(i) 18 U.S.C. 844(f) or (i) (relating to explosives or arson),

(ii) 18 U.S.C. 922(l) (relating to the illegal importation of firearms),

(iii) 18 U.S.C. 924(n) (relating to illegal firearms trafficking),

(iv) 18 U.S.C. 1952 (relating to traveling in interstate commerce in aid of racketeering enterprises insofar as they concern liquor on which Federal excise tax has not been paid);

(v) 18 U.S.C. 2341-234 6 (trafficking in contraband cigarettes);

(vi) Section 38 of the Arms Export Control Act, as added by Public Law 94-329, section 212(a)(1), as amended, 22 U.S.C. 2778 (relating to the importation of items on the U.S. Munitions Import List), except violations relating to exportation, in transit, temporary import, or temporary export transactions;

(vii) 18 U.S.C. 1961 insofar as the offense is an act or threat involving arson that is chargeable under State law and punishable by imprisonment for more than one year; and

(viii) Any offense relating to the primary jurisdiction of Bureau of Alcohol, Tobacco, Firearms, and Explosives that the United States would be obligated by a multilateral treaty either to extradite the alleged offender or to submit the case for prosecution if the offender were found within the territory of the United States;

(b) Investigate, seize, and forfeit property involved in a violation or attempted violation within the investigative jurisdiction set out in paragraph (a), under 18 U.S.C. 981 and 982;

(c) Subject to the limitations of 3 U.S.C. 301, exercise the authorities of the Attorney General under section 38 of the Arms Export Control Act, 22 U.S.C. 2778, relating to the importation of defense articles and defense services, including those authorities set forth in 27 CFR part 47; and

(d) Perform any other function related to the investigation of violent crime or domestic terrorism as may be delegated to the Bureau of Alcohol, Tobacco, Firearms, and Explosives by the Attorney General.

Figure 2.3: Specific Functions of the BATFE

The Director of the Bureau of Alcohol, Tobacco, Firearms, and Explosives shall:

(a) Operate laboratories in support of Bureau activities; provide, with or without cost, technical and scientific assistance, including expert testimony, to Federal, State, or local agencies; and make available the services of the laboratories to foreign law enforcement agencies and courts under procedures agreed upon by the Secretary of State and the Attorney General;

(b) Operate the National Explosives Licensing Center to review applications for explosives licenses and permits; determine the eligibility of applicants; issue licenses and permits on approved explosives applications; coordinate with field offices the inspection of applicants, licensees, and permittees; and maintain an explosives license and permit database;

(c) Operate the National Firearms Licensing Center to review applications for firearms licenses; determine the eligibility of applicants; issue licenses on approved firearms applications; coordinate with field offices the inspection of applicants and licensees; and maintain a firearms license database;

(d) Maintain and operate the National Firearms Registration and Transfer Record (NFRTR), pursuant to section 5841 of the Internal Revenue Code of 1986, 26 U.S.C. 5841, as a registry of all National Firearms Act (NFA) firearms in the United States that are not in the possession or under the control of the United States;

(e) Maintain and operate the Arson and Explosives National Repository, a national repository of information on incidents involving arson and the suspected criminal misuse of explosives, under 18 U.S.C. 846(b);

(f) Maintain and operate the National Tracing Center to process requests from Federal, State, local, and foreign law enforcement agencies for the tracing of crime guns; and collect and analyze trace data, out-of-business records, reports of firearms stolen or lost from the inventories of licensees or interstate shipments, and multiple sales reports contained in the Firearms Tracing System (FTS), under 18 U.S.C. chapter 44;

(g) Establish, maintain and operate an Explosives Training and Research Facility to train Federal, State, and local law enforcement officers to investigate bombings and explosions, properly handle, utilize, and dispose of explosives materials and devices, train canines as explosives detection canines, and conduct research on explosives, as authorized by section 1114 of the Homeland Security Act of 2002;

(h) Pay awards for information or assistance and pay for the purchase of evidence or information as authorized by 28 U.S.C. 524;

(i) Subject to applicable statutory restrictions on the disclosure of records of information:

(1) Release information obtained by the Bureau and Bureau investigative reports to Federal, State, and local officials engaged in the enforcement of laws related to alcohol, tobacco, arson, firearms, and explosives offenses;

(2) Release information obtained by Bureau and Bureau investigative reports to Federal, State, and local prosecutors, and State licensing boards, engaged in the institution and prosecution of cases before courts and licensing boards related to alcohol, tobacco, arson, firearms and explosives offenses;

(3) Authorize the testimony of Bureau officials in response to subpoenas or demands issued by the prosecution in Federal, State, or local criminal cases involving offenses under the jurisdiction of the Bureau; and

(4) Except as provided in paragraph (i)(1) of this section, authorize all other production of information or testimony of Bureau officials in response to subpoenas or demands of courts or other authorities as governed by subpart B of part 16 of this chapter.

History

According to Jeffrey Bumgarner, "the Bureau of Alcohol, Tobacco, Firearms, and Explosives (ATF) is one of the most significant and recognizable law enforcement elements of the Treasury Department's law enforcement history."[5] To others it is considered a very controversial agency, one that has consistently taken away the rights of Americans, particularly in regard to the Second Amendment.[6] Regardless, one thing is clear; its original focus on alcohol and, later, tobacco has taken a back seat to a more recent focus on firearms and explosives. This highlights the fact that the history of this agency is just as complex as its name would suggest; but in tracing its history, one comes to understand why the agency is responsible for enforcing such a volatile mix of materials.

The earliest precursors of the BATFE can be found in a story very similar to the one detailed regarding the U.S. Marshals Service. In the wake of the Revolutionary War, Alexander Hamilton devised a strategy to make the national government more powerful by absorbing the war time debt of the states. He then needed a means to pay for the new federal debt, and this was accomplished through a tax on spirits. This, then, was the trigger for the Whiskey Rebellion, to which the president, an army of 10,000 soldiers, and a U.S. marshal responded. From that time forward until the Civil War, the use of this type of taxation to raise revenue became common. The enforcement of these laws, however, became evidently necessary if these forms of taxation were to ever have any success.

After the Civil War commenced, the United States found itself in dire need of revenue to fund the war.[7] In order to ensure these taxes were collected, the U.S. Congress created the Office of Internal Revenue within the U.S. Department of the Treasury, effective July 1, 1862. Over the ensuing year, the new office found it difficult to enforce the law when tax violations were discovered, so a further request for assistance was made to Congress. The following year, Congress authorized the Office of Internal Revenue to hire "three detectives to aid in the prevention, detection and punishment of tax evaders."[8] Under the Department of the Treasury, tax collection and tax enforcement were now consolidated, but it was the enforcement side of the equation that would eventually lead to the creation of the Bureau of Alcohol, Tobacco, and Firearms.

The Office of Internal Revenue was noted for enforcing revenue laws in the "Whiskey Ring" of 1875 that would ultimately save the federal government millions of dollars in liquor taxes.[9] Other similar cases would arise over the following decades and well into the next century. However, all of this would begin to change when the Anti-Saloon League and the Woman's Christian Temperance Movement, among others, finally had their way, and a whole country would attempt what President Herbert Hoover once called "the Noble Experiment."[10] Thus, the more modern development of the BATFE actually had its roots in the American era of Prohibition.

After the passage of the Volstead Act and the ratification of the Eighteenth Amendment to the United States Constitution, Prohibition went into effect. On January 16, 1920, it was no longer legal to manufacture, sell, or transport alcoholic beverages. In order to respond to the issues America would now face, the Prohibition Unit was created within the Bureau of Internal Revenue.[11] On April 1, 1927, the unit was rolled out from underneath the Bureau of Internal Revenue and became its own independent agency under the Department of the Treasury with a brand new name: the Bureau of Prohibition.

On July 1, 1930, the Hoover Administration transferred the Bureau of Prohibition from the Department of the Treasury to the Department of Justice. This reoriented the mission of the Bureau of Prohibition to focus more heavily on law enforcement rather than tax enforcement. Regardless, with the country's dissatisfaction with Prohibition and the election of President Franklin D.

Roosevelt, who had campaigned for the repeal of Prohibition, this move lost much of its impetus. In fact, after Roosevelt became president, while waiting for the ratification of the Twenty-First Amendment, which would repeal the Eighteenth Amendment, the Bureau of Prohibition was temporarily absorbed into the Bureau of Investigation and became the Alcohol Beverage Unit. Once Prohibition was repealed, there was no longer a function for the unit, so it was removed in March of 1934 and became the Alcohol Tax Unit (ATU) of the Bureau of Internal Revenue, under the Department of the Treasury.[12] The agency had come full circle.

The Alcohol Tax Unit remained busy over the next two decades, pursuing the old moonshiners from the Prohibition-era who had refused to stop selling their product. Although it was no longer illegal to manufacture and sell alcohol, it had to be under government license, and licensees were required to pay taxes. In addition, many counties in the South refused to abide by the repeal of Prohibition laws and either continued their preexisting Prohibition laws or passed new ones to continue Prohibition, making for many dry counties in the South. Illegal importation of alcohol into dry counties from wet counties created a miniature version of past opportunities for moonshiners and the Alcohol Tax Unit remained busy in the Southern states.

One other responsibility that the Alcohol Tax Unit had picked up in 1934 was the investigation of firearm sales. During his election in 1932, President Franklin D. Roosevelt had become the target of an assassination. Although he was not harmed in the shooting, Chicago Mayor Anton Cermak was killed. After entering office in March of 1933, Roosevelt's attention was first focused on the repeal of Prohibition and economic recovery. Once those were underway after the famous 100 days, he turned his attention in the fall of 1933 and spring of 1934 to the issue of crime.[13]

Concerned with the problem of guns, especially those associated with gangsters and mob bosses, a flurry of bills entered Congress from the White House. One of the bills that eventually saw passage was the National Firearms Act.[14] That was the first federal gun control law. As outright gun bans were considered violations of the Second Amendment, various machine guns, short-barreled rifles and shotguns, grenades, and bombs were identified as items that required registration of ownership and taxation. The agency that made the most sense to enforce these laws was the Alcohol Tax Unit.

The Alcohol Tax Unit remained firmly established in the Bureau of Internal Revenue until the early 1950s. In 1952, the Bureau of Internal Revenue became the now more familiar Internal Revenue Service.[15] The year before that, in 1951, the Alcohol Tax Unit was changed to the Alcohol and Tobacco Tax Division (ATTD), largely in recognition of the increased regulation of tobacco products and because the wide array of tobacco taxes created situations for abuse similar to those of alcohol taxes. The name change reflected their new responsibility of enforcing federal tobacco taxes, as well.

The registration and taxation of firearms was not really a primary function for the ATTD during the 1950s and early 1960s. When street crime began to rise in the early 1960s, more attention was paid to gun violations. What greatly changed the dynamic, however, was the second major piece of gun control legislation in America's history, and that was the Gun Control Act of 1968.[16] This legislation removed the requirement that citizens register their weapons as it was considered a violation of the Second Amendment. Instead, it focused more stringently on the interstate commerce of firearms and prohibited the interstate transfer of firearms except among those individuals who were licensed manufacturers of firearms, dealers, or importers. Once this occurred, it was the enforcement of registration and taxation laws of firearms dealers that became a more central focus of the ATTD.

Two years later, Congress passed the Organized Crime Control Act of 1970, aimed at dealing with organized crime groups such as the mafia and drug dealers. Title XI of the act was related to explosives, allowing for the federal government to closely regulate the explosives industry, especially in regard to various chemicals that were used in arsons and bombings. It also made these two offenses federal crimes, thus allowing for the enforcement of criminal violations related to the regulatory laws. Although the secretary of the Treasury and the attorney general of the Department of Justice were given concurrent jurisdiction in the investigation of arsons and bombings that violated federal laws, the primary responsibility was given to the ATTD of the Internal Revenue Service.

It was the importance of the regulation of interstate commerce in firearms that became the impetus for another change in the placement of the agency and its name. On July 1, 1972, the Treasury Department issued Order Number 221, which transferred the ATTD out from under the Internal Revenue Service and made it its own bureau. Hence, now that it was a bureau, it was necessary to call it that. And, coupled with the fact that enforcing the Gun Control Act of 1968 was one of its central missions, the new name of the agency became: The Bureau of Alcohol, Tobacco, and Firearms (ATF).

In order to deal with the transition from being a tax unit to its own independent bureau, Rex D. Davis was appointed the first director by President Nixon. Davis was a veteran of World War II, having served as a bombardier, who, after the war, went to work for the Department of the Treasury. He became the head of the division in 1970 and was in a good position to care for the agency's transition to bureau status. While in office, Davis focused heavily on the federal firearms and explosives laws. But the reality remained that revenue collection from alcohol and tobacco products was still an important part of the duties of the Bureau of Alcohol, Tobacco, and Firearms, so much so that the ordering of the three focal areas in their name appeared to be in the proper order. In fact, Director Davis once commented after retirement that "When our law enforcement officers were asked who they were, they would say Treasury agents,"[17] to hide the less glamorous fact that they were, in many ways, glorified tax collectors. It would appear to have remained that way for the following two decades, but once again things would change with a series of bombings that began to highlight the one responsibility the ATF did not have in its bureau name—explosives.

On February 26, 1993, at approximately 12:18 p.m., an explosion rocked the World Trade Center complex in New York City. This was the first attack on the World Trade Center committed by international terrorists who saw the center and New York City as the embodiment of all that was wrong with capitalist America. Special agents from the ATF, located in the nearby Field Division head-quarters, immediately responded to the scene, along with other federal, state, and local investigators.[18] While the Federal Bureau of Investigation took the lead because of the terrorist nature of the attack, the ATF had a crucial role as they were the federal agency responsible for investigating bombings. In addition, because of the fact the bombing occurred in New York City, the New York City Police Department also played a major role in the investigation. These three agencies set up a temporary command post and began working together to develop a coordinated response to the crisis. This included the deployment of both the ATF's National Response Team (NRT) and their Mobile Communications Center.

The National Response Team consisted of 13 special agents, 2 explosive enforcement officers, and 3 forensic chemists. They began conducting a site evaluation and developed a strategy for sifting through the five stories of wreckage. They traced the bomb to the B2 Parking level, determining that after detonation it caused severe blast damage several levels above and several levels below. Initial chemical analysis detected traces of nitrates, a chemical found in explosives. ATF Explosives Officer Joseph Hanlin and members of the New York City Police Department's bomb squad then entered the wreckage and found the vehicle used to transport the explosives. Within days of painstakingly sifting through the debris, agents found the vehicle identification number (VIN) of the van, which ultimately would lead to the arrest of the terrorists. The status of the ATF's National Response Team and their expertise with explosives had helped to solve the case.

Two years later, on April 19, 1995, another bombing would once again bring an important response from the ATF, and that was the bombing of the Alfred P. Murrah Federal Building—the Oklahoma City Bombing. At 9:02 a.m., 5,000 pounds of ammonium nitrate fertilizer in a Ryder rental truck exploded and 168 people were killed. Until September 11, 2001, it was the deadliest act of terrorism ever committed on United States soil. Once again, a National Response Team from the ATF responded and would become part of the investigation because of the explosives used. This would play out again in the Atlanta Olympics bombing in 1996, the Otherside Lounge bombing in Atlanta in 1997, and the abortion clinic bombings in 1998. The investigation of explosives had become an integral part of the mission of the ATF.

The events of September 11, 2001, had a profound impact on the nation, and it would have repercussions for the ATF as well. Special agents in New York City were some of the first responders to the World Trade Center attacks on that day, and they assisted in the response like many of the other federal agencies. While they did not take a lead in the investigation, they would be affected by its aftermath. President George W. Bush began contemplating changes to the Administration, which would ultimately lead to the creation of the Department of Homeland Security, and many agencies responsible for criminal investigations wondered where they would fall under the organizational restructuring.

Much of this decision making was predicated on the mission of the agency itself. One issue that arose for the ATF was in regard to the investigation of bombings and which federal agency had the lead. In cases of bombings, ATF would lead the investigation, but in all acts of terrorism, the Federal Bureau of Investigation would lead. Hence, like the first World Trade Center bombing, the Oklahoma City bombing, and the attacks on 9/11, because they were terrorist attacks (foreign and domestic), the FBI took the lead, but the ATF assisted. Since this working relationship had become so closely associated over the last two decades of the twentieth century, many had even contemplated rolling the ATF into the FBI or at least moving the ATF under the Department of Justice.[19] Then, with the creation of the Department of Homeland Security, the organizational home of the ATF had become questionable.

In January of 2003, with the passage of the Homeland Security Act of 2002, the ATF was moved from the Department of the Treasury and placed under the Department of Justice. The agency remained an independent bureau in the transfer, but it did receive a slight change in name. The name was changed to reflect the one area of responsibility that had become such an integral part of their mission but was not reflected in their name: the Bureau of Alcohol, Tobacco, Firearms, and Explosives. The agency, however, decided to retain the acronym for their agency as the more familiar ATF, rather than expanding it to ATFE. In addition, when the move occurred, the tax and trade functions of the ATF remained with the Department of the Treasury and were placed under the responsibility of the newly formed Alcohol and Tobacco Tax and Trade Bureau.[20]

In light of the post 9/11 terrorist attacks, it has been clarified that "As a law enforcement agency within DOJ, ATF's first priority is preventing terrorist attacks within the United States."[21] As William J. Krouse of the Congressional Research Service notes, the ATF is "responsible for countering the illegal use and trafficking of firearms and explosives, and the criminal diversion of alcohol and tobacco products as an illegal source of funding for terrorist activities."[22] In fact, Krause points out that ATF agents, in the course of their tobacco bootlegging investigations, have uncovered some of these operations as part of terrorist financing operations. Despite the movement toward preventing and investigating terrorism, however, Krouse explains "the lion's share of ATF's resources are allocated to its firearms compliance and investigations program" and that their primary goal has been the "reduction of firearms-related violence."[23]

The BATFE clearly has a unique history, one that, when reviewed closely, clears up the matter of why four such uniquely differing materials create today's Bureau name and mission. However, the history of the ATF has not been without controversy, and in fact, the ATF has usually been one of the most targeted federal law enforcement agencies for criticism and derision.[24] One of the controversies centers on the case of Ruby Ridge in 1992, which involved an ATF-initiated case of firearms violations that led to a standoff with Randy Weaver and resulted in the death of a U.S. marshal, as well as Weaver's wife and son. A second incident was the Waco Siege of the Branch Davidian religious compound near Waco, Texas, that began as an ATF-initiated raid for gun violations. When agents entered, six Branch Davidians were killed, as were four ATF agents. It was the worst loss in the ATF's history and both the raid and the 51-day standoff that ultimately ended in the compound being burned down (although this part of the operation was carried out by the FBI) remains controversial to this day.

There have been other controversies with the BATFE, generally centered on their firearms investigations, including some undercover operations that focused on gun show sales. Cases in 2004 and 2005 in Virginia and Pennsylvania surfaced through congressional hearings regarding allegations of harassment, intimidation, and verbal abuse directed toward citizens who purchased firearms at gun shows, where BATFE demanded to see the paperwork and tried to persuade these individuals not to purchase firearms at gun shows in the future. The most recent controversy has also centered on firearms, but in this case it was the result of gun-walking operations between 2006 and 2011. In these operations, nicknamed "Fast and Furious," the BATFE was allowing firearms to be sold in undercover operations to drug traffickers who were taking them into Mexico in order to allegedly track them to the various drug cartels in order to identify them and bring them to justice. When Border Patrolman Brian Terry was killed with one of the weapons that had been allowed to walk, congressional hearings ensued. As a result of the hearings, the House of Representatives voted to hold Attorney General Eric Holder in contempt of court, but no formal charges were filed against him.

So, while Jeffrey Bumgarner may be correct in saying that "the Bureau of Alcohol, Tobacco, Firearms, and Explosives (ATF) is one of the most significant and recognizable law enforcement elements of the Treasury Department's law enforcement history,"[25] it has also been one of the most controversial.

Who Gets Hired

Special Agents

BATFE special agents are highly trained officers who investigate possible violations of federal laws concerning firearms, explosives, arson, alcohol, and tobacco. Agents rely on surveillance tactics, interviews, search warrants, and searches for physical evidence as a way to gather evidence. Arrests may be made at the completion of an investigation, with possible prosecution. Agents must complete investigative case reports and, if needed, testify for the government either in a court setting or before a grand jury.[26]

To become an agent, an applicant must be a U.S. citizen and, if male, must be registered with Selective Service. Applicants must be at least 21 years of age but not older than 36 at the time of appointment. They must possess a current driver's license. Once an applicant has completed the BATFE special agent application questionnaire, they must pass the BATFE special agent exam and assessment test. Once this is done, the applicant must take part in a field panel interview. In addition, a writing sample will be required. All successful candidates must comply with the BATFE's drug policy. They must take and pass a medical examination and meet set vision requirements. These require that candidates have normal depth perception and peripheral vision and have the ability to distinguish shades of color.

Investigators

BATFE investigators conduct inspections to help identify evidence of falsification of records or inventories. They also conduct interviews, inspect buildings, and perform background investigations to determine if those seeking licensure are suitable to do so. If violations are discovered, investigators report those to special agents for any further action.[27] To be an investigator, candidates must meet the same requirements as those listed above.

Professional and Technical Support

Many types of support professional and technical employees are hired at BATFE who seek to assist the agents in their duties. The agency has many attorneys who provide legal advice to the Bureau, both in Washington D.C. and in field offices around the country. The forensic chemists help to examine evidence, while auditors take part in audits in criminal investigations. Intelligence research specialists help to collect and analyze evidence for investigations involving terrorist activities. Administrative personnel serve to advise agency officials on personnel matters such as hiring or benefits.[28]

Internships

The Student Temporary Employment Program (STEP) in the BATFE provides students with the opportunity to gain experience in many fields that may not be related to their academic field of study. Job opportunities for students in this program provide temporary employment ranging from summer positions to longer-term positions that students may hold as long as they are enrolled at least half-time in an accredited academic institution.[29]

BATFE also has developed a student volunteer program for students to explore career options in an unpaid setting. Students in this program are exposed to the federal work environment and can develop office and professional skills while learning about the mission and responsibilities of the BATFE. Students in this program may or may not be assigned duties which relate to their course of academic study.[30]

Budgets

Table 2.1 shows the congressional allocations for the BATFE. It shows that the agency's budget has remained fairly constant over this time period.

Table 2.1	Budget Authority (In Billions of Dollars)
2011 enacted	$1.413
2012 enacted	$1.152
2013 request	$1.153
2014 request	$1.230

Source: United States Department of Justice, Fiscal Year 2014 Budget and Performance Summary, available at http://www.justice.gov/jmd/2014summary/.

Organization

BATFE is housed within the U.S. Department of Justice and is headquartered in Washington, D.C., although it has 25 domestic field offices throughout the U.S. and its territories. In 2013, there were 2,402 special agents, 791 investigators, and other administrative, professional, and technical personnel for a total of 4,719 total employees.[31]

BATFE also has an Office of International Affairs, which details the agency's international activities. The goal of the office is to coordinate BATFE's international activities, such as requests from foreign nations for assistance and training or help with criminal investigations related to firearms trafficking or illicit tobacco products. The International Affairs Team, made up of special agents and other professionals, provide expertise to foreign nations on issues related to firearms and explosives. Through the international offices, BATFE is more effective in their goals of halting illegal firearms trafficking and combating the activities of violent criminal gangs on a global scale. The office also serves as a contact to international organizations such as the UN and the Organization of American States in efforts to combat illicit firearms trafficking. During Fiscal Year 2013, ATF had 14 international offices in 8 countries, including offices in Canada, Mexico, Colombia, and Iraq. There are also regional firearms advisors based in San Salvador and serving El Salvador, Guatemala, Nicaragua, Panama, Belize, Honduras, and Costa Rica.[32]

Leader

The current BATFE acting director is B. Todd Jones. Todd Jones was one of the first five U.S. attorneys confirmed by the U.S. Senate on August 7, 2009. This is the second time Jones has served as United States attorney—President Clinton appointed him to the position in 1998, and he served in that capacity until January 2001. Jones also has served as an assistant U.S. attorney in the District of Minnesota. Prior to becoming U.S. attorney in 2009, Jones was a partner with a major national law firm in Minneapolis, where his practice focused on criminal defense and complex business litigation. He is also a fellow of the American

College of Trial Lawyers. Attorney General Eric Holder appointed Jones to serve as chair of the Attorney General Advisory Committee (AGAC). This body, consisting of 18 United States attorneys from around the country, is responsible for advising the attorney general on a broad array of Department of Justice policy issues.

Jones received his J.D. from the University of Minnesota Law School in 1983 and his B.A. from Macalester College in 1979. Following admission to the Minnesota Bar, he went on active duty in the United States Marine Corps, where he served as an infantry officer with the First Marine Division and subsequently as both a trial defense counsel and prosecutor in a number of courts-martial proceedings. In 1989, he left active duty and returned to Minnesota with his family. He was recalled to active duty for Operation Desert Storm in 1991.

Most recently, Jones has been asked by Attorney General Holder to serve as the acting director of the Bureau of Alcohol, Tobacco, Firearms, and Explosives (BATFE). As the acting director, Jones is responsible for leading an agency of men and women charged with carrying out the laws related to firearms, explosives, arson, and alcohol and tobacco trafficking.

For Jones, public service has always been important, whether it has been as a U.S. Marine Corps officer, working pro bono matters while in private practice, or with the Department of Justice. As he explains, "All of us who are lawyers should understand that a professional life in the law is, in fact, essentially a life of service to others. It is a duty we have as citizens, professionals and members of the Bar."[33]

What They Do

Alcohol and Tobacco Diversion/Smuggling

BATFE works to reduce alcohol smuggling and contraband cigarette trafficking as a way to reduce the possibilities that criminal and terrorist organizations may be using the profits from these activities for criminal purposes. Reducing smuggling can also combat the loss of significant tax revenue for the states.[34]

The BATFE tries to identify and arrest anyone who is trafficking in contraband cigarettes and illegal liquor. When they are discovered, the BATFE attempts to seize the assets that could be used by illegal groups to enhance their profits. Agents also assist local, state, and other federal law enforcement agencies investigate trafficking of contraband cigarettes and liquor in their jurisdictions.[35]

Arson and Explosives Enforcement

In the Safe Explosive Act, Congress made the BATFE more responsible for overseeing the explosives industry in the U.S. The act gave the BATFE the power to investigate all thefts and loss of explosives as well as to require background checks for all of those people seeking licenses to sell explosives. It is hoped that it will be more difficult for those people who are prohibited from owning explosives from doing so. The law mandates that BATFE agents inspect explosive licensees every three years as a way to guarantee that all explosive materials are properly stored and accounted.[36]

The BATFE is also the agency responsible for enforcing the federal laws concerning the manufacture, importation, and distribution of destructive devices (bombs), explosives, and arson. Over the years, the BATFE has become the nation's primary source for information and knowledge on explosives and arsons. To accomplish its task, the BATFE uses accelerant and explosives detective canines, certified explosives specialists, certified fire investigators, criminal investigative analysis, explosives enforcement officers, explosives research and development, the International and National Response Teams, the U.S. Bomb Data Center, and the Bomb Arson Tracking System.[37]

Accelerant and Explosive Detection Canines

One way BATFE agents investigate arsons and explosives is with use of canines that have been trained to detect explosives, residue, and post-blast evidence. The canines are also trained to find accelerants that are often undetected by humans. Moreover, the dogs are trained to detect firearms and ammunition that have been hidden in containers, in vehicles, on people, and even buried underground. BATFE provides the detection canine dogs to law enforcement around the U.S. and in other countries as a means to assist them to combat terrorism. To date, BATFE has certified over 300 canines and deployed them to 13 different countries. The agency has 21 BATFE agents working with the explosives detection canines.[38]

Certified Explosives Specialists

Some BATFE agents are trained to be certified explosives specialists, who then become BATFE's experts in explosives-related matters. These agents are trained to investigate all types of explosives and the disposal of explosive materials, as well as any other possible violations of the federal laws concerning explosives. Their duties also include conducting explosives recovery and disposal; maintaining knowledge of common military, commercial, and homemade explosives; providing support for special events; maintaining expertise on packaging explosives samples; providing explosives training; and assisting industry operations investigators.[39]

Certified Fire Investigators

The BATFE certified fire investigators seek out the origin and cause of fires. They use scientific and engineering-based technology, in addition to computer software programs and mathematical equations to describe both the chemical and the physical behavior of different fires. They also provide expert testimony in court, if needed.[40]

Explosives Enforcement Officers

Explosives enforcement officers (EEOs) have technical expertise in bomb disposal and explosives. Their responsibilities include providing technical advice on regulations pertaining to the storage, handling, and disposal of explosives; assessing the vulnerability of infrastructure; constructing copies of explosive devices; reporting on explosive, incendiary, and destructive devices for court hearings; providing expert testimony for trials; creating safe disassembly procedures for explosive and incendiary devices; conducting explosive destruction operations; providing operational and training support to state, local, national, and international agencies; providing underwater explosives dive and recovery operations; preparing research studies and analyses of explosives-related equipment; and preparing for special national security events.[41]

International Response Team

Foreign governments may request that BATFE agents provide technical/forensic assistance in investigating incidents involving arson or explosives. The International Response Team (IRT) is comprised of four supervisory special agents, fire specialists, and explosives specialists who have post-blast expertise. Explosives technology experts and forensic chemists may also be involved, depending on the circumstance. The IRT often travels to the other country to assist in the investigation.[42]

National Response Team

The BATFE has a national response team that assists federal, state, and local law enforcement agencies investigate possible incidents of arson and explosives. The National Response Team (NRT) is comprised of special agents with the expertise in explosives who are able to travel to any location in the U.S. within 24 hours. The team also has technical and legal advisors and response vehicles to provide logistical support. Often, the NRT works closely with state and local investigators to reconstruct the scene, identify the seat of the blast or origin of the fire, and determine the possible cause. If it is a criminal event, NRT members gather evidence for a possible criminal prosecution.[43]

U.S. Bomb Data Center

The U.S. Bomb Data Center was originally established by congressional mandate in 1996 to serve as a national collection center for information regarding arson and explosives incidents throughout the country. The Center gathers information from different sources such as the BATFE, the FBI, and the U.S. Fire Administration and makes it available to scholars, fire departments, the public, and other law enforcement agencies for statistical analysis and investigative research.

The mission of the U.S. Bomb Data Center is to collect statistics on arson and explosives from all available sources on the federal, state, and local levels. In addition to maintaining a database, the Center provides information on current arson and explosives issues to federal, state, and local law enforcement agencies and fire departments. They track trends and patterns related to arson and misuse of explosives. The Center increases the communication among investigators working to solve similar types of cases related to arson and explosives.[44]

Bomb Arson Tracking System

The BATFE developed the Bomb Arson Tracking System (BATS) as part of the United States Bomb Data Center. This allows state and local law enforcement agencies to track and share information about bombings, arsons, and explosives. This way, agencies can be more effective in solving arsons and bombings that occur. They can also track national trends and patterns regarding arsons and bombings. Information on bombings and explosives can be shared between international law enforcement agencies through DFuze, BATFE's international bombing database.

The BATFE maintains a database called TEDAC, or the Terrorist Explosive Device Analytical Center. The deputy director of TEDAC is a BATFE supervisory special agent. BATFE works closely with other highly trained individuals such as FBI agents, intelligence analysts, and explosives specialists to analyze and track improvised explosives devices (IED) triggering mechanisms that are used in Iraq and Afghanistan. TEDAC personnel also maintain a database on explosives that identifies and tracks different components that are used in the IED triggering devices by terrorists.[45]

Firearms

BATFE recognizes that firearms play a key role in violent crimes and investigates those crimes and enforces the federal laws pertaining to firearms. Their investigative priorities focus on armed violent offenders and career criminals, narcotics traffickers, narco-terrorists, violent gangs, and domestic and international arms traffickers. BATFE agents investigate these offenders in an effort to reduce violent crime and in turn enhance the public's safety. BATFE also works to increase state and local awareness of the federal laws.

As a way to reduce the illegal use of firearms, BATFE is responsible to grant firearms licenses. They conduct firearms licensee qualification and compliance inspections to ensure the laws are being followed for selling of weapons. The Federal Firearms Licensee Inspections verify that licensees are complying with the Gun Control Act. Agents also teach licensees about the proper way to keep records on gun sales. They oversee gun purchases so that those who buy guns illegally are apprehended.[46]

Agents verify that provisions of the National Firearms Act (NFA) are being followed. This law requires that firearm makers, importers, and manufacturers register firearms they make or import with BATFE, and that BATFE approves all NFA firearms transfers. The NFA also imposes a tax on the making and transfer of NFA firearms and requires manufacturers, importers, and dealers to pay a special occupational tax.

BATFE agents also oversee the Brady Act Enforcement Strategy. The Brady Handgun Violence Prevention Act (otherwise known as the Brady Bill) requires that gun purchasers have a background check through the National Instant Criminal Background Check System (NICS). The NICS record check process is performed by the FBI, but the BATFE investigates and enforces violations of the Brady Act.

Firearms are traced through the National Tracing Center (NTC), the Nation's only firearms tracing facility. They are able to trace guns used in crimes as a way to help federal, state, local, and international law enforcement agencies. Through the analysis of crime guns, ATF helps federal, state, local, and international law enforcement to identify sources of guns used in crimes.

BATFE also oversees the National Integrated Ballistic Information Network (NIBN) that allows the BATEF to deploy the Integrated Ballistics Identification System (IBIS) equipment to federal, state, and local law enforcement agencies so they can image and compare crime gun evidence. The equipment in IBIS equipment allows firearms technicians to gather digital images of the markings made by a firearm on bullets and cartridge casings.

BATFE also leads the attorney general's Violent Crime Impact Teams (VCITs). Located in 29 cities across the country, these teams work to reduce the number of homicides and other violent crimes committed with firearms. The VCIT members assist state and local authorities by providing investigative help if weapons were used in a crime and interviewing those involved to determine the source of the firearms. They also work to remove career criminals from the streets. They use techniques such as undercover operations and confidential informants to infiltrate violent groups. The VCIT pursues those violent criminals through geographic targeting, proactive investigation, and prosecution. When needed, VCITs investigate corrupt federal firearms licensees (FFLs).[47]

Compliance Inspections of Licensed Gun Dealers

BATFE agents inspect federal firearms licensees as a way to monitor their compliance with the Gun Control Act and to prevent the diversion of firearms from legal to illegal channels of commerce. BATFE special agents are authorized to inspect the inventory and records of a federal firearms licensee without search warrants under certain circumstances.[48] By inspecting the firearms transfer records, BATFE investigators can generate vital leads in homicide and other criminal investigations. In addition, by inspecting the records, BATFE investigators are sometimes able to uncover evidence of FFLs transferring firearms illegally.[49]

Project Gunrunner

Violence associated with firearms has increased sharply on the Southwest border with Mexico in recent years, the result of drug trafficking organizations (DTOs) that are competing for control of key smuggling corridors into the U.S. During FY 2006 and 2007, BATFE assigned approximately 100 special agents and 25 investigative officers to a new initiative known as "Project Gunrunner." The intent of the program was to disrupt the illegal flow of guns from the U.S. into Mexico. In FY 2007, BATFE agents in the program investigated 187 firearms trafficking cases and recommended 465 defendants for prosecution.[50]

ATF has seized thousands of weapons from drug runners in the past few years. Of the weapons seized between 2005-2007, it was discovered that the most frequently used weapons by drug traffickers include 9mm pistols, .38 Super pistols, 5.7mm pistols, .45-caliber pistols, AR-15 type rifles; and AK-47 type rifles.[51]

Criminal Investigative Analysis

Beginning in the mid-1980s, the BATFE has placed special agent/criminal profilers with the FBI's National Center for the Analysis of Violent Crime, or NCAVC. The Center provides investigative support, research, and training to law enforcement agencies nationally and overseas. The Center provides the BATFE with a behavioral profiler who helps to analyze violent crimes, including bombings and arsons. They examine crime-scene behavior, victim statements, witnesses, and suspects. They also rely on analyses of the personalities of known offenders. A geographic profiler analyzes the locations of any crimes that may be connected to the one being investigated and attempts to predict the most likely location where an offender would live. NCAVC personnel often publish articles as a means to educate law enforcement officers on these areas.[52]

Violent Crime and Gangs

In recent years, the BATFE has dedicated resources to investigating the criminal activities of violent street gangs, which often includes gun-related violence and trafficking.[53] BATFE instituted Project Safe Neighborhoods (PSN) as a way for BATFE agents to investigate violent firearms offenders, who often turn out to be gang members. As part of Project Safe Neighborhoods, BATFE works with attorneys from the Department of Justice, other federal law enforcement agencies, and state, local, and tribal authorities to investigate and prosecute offenders who carry out armed violent crimes.

Gang members are tracked through the National Gang Targeting, Enforcement, and Coordination Center (GangTECC). This is a new national anti-gang task force located in the Department of Justice that is geared toward dismantling the most violent gangs in the U.S. The Center helps law enforcement agencies exchange strategies and information about gang membership and activities more easily. The Center also helps to initiate and coordinate gang-related investigations and possible prosecutions. In doing so, they are helping law enforcement have a better understanding of the national gang problem. With that, more appropriate countermeasures can be suggested.

Conclusion

It is clear that the agents from the Bureau of Alcohol, Tobacco, Firearms, and Explosives have been granted the responsibilities and powers to investigate those who choose to break the laws on alcohol, tobacco products, weapons, and explosives. Like all other law enforcement groups, they work diligently to keep our neighborhoods safe from those who choose to break these laws.

Key Terms

Law Enforcement Information
Sharing Program
Volstead Act/Prohibition
Eighteenth Amendment
Prohibition Unit
Alcohol Tax Unit
National Firearms Act
Gun Control Act of 1968
Order Number 221
Rex D. Davis
National Response Team
Ruby Ridge
Fast and Furious
special agents
investigators
Student Temporary Employment
Program
Office of International Affairs

B. Todd Jones
Safe Explosives Act
accelerant and explosive detection
canines
certified explosives specialists
certified fire investigators
explosives enforcement officers
International Response Team
U.S. Bomb Data Center
Bomb Arson Tracking System
Terrorist Explosives Device
Analytical Center
National Integrated Ballistics
Information Center
Violent Crime Impact Team
Project Gunrunner
National Gang Targeting, Enforce-
ment, and Coordination Center

Review Questions

1. What are the primary responsibilities of the BATFE?

2. Describe the history of the BATFE.

3. How did Prohibition affect the BATFE?

4. Explain how the agency became responsible for enforcing federal gun laws.

5. What was the role of the BATFE in the explosions at the World Trade Center in 1993 and the Alfred P. Murrah Federal Building in 1995?

6. What are some controversies surrounding BATFE?

7. What are the qualifications to be hired as a special agent in BATFE?

8. Describe the budgets for BATFE.

9. How is BATFE organized?

10. What techniques do BATFE agents use to regulate guns and firearms?

Endnotes

1. Bureau of Alcohol, Tobacco, Firearms, and Explosives: Strategic Plan—Fiscal Years 2010-2016, available at http://www.atf.gov/publications/general/strategic-plan/index.html.

2. Krouse, William J. "The Bureau of Alcohol, Tobacco, Firearms and Explosives (ATF): Budget and Operations." Washington, D.C.: Congressional Research Service, August 6, 2009, available at http://fas.org/sgp/crs/misc/R41206.pdf.

3. Krouse, "The Bureau of Alcohol, Tobacco, Firearms and Explosives (ATF): Budget and Operations."

4. Bureau of Alcohol, Tobacco, Firearms and Explosives: Mission, Vision and Values; available at http://www.atf.gov/about/mission/.

5. Bumgarner, Jeffrey B. (2006). *Federal Agents: The Growth of Federal Law Enforcement in America*. Westport, CT: Praeger, p. 84.

6. Moore, James. (2001). *Very Special Agents: The Inside Story of America's Most Controversial Law Enforcement Agency — The Bureau of Alcohol, Tobacco, and Firearms*. Champaign, IL: University of Illinois Press; Vizzard, William J. (1997). *In the Cross Fire: A Political History of the Bureau of Alcohol, Tobacco and Firearms*. Boulder, CO: Lynne Rienner Publishers.

7. Bureau of Alcohol, Tobacco, Firearms, & Explosives. (2012). History of the ATF. Available online at http://www.atf.gov/; Kurian, George T. (1998). *A Historical Guide to the U.S. Government*. New York: Oxford University Press.

8. Kurian, *A Historical Guide*, p. 39.

9. Kurian, *A Historical Guide*.

10. Burns, Ken & Lynn Novick. (2011). *Prohibition*. Washington, D.C.: PBS.

11. Bureau of Alcohol, Tobacco, Firearms, & Explosives, History of the ATF; Kurian, *A Historical Guide*.

12. Kurian, *A Historical Guide*.

13. Burroughs, Bryan. (2009). *Public Enemies: America's Greatest Crime Wave and the Birth of the FBI, 1933-34*. New York: Penguin.

14. Bureau of Alcohol, Tobacco, Firearms, & Explosives. (2012). History of the National Firearms Act. Available online at http://www.atf.gov/firearms/nfa/.

15. Internal Revenue Service. (2012). Brief History of IRS. Available online at http://www.irs.gov/uac/Brief-History-of-IRS.

16. Bureau of Alcohol, Tobacco, Firearms, & Explosives, History of the National Firearms Act; Ludwig, Jens & Philip J. Cook. (2003). *Evaluating Gun Policy: Effects on Crime and Violence*. Washington, D.C.: Brookings Institution Press.

17. Larson, Erik. (1994). *Lethal Passage*. New York: Crown Publishers, p. 135.

18. Bureau of Alcohol, Tobacco, Firearms & Explosives. (2008). World Trade Center Terrorist Bombing Investigation 15th Anniversary — February 26, 1993. Available online at http://www.atf.gov/press/releases/2008/02/022708-atf-wtc-bombing-investigation-anniversary.html.

19. See, for instance, the *Time Magazine* article Emery, Theo. (2009). "It's Official: The ATF and FBI Don't Get Along." *Time*. Available online at http://www.time.com/time/nation/article/0,8599,1932091,00.html.

20. Bureau of Alcohol, Tobacco, Firearms, & Explosives, ATF Homepage; Krouse, William J. (2011). *The Bureau of Alcohol, Tobacco, Firearms, and Explosives (ATF): Budget and Operations for FY 2011*. Washington, D.C.: Congressional Research Service.

21. Krouse, *The Bureau of Alcohol, Tobacco, Firearms, and Explosives (ATF): Budget and Operations for FY 2011*, p. 1.

22. Krouse, *The Bureau of Alcohol, Tobacco, Firearms, and Explosives (ATF): Budget and Operations for FY 2011*, pp. 1-2.

23. Krouse, *The Bureau of Alcohol, Tobacco, Firearms, and Explosives (ATF): Budget and Operations for FY 2011*, p. 2.

24. Moore, *Very Special Agents*; Vizzard, *In the Cross Fire*.

25. Bumgarner, *Federal Agents*, p. 84.

26. Bureau of Alcohol, Tobacco, Firearms and Explosives: Special Agents, available at http://www.atf.gov/content/Careers/careers-at-ATF/special-agent.

27. Bureau of Alcohol, Tobacco, Firearms and Explosives: Industry Operations Investigators, available at http://www.atf.gov/content/Careers/careers-at-ATF/industry-operations-investigator.

28. Bureau of Alcohol, Tobacco, Firearms and Explosives: Professional/Technical, available at http://www.atf.gov/content/Careers/careers-at-ATF/professional-and-technical.

29. Bureau of Alcohol, Tobacco, Firearms and Explosives: Internships, available at http://www.atf.gov/content/Careers/careers-at-ATF/internships.

30. Bureau of Alcohol, Tobacco, Firearms and Explosives: Internships, available at http://www.atf.gov/content/Careers/careers-at-ATF/internships.

31. Bureau of Alcohol, Tobacco, Firearms and Explosives, Fact Sheet: Facts and Figures (FY 2011), available at http://www.atf.gov/publications/factsheets/factsheet-staffing-and-budget.html.

32. ATF—Bureau of Alcohol, Tobacco, Firearms and Explosives—International Offices, available at http://www.atf.gov/content/international-offices.

33. ATF—Bureau of Alcohol, Tobacco, Firearms and Explosives. (2012). ATF Acting Director B. Todd Jones. Available at http://www.atf.gov/content/About/ATF-executive-staff.

34. Krouse, "The Bureau of Alcohol, Tobacco, Firearms and Explosives (ATF): Budget and Operations."

35. "ATF—Bureau of Alcohol, Tobacco, Firearms and Explosives—Alcohol and Tobacco Diversion/Smuggling," available at http://www.atf.gov/content/alcohol-and-tobacco.

36. Krouse, "The Bureau of Alcohol, Tobacco, Firearms and Explosives (ATF): Budget and Operations."

37. ATF—Bureau of Alcohol, Tobacco, Firearms and Explosives—Arson and Explosives Enforcement, available at http://www.atf.gov/content/Arson/arson-explosives-enforcement; Krouse, "The Bureau of Alcohol, Tobacco, Firearms and Explosives (ATF): Budget and Operations."

38. ATF—Bureau of Alcohol, Tobacco, Firearms and Explosives—Accelerant and Explosives Detection Canines, available at http://www.atf.gov/content/Explosives/explosives-enforcement/accelerant-and-explosives-detection-canines.

39. ATF—Bureau of Alcohol, Tobacco, Firearms and Explosives—Certified Explosives Specialists, available at http://www.atf.gov/content/Explosives/explosives-enforcement/certified-explosives-specialists.

40. ATF—Bureau of Alcohol, Tobacco, Firearms and Explosives—Certified Fire Investigators, available at http://www.atf.gov/publications/factsheets/factsheet-certified-fire-investigators.html.

41. ATF—Bureau of Alcohol, Tobacco, Firearms and Explosives—Explosives Enforcement Officers, available at http://www.atf.gov/content/Explosives/explosives-enforcement/explosives-enforcement-officers.

42. ATF—Bureau of Alcohol, Tobacco, Firearms and Explosives—International Response Team, available at http://www.atf.gov/content/Explosives/explosives-enforcement/international-response-team.

43. ATF—Bureau of Alcohol, Tobacco, Firearms and Explosives—National Response Team, available at http://www.atf.gov/content/Explosives/explosives-enforcement/national-response-team.

44. ATF—Bureau of Alcohol, Tobacco, Firearms and Explosives—U.S Bomb Data Center, available at http://www.atf.gov/content/Explosives/explosives-enforcement/US-bomb-data-center/US-bomb-data-center-FAQs.

45. ATF—Bureau of Alcohol, Tobacco, Firearms and Explosives—BATS, available at http://www.atf.gov/content/bomb-arson-tracking-system-bats.

46. ATF—Bureau of Alcohol, Tobacco, Firearms and Explosives—Firearms Enforcement, available at http://www.atf.gov/content/Firearms/firearms-enforcement.

47. Krouse, "The Bureau of Alcohol, Tobacco, Firearms and Explosives (ATF): Budget and Operations."

48. Krouse, "The Bureau of Alcohol, Tobacco, Firearms and Explosives (ATF): Budget and Operations."

49. Krouse, "The Bureau of Alcohol, Tobacco, Firearms and Explosives (ATF): Budget and Operations."

50. Krouse, "The Bureau of Alcohol, Tobacco, Firearms and Explosives (ATF): Budget and Operations."

51. Embassy of the United States, Mexico. "Borders and Law Enforcement: Project Gunrunner." Available at http://www.usembassy-mexico.gov/eng/texts/et080116eTrace.html.

52. ATF—Bureau of Alcohol, Tobacco, Firearms and Explosives—Criminal Investigative Analysis, available at http://www.atf.gov/explosives/programs/crimina-investigative-analysist/.

53. Krouse, "The Bureau of Alcohol, Tobacco, Firearms and Explosives (ATF): Budget and Operations."

3

U.S. Postal Inspection Service

The U.S. Postal Inspection Service is one of the oldest federal law enforcement agencies in the nation. Founded by Benjamin Franklin, the Postal Inspection Service is the enforcement arm of the U.S. Postal Service. Agents help to prevent criminals from attacking the postal system, misusing it for fraud, or to otherwise threaten the American public.[1]

Their mission is threefold. First, they support and protect the U.S. Postal Service, including its infrastructure, its employees, and its customers. Second, they enforce federal laws that protect the nation's mail system from illegal or dangerous use. Finally, agents ensure the public's trust in the mail so that customers feel safe in sending correspondence and messages through the postal system.[2] As such, the jurisdiction of the Postal Inspection Service covers any offenses that may adversely affect the mail, the postal system, or its employees.[3]

According to the Postal Inspection Service, their strategic plan includes four components, which are to protect employees, facilities, infrastructure, customers, and the U.S. mail; to prevent criminal attacks to the Postal Service and the U.S. mail by improving intelligence gathering and implementing enhanced security strategies; to enforce criminal laws, civil statutes, and postal policies to preserve public trust in the U.S. Postal Service, its brand, and the U.S. mail; and to prepare the organization by continuously developing its workforce, deploying emerging technologies, standardizing organizational processes, and improving communications.[4]

45

The agency oversees the safety of over 700,000 Postal Service employees and billions of pieces of mail that are transported through the air, land, rail, and sea throughout the world each year. Postal inspectors take the lead and sometimes assist in joint federal and state investigations. In recent years, postal inspectors have investigated cases that involved ricin, anthrax, and other toxic substances sent through the mail.

According to 39 USC §204, the chief postal inspector shall be appointed by, and serve at the pleasure of, the postmaster general. Moreover, the Postal Service, according to 39 U.S.C. §404, is to investigate postal offenses and civil matters relating to the Postal Service and to offer and pay rewards for information and services in connection with violation of the postal laws. The specific responsibilities of the postal inspectors are found in 18 U.S.C. §3061, as shown in Figure 3.1.

Figure 3.1: Statutory Authority of U.S. Postal Inspectors

(a) Subject to subsection (b) of this section, Postal Inspectors and other agents of the United States Postal Service designated by the Board of Governors to investigate criminal matters related to the Postal Service and the mails may—

(1) serve warrants and subpoenas issued under the authority of the United States;

(2) make arrests without warrant for offenses against the United States committed in their presence;

(3) make arrests without warrant for felonies cognizable under the laws of the United States if they have reasonable grounds to believe that the person to be arrested has committed or is committing such a felony;

(4) carry firearms; and

(5) make seizures of property as provided by law.

(b) The powers granted by subsection (a) of this section shall be exercised only—

(1) in the enforcement of laws regarding property in the custody of the Postal Service, property of the Postal Service, the use of the mails, and other postal offenses; and

(2) to the extent authorized by the Attorney General pursuant to agreement between the Attorney General and the Postal Service, in the enforcement of other laws of the United States, if the Attorney General determines that violations of such laws have a detrimental effect upon the operations of the Postal Service.

(c)

(1) The Postal Service may employ police officers for duty in connection with the protection of property owned or occupied by the Postal Service or under the charge and control of the Postal Service, and persons on that property, including duty in areas outside the property to the extent necessary to protect the property and persons on the property.

(2) With respect to such property, such officers shall have the power to—

(A) enforce Federal laws and regulations for the protection of persons and property;

(B) carry firearms; and

(C) make arrests without a warrant for any offense against the United States committed in the presence of the officer or for any felony cognizable under the laws of the United States if the officer has reasonable grounds to believe that the person to be arrested has committed or is committing a felony.

(3) With respect to such property, such officers may have, to such extent as the Postal Service may by regulations prescribe, the power to—

(A) serve warrants and subpoenas issued under the authority of the United States; and

(B) conduct investigations, on and off the property in question, of offenses that may have been committed against property owned or occupied by the Postal Service or persons on the property.

(4)

(A) As to such property, the Postmaster General may prescribe regulations necessary for the protection and administration of property owned or occupied by the Postal Service and persons on the property. The regulations may include reasonable penalties, within the limits prescribed in subparagraph (B), for violations of the regulations. The regulations shall be posted and remain posted in a conspicuous place on the property.

(B) A person violating a regulation prescribed under this subsection shall be fined under this title, imprisoned for not more than 30 days, or both.

History

The U.S. Postal Inspection Service is often considered the oldest of the federal law enforcement agencies because of the fact that it dates back to the origins of the United States Post Office during the colonial era. In 1737, Benjamin Franklin was appointed as one of two deputy postmasters general and was given the task of "regulating the several post offices and bringing the postmasters to account."[5] He was instrumental in establishing the postal routes, determining how the system would run, and establishing the postage fees based on the size and distance an item was to be delivered. When America gained its independence, Benjamin Franklin remained integrally involved in the progress and development of the postal system.

In 1772, Postmaster Benjamin Franklin created the position of "surveyor" because he could no longer single-handedly regulate and audit post offices. These same surveyors would become instrumental in the American Revolutionary War, for they were key to keeping the lines of communication open.

On July 26, 1775, the Second Continental Congress created the United States Post Office in Philadelphia, Pennsylvania, under the guidance of Benjamin Franklin.[6] William Goddard was named the first surveyor of the reestablished United States Postal Service. Goddard, like Franklin, had worked as a printer and publisher in Rhode Island before joining Franklin in Philadelphia, where he started a pro-independence newspaper. When the U.S. Post Office was officially created, Franklin held the position of postmaster for one year and appointed Goddard as the first surveyor.

In 1789, after the ratification of the new United States Constitution, Congress implemented its right under Article One, Section 8, "to establish Post Offices and post Roads." The U.S. Post Office at that time already had 75 post offices and over 2,000 miles of posted roads. The number of personnel at the time consisted of the postmaster general, an inspector of dead letters, a couple of surveyors, and several dozen post riders. Congress converted all of this into the Office of Postmaster General on a temporary basis and then made it a permanently established agency in the year 1792. The position of surveyor continued with the reorganization, and they were given more authority for investigating crimes against the U.S. mail, especially under the statute that made it a crime punishable by death to steal the mail.

The U.S. Post Office grew very little during the rest of the 1790s, but when Thomas Jefferson became president of the United States, closer attention was paid to its importance. One major change occurred in 1801, when the title of surveyor was changed to that of "special agent." This was one more change in a slow evolution that would firmly establish the United States Postal Inspection Service in the future.

When the British invaded the United States of America in 1812, once again the U.S. Postal special agents played a role in America's defense. As a result of their constant movement along posted roads, they were able to provide intelligence regarding the movements of the British fleet along the Potomac River.

In 1829, the special agents were to be reorganized under a newly formed organization within the United States Post Office.[7] Preston S. Loughborough, who was a framer of Kentucky's first constitution, became the first chief postal inspector. He worked to establish the dynamics of the new organization by creating the Office of Instruction and Mail Depredation, which would serve as the investigative branch of the U.S. Post Office. While the director was named the chief postal inspector, the investigators retained the title of special agents.

The Office of Instruction and Mail Depredation slowly grew during the next two decades, and by 1853, the number of special agents stood on 18. They were assigned to specific regions of the United States, as well as the territories, and their duties include reporting on the conditions of steamboats, stagecoaches, railroads, and horses that were used to transport the mail. They also visited mail distribution offices and examined postal accounts as auditors.

When the American Civil War began in 1861, the special agents once again were called to assist the country in wartime.[8] As agents of the United States government, they were pulled from southern states that had seceded from the Union, and they were then placed in various northern states in order to maintain military post offices as well as military routes during the war. In the wake of the war, the chief postal inspector and his special agents were tasked with the job of returning to the southern states in order to reestablish post offices and routes during Reconstruction. This proved to be a difficult task, for while many of the cases the special agents became involved with were some form of fraud committed against the federal government, many of the issues they dealt with were simply frauds being committed by way of the United States mail. Because these crimes presented no direct injury to the United States government, the special agents had no jurisdiction. Fraud was wide-spread in the South during the late 1860s, and there wasn't anything they could do.

Congress began debating this very topic in the early 1870s, as to whether or not the U.S. government could regulate the postal system based on how the post system was used. If someone used the government's postal system for a crime, it was reasoned that they should be punishable under federal law. In 1872, as part of a larger reorganization effort regarding the post office, the Mail Fraud Act was passed. It was now a crime to mail material that was intended to carry out "any scheme or artifice to defraud."[9] This meant that the special agents of the Office of Instructions and Mail Depredation now had concurrent jurisdiction with the states to investigate and arrest those who would use the U.S. mail to commit fraud.

The following year, in 1873, there was a movement to further the federal reach of the special agents by making it illegal to use the postal system for the delivery of obscene material. One man was at the forefront of this movement and his name was Anthony Comstock.[10] Comstock was born in New Canaan, Connecticut on March 7, 1844. At the age of 19 he enlisted in the Union Army and fought with Company H, 17th Connecticut Infantry until the war's end. Moving to New York City, he found a job as a businessman, but he was appalled at the level of vice he found in the city. He joined the Young Men's Christian Association and advocated for greater public morality. Frustrated with the slow movement of the association but gaining a strong following, he decided to create his own organization, the New York Society for the Suppression of Vice. The NYSSV was an organization dedicated to monitoring public morality and ensuring that laws supporting morality were enforced or, where the law was seen as lacking, support their creation. Typically, the organization would monitor the local newsstands to ensure they were not selling anything that would violate the current obscenity laws. In other cases, Comstock and his organization pushed for new obscenity laws.

Comstock envisioned laws written largely against obscenity, so he knew he had to try and influence the United States Congress, not just the New York legislature. Recognizing that the Mail Fraud Act would allow the federal government to regulate a crime committed through the postal system, in this case fraud, Comstock began his politics to make the use of this same regulation to control another crime using the postal system—obscenity. The same year that he formed his New York Society for the Suppression of Vice, 1873, he also managed to influence Congress to pass a law that made it illegal to deliver or transport "obscene, lewd, and or lascivious material," including any literature or device used for the purposes of birth control. The federal law was named the Comstock Act, and it amended the Post Office Act. As 24 states also passed similar laws, these laws became collectively known as the *Comstock Laws*.

Comstock, a firm advocate of the laws that now bore his name, was ever dissatisfied with the lack of enforcement, or at least the lack of enforcement he perceived to be taking place. So, he decided to take the law into his own hands, literally. He used his New York political connections and managed to land a position with the New York Post Office as a special agent. Comstock was now enforcing the laws he helped to create. Comstock relished the position, for he was able to inspect the mail for any type of pornography, birth control devices, abortion devices, or related literature; seize it, obtain warrants, and arrest the individuals who sent the material through the U.S. mail. He did so for the next 40 years, and in that time he would see numerous challenges to the laws he helped to create.

In 1880, new issues related to mail fraud would arise, and more changes to the Post Office Act would be made by the U.S. Congress.[11] In the post-Civil War era, America witnessed a rise in the use of confidence games to swindle people out of their money—so-called confidence games because the swindler typically found some means to gain the confidence of the individual they were swindling before actually taking their money. These scams were also known in slang terms as "green goods scams" for their ability to get the green goods—money. As a number of these types of scams and bogus offers were being conducted through the U.S. mail, Congress passed an amendment to the Mail Fraud Statue to include these types of crimes. Along with the new law, the names of those enforcing the laws would also be changed by Congress. The U.S. Post Office was authorized to change the name of their special agents to that of post office inspectors. This was done to bring them more in line with the title given to the director of the postal inspectors—the chief postal inspector.

The following year, the post office inspectors found themselves investigating the infamous Billy the Kid. Inspector Robert Cameron wrote to Col. D.B. Parker, chief postal inspector of the Post Office Department, on January 11, 1881:

> On my recent trip to New Mexico, I stopped at Santa Fe to learn as much as possible in regard to the mail robbers who had recently been arrested and their doings . . . William Bonney (alias, the Kid) is held for murder. He is supposed to have killed some 11 men, but that is an exageration [sic]; four or five would be quite enough. He is about 21 or 23 years of age, born in New York City, and a graduate of the streets. I think his principle [sic] business has been stealing cattle and raiding in Old Mexico, and there robbing stores and valuables from wealthy ranchmen. He has probably done something in the line of stage robbing, but refuses to say anything about it, denying all knowledge of the business.[12]

Although the post office inspectors did not bring Billy the Kid to justice, they were very active protecting the mail and investigating mail fraud in the farthest reaches of the American West—so much so, they ended up the derision of one editorial in the *Tombstone Epitaph*, located near the famous gunfight at the OK Corral. In the editorial, it noted: "A typical Post Office Inspector is a man past middle age—spare, wrinkled, intelligent, cold, passive, noncommittal, with eyes like a codfish, polite in contact but, at the time, nonresponsive; calm, and as damnably composed as a concrete post or a plaster of Paris case; a petrification with a beard of feldspar and without charm or the friendly germ; minus passion or a sense of humor. Happily, they never reproduce and all of them finally go to hell."[13] Apparently they were good at their job, hence the derision of those on the other side of the law.

As the U.S. post office inspectors entered the twentieth century, new challenges would face them over the next 100 years, and the risks and dangers of the job only seemed to increase. Although they had gone the first hundred years with no one killed in the line of duty, in the second hundred they were not so fortunate. On September 23, 1909, the service lost its first post office inspector—Charles Fitzgerald. According to the record, Post Office Inspector Fitzgerald "was shot and killed in Clinton, Mississippi, by a deputy post master whose post office had a shortage of funds. The post master asked Inspector Fitzgerald not to report the shortage and then shot him in the side when he refused. The suspect was convicted of Inspector Fitzgerald's murder and sentenced to life in prison."[14] Since then, another 12 postal inspectors have been killed in the line of duty with the last one, Robert F. Jones, dying on July 14, 2000, in a training accident.[15]

As the post office inspectors moved into the twentieth century, they still found vestiges of the nineteenth century a part of their investigations. In fact, it is noted that the U.S. postal inspectors investigated the last stagecoach robbery and the last great train robbery.[16] On December 5, 1916, Fred M. Searcy was driving the mail stage (technically not a stagecoach as it was a mail wagon pulled by two horses) when he was robbed and murdered. The perpetrator, Ben Kuhl, was apprehended within five days of the crime and a palm print was used to help convict him to a lengthy sentence in prison; he was not released until 1945.[17] In the case of the train robbery, three brothers, the D'Autremont brothers, having heard a particular train was hauling a half-million dollars in gold, decided to rob the Southern Pacific train on October 11, 1926. Using dynamite, they blew the mail car apart and ultimately killed three railroad employees and a mail clerk. There were no riches in gold onboard the train and the brothers fled sparking a manhunt for the murderers that would span three and one-half years before they were caught, tried, and sentenced to prison for life.[18]

The seriousness of the twentieth century, however, was revealed further in what began to occur in the early 1920s. In a period of two years—from 1920 to 1921—36 major mail robberies were committed, with the thefts totaling more than $6 million.[19] Postmaster General Will H. Hays issued an order directing that some 50,000 guns and 2 million rounds of ammunition be distributed and also offered a maximum reward of $5,000 for mail robbers—*dead or alive!* Postal inspectors recovered more than half of the stolen amount, arrested 123 people and, with the exception of a few who were discharged or acquitted, helped ensure that the remainder served long penitentiary terms. In the detection and apprehension of the bandits, postal inspectors served notice to the underworld that they would *never* give up if the mail was tampered with and, whether it took a week or a year, swift and sure justice would await criminals in the federal courts.

The U.S. post office inspectors played a role in bringing another famous outlaw, Alvin Karpis, to justice. According to the *Annual Report of the Postmaster General* for the fiscal year ending June 30, 1936:

> On the afternoon of Nov. 7, 1935—in a spectacular machine-gun holdup of an Erie Railroad mail train at Garrettsville, OH, Karpis and four other men stole Registered Mail containing $34,000 in currency and $11,650 in bonds. Karpis was found by Post Office Inspectors to have been the leader of the bandits . . .

In March 1936 . . . Inspectors and a member of the Kansas State police apprehended one of the gang. Several weeks later, Karpis and two more of the gang
were arrested . . . Inspectors have identified . . . the fifth bandit, and they hope
to take him into custody in the near future."[20]

The post office inspectors were called upon, over the following decades,
to take on additional duties that they appeared well equipped to handle. When
the nation's gold reserves were transferred from New York City to Fort Knox,
Kentucky, the U.S. post office inspectors were charged with guarding the ship-
ment. Later, in 1958, when the Hope Diamond was shipped by U.S. mail from
the estate of Evalyn Walsh McLean to the Smithsonian in Washington, D.C., it was
the postal inspectors who guarded it along the mail route. In addition, during
World War II, the post office inspectors were called upon to organize and protect
the delivery of the U.S. mail to American soldiers around the world fighting on
the front lines.

A number of organizational reforms occurred after World War II. In 1947,
when the Chief Postal Inspector Jess M. Donaldson was appointed as the postmaster general, changes to better his former organization were soon implemented.
In 1954, one minor change was made to their titles. Instead of post office inspectors, their title was changed to postal inspectors, in order to deemphasize their
role at post office facilities and recognize their responsibilities throughout the
entire postal system. While most of the changes made were minor and more sub-
tle, the organizational changes that occurred from 1970 to 1971 had a profound
impact on the future of the U.S. postal inspectors.

In 1970, Congress passed the Postal Reorganization Act of 1970, and its provisions went into effect in 1971. The Bureau of the Chief Postal Inspector became
the United States Postal Inspection Service, the name it bears today. A whole new
branch of the Postal Inspection Service was added—the U.S. Postal Police Force.
While the U.S. postal inspectors had long been considered the "silent investigators,"[21] it was determined that a more highly visible deterrent was needed at
some of the high-risk post offices and facilities found in major cities across the
United States. Thus, a uniformed arm of the U.S. Postal Inspection Service was
created and these officers became known as postal police officers.[22] In addition,
the Reorganization Act allowed for women to be hired as U.S. postal inspectors,
and on September 25, 1971, Janene Gordon was appointed as the first female
postal inspector.[23]

Over the following three decades, the U.S. postal inspectors were given more
authority to investigate child pornography being sent through the U.S. mail; they
investigated widespread white-collar crime on Wall Street that included insider
trading and check-kiting operations; and they assisted in the investigation that
led to the arrest of the Unabomber, Ted Kaczynski. It was, however, in the wake
of the 9/11 terrorist attacks that the U.S. Postal Inspection Service would face its
greatest challenge, and that was investigating the anthrax attacks. Occurring one
week after the 9/11 attack, letters containing anthrax spores were mailed to the
offices of members of the U.S. Senate and the media. Eventually the anthrax killed
5 people, including 2 postal employees, and made another 17 sick. Because the
U.S. mail was used for these attacks, the U.S. Postal Inspection Service played a

major role in the investigation; however, because it was considered a terror-ist attack, the Federal Bureau of Investigation was the lead investigative agency. Although suspects were generated, no one was ever brought to justice for the anthrax attacks.[24]

Who Gets Hired

There are approximately 4,000 employees in the Postal Inspection Service; 1,200 of them are criminal investigators. There is also an armed uniformed division, which employs approximately 1,000 personnel, forensic laboratories, and a com-munications system. There are also approximately 1,000 technical and adminis-trative support personnel. New recruits attend a training program through the USPIS Training Academy (the Career Development Unit) in Potomac, Maryland.

Budgets

Unlike the other federal law enforcement agencies featured in this book, the U.S. Postal Inspection Service is unique because of the relationship between the U.S. government and the U.S. Postal Service. The USPS is an independent agency of the United States government, which means, technically, it receives no budge-tary assistance from the federal government. The federal government can regu-late the industry, and it will often mandate how funds raised from the cost of stamps, shipping, etc. are distributed (e.g., pensions, health care benefits, etc.), but because they are independent they do not have to request or report their annual budget to Congress. As a result, there is limited budget data for the U.S. Post Office, and what budget data does exist is unclear in regard to the annual budget for the U.S. Postal Inspection Service.

Organization

There are approximately 1,500 postal inspectors stationed throughout the United States and overseas. They are responsible for enforcing over 200 federal laws related to possible crimes of fraud or misuse of the U.S. mail and postal system.[25]

The Postal Police Force was created in the Postal Reorganization Act of 1970. This law created a uniformed police force of approximately 650 officers that patrol in some postal facilities in major metropolitan areas throughout the coun-try. These uniformed officers provide a visible deterrent to criminal acts and also are able to respond quickly to emergencies that may occur, such as disturbances, assaults, or thefts, especially if they seem to threaten the safety of the employees or customers. They also provide perimeter security for the facilities, escort valu-able mail shipments, and carry out other protective functions. The officers have the power to make arrests, if needed.

Plain clothes investigators, called postal inspectors, enforce laws related to the mail or employees, such as assaults, bombs, counterfeit stamps, or delay of the mail, among others.[26] These are federal law enforcement officers who carry firearms, make arrests, serve search warrants, and serve subpoenas. The inspectors work closely with other law enforcement agencies to investigate cases and with U.S. attorneys and local prosecutors when needed to prepare cases for court.

The Postal Inspection Service also operates a state-of-the-art forensic crime laboratory that houses forensic scientists and other technical specialists who assist inspectors to analyze evidence needed to identify a suspect charged with wrongdoing. They can also provide expert testimony as needed in any cases brought to trial.[27] Working in the laboratory are forensic scientists and technical specialists who are trained to examine both physical and digital evidence. Their mission is to provide both scientific and technical expertise for the investigations conducted by the USPIS. While the main office is housed in Dulles, Virginia, there are also many satellite offices in locations around the United States that primarily investigate computer forensics. The investigators in the laboratory have an integral role in identifying, apprehending, prosecuting, and convicting those individuals who may be responsible for committing offenses against the postal service.

The Laboratory Services are divided into four units. The first, the Questioned Documents Unit, provides technical assistance to investigators who need documents authenticated. The Fingerprint Unit looks for latent prints on documents to determine who has handled evidence. They sometimes testify in court as to what they found. The personnel in the third unit, the Physical Sciences Unit, conduct chemical analyses on documents or even examine bomb debris or other trace evidence from crime scenes. Experts in the Chemistry Section often test for controlled substances such as cocaine, heroin, LSD, amphetamines, or marijuana. Finally, experts in the Digital Evidence Unit are responsible for the collection, preservation, and examination of computer digital evidence that is related to investigations.[28]

Leader

Guy Cottrell was appointed as the 38th chief postal inspector of the U.S. Postal Inspection Service in July 2010. Chief Cottrell oversees all operations of the Postal Inspection Service, including National Headquarters offices, 18 field divisions, 2 service centers, and the National Forensic Laboratory. The offices are staffed by more than 1,400 postal inspectors, about 700 postal police officers, and approximately 600 support personnel. Chief Cottrell also serves as chairman of the Universal Postal Union's Postal Security Group.

Prior to his appointment, Chief Cottrell served as deputy chief inspector at National Headquarters, where he oversaw all national security programs for the Postal Service. As a native of West Virginia who grew up in New Orleans, Cottrell joined the Postal Service in 1987 when he became a letter carrier there. In 1991, Chief Cottrell became a postal inspector at the New Orleans Division, where he investigated internal and external mail theft throughout Louisiana and southern Mississippi.

Since that time, Chief Cottrell has held a number of management positions in major metropolitan areas, including his appointment as inspector in charge of the Postal Inspection Service's Washington field office during the anthrax investigation.

In 2008, Chief Cottrell served as inspector in charge of the Security & Crime Prevention and Communications Group, where he guided the Postal Inspection Service toward a risk- and management-analysis platform, streamlined security-related programs, and implemented numerous cost-effective and innovative solutions. His group produced security and crime prevention publications and videos and overhauled the Postal Inspection Service's external Web site.

Chief Cottrell holds a Bachelor's degree in psychology from the University of New Orleans.

What They Do

The USPIS has many functions when it comes to protecting the U.S. mail service and those who use it. Table 3.1 provides information on their major roles and the number of arrests and convictions for offenses related to them.

Table 3.1   **Investigative Categories for USPIS, FY 2012**

	Arrests and Indictments	Convictions
Mail theft by nonemployees and contractors	3,158	2,321
Mailings of controlled substances	2,299	1,169
Mail fraud	1,406	738
Money laundering	240	174
Assaults and threats	235	160
Child exploitation, mailing of obscene matter, and sexually oriented advertisements	153	86
Burglary	85	67
Robbery	69	55
Revenue fraud	66	43
Non-mailable, restricted, and perishable matter	66	42
Vandalism and arson	35	32
Suspicious substances	19	15
Suspicious items	14	17

Source: "Behind the Badge: U.S. Postal Inspection Service Annual Report, FY 2012," available at https://postalinspectors.uspis.gov/radDocs/pubs/AnnualReport%20FY%202012.pdf.

USPIS activities have been categorized into seven functions. The first is to investigate fraud committed through the mail. Federal law makes it illegal to use the mail system to commit fraud against consumers, businesses, or government. This can include mail fraud, bank fraud, identity theft, credit card fraud, wire fraud, or Internet computer fraud. Mail fraud is often a component in white collar crimes such as some Ponzi schemes, 419 frauds, or any other crimes in which the mail system is used to commit the fraud.

If the mail system is used as part of any crime, it is considered to be mail fraud. Mail fraud schemes can include franchise fraud (where criminals describe "investment" opportunities that seem so good that inexperienced victims agree to participate)[29] and phony job opportunities with guaranteed job placement for those with little or no previous job experience or special skills or above average wages.[30] Pyramid schemes are also a form of mail fraud,[31] as are schemes to mail letters with less postage than required.[32] Financial fraud includes "900" telephone number fraud,[33] advance-fee loan schemes,[34] charity fraud,[35] credit card fraud,[36] schemes that charge money for services that the government provides for free,[37] and others. Some fraud relates to illegal sweepstakes and lotteries, such as chain letters.[38] Another example is the free-prize scheme in which a person is notified by mail that he has won a free prize, which will be sent when the shipping and handling fees are sent.[39]

As a way to address new financial crime schemes such as money laundering, online fraud, and bank fraud, the USPIS created the Financial Industry Mail Security Initiative (FIMSI). This agency includes not only members from USPIS but also security and retail managers, prosecutors, and representatives from the mailing industry. To help in this project, 17 Financial Crimes Task Forces were established throughout the country to gather information, make arrests, and execute search warrants. They also created two Identity Theft Economic Crimes Task Forces.[40]

The second function of the USPIS is performed by the External Crime and Violent Crime Teams, who investigate the possible theft of U.S. mail by non-employees, assaults of any postal employees, and the possible theft of property belonging to the postal system or postal personnel. The purpose of this function is to help to maintain the public's trust in the mail system.

The third function of the United States Postal Inspection Service is to investigate mailings of prohibited materials, ranging from narcotics, child pornography, and sexually prohibited materials to hazardous materials such as mail bombs and nuclear, biological, or chemical weapons. The Dangerous Mail Investigations Program helps to screen the mail to keep employees and the public safe. In FY 2011, postal inspectors were called to investigate 3,572 suspicious powders and liquids in packages.[41]

The fourth function of the USPIS is Aviation and Homeland Security. The organization helps to guarantee the safe and protected transportation of mail and seeks to prevent anything that may endanger the security of the homeland via the mail system. These teams conduct regular security audits as a way to ensure that the postal service facilities are secure from crimes such as theft as well as from harms done by either natural or manmade disasters.

The fifth function of USPIS revolves around investigation of revenue-related offenses. The USPIS investigates cases in which there are concerns about fraudulent practices being carried out by businesses or consumers that mail items without the proper postage or with counterfeit postage. This may also include actions that are geared toward defrauding the USPS of revenue.

The sixth function of the USPIS is to carry out international investigations to assure global security of the mail system. This function helps to ensure that the mail system is safe and secure for international businesses that use the system. In order to do this, the USPIS maintains investigators in offices in locations around the world for easier intelligence gathering.

The seventh function of the USPIS is to conduct joint task force investigations. The USPIS frequently takes part in joint task force investigations with other agencies in cases where federal laws related to the mail service have been violated. These cases cover a wide variety of offenses and involve many other law enforcement agencies in the federal government.

In addition to these functions, the USPIS has implemented 2 SMRT 4U, a campaign aimed at teenaged girls, who are most often the targets of sexual predators online. The program is intended to educate teens about how to chat and post online personal information wisely.[42] In 2011, postal inspectors identified 45 children who were being sexually abused by adults, who sometimes took photographs of the abuse.[43]

Officials from the Postal Inspection Service also work with members of another vulnerable population, the elderly, to prevent their victimization. In 2013, the Postal Inspection Service worked jointly with AARP to help older citizens be more aware of fraudulent foreign lottery scams. The program, called "Dollars and Sense—Rated A for All Ages," was intended to educate customers and to help prevent them from becoming the victims scams and to provide them with information on what to do if they became the victims of scams. As part of the program, the Inspection Service also presented educational news segments related to fraudulent foreign lottery scams in multiple broadcast markets.[44]

In another attempt to protect the public from becoming victimized, the Inspection Service instituted the Consumer Alert News Network (CANN), on which they air 12 news stories each month that feature fraud investigations. These may include bogus job offers, sweepstakes scams, or phony charities. In the reports, inspectors and victims talk about the scams and how to identify them.[45]

The USPIS sponsors other tools to educate consumers regarding fraudulent schemes by use of the mail. These are carried out by inspection service public information officers and public information representatives, who provide information to the media and customers about methods criminals use to exploit citizens. The Postal Inspection Service co-sponsors National Consumer Protection Week to help educate the public in different ways. They sponsor Shred Day events to allow customers to shred documents that include personal information as a way to prevent mail fraud and identity theft. [46]

In 2011, The USPIS assisted 57,000 victims of postal-related crimes in some way. They educated victims about their rights, informed them of services available to provide assistance, and apprised victims of the status of their cases. To do this, the USPIS often works with the Office of Victims of Crime, found within the Department of Justice.[47]

Conclusion

U.S. postal inspectors investigate any crime in which the U.S. mail is used to further a criminal act, regardless of whether it began in the mail or another way. Their work ensures that our postal employees are safe and the items we place in the system arrive safely.

Key Terms

Office of Postmaster General
Preston S. Loughborough
Office of Instruction and Mail
  Depredation
Mail Fraud Act
Post Office Act
Anthony Comstock
Comstock Act

Comstock Laws
Billy the Kid
Alvin Karpis
Postal Reorganization Act of
  1970
Postal Police Force
postal inspectors
Guy Cottrell

Review Questions

1. What are the three distinct missions of the Postal Inspection Service?

2. What are the four components of the Postal Inspection Service?

3. Describe the history of the Postal Inspection Service.

4. Why is Benjamin Franklin's name associated with the Postal Inspection Service?

5. Who is Anthony Comstock and what role did he play in the creation of the Postal Inspection Service?

6. What are the qualifications of those hired to be criminal investigators in the Postal Inspection Service?

7. Describe the organization of the Postal Inspection Service.

8. Describe the laboratory services of the Postal Inspection Service.

Endnotes

1. United States Postal Inspection Service, "Mission Statement," available at https://postal inspectors.uspis.gov/aboutus/mission.aspx.
2. United States Postal Inspection Service, "'900' Telephone Number Fraud," available at https://postalinspectors.uspis.gov/investigations/MailFraud/fraudschemes/financialfraud/Phone900.aspx; USPIS, "Mission Statement."
3. USPIS, "Mission Statement."
4. U.S. Postal Inspection Service (2012) Annual Report FY 2011, available online at https://postalinspectors.uspis.gov/radDocs/pubs/AnnualReport2011.pdf.
5. U.S. Postal Inspection Service. (2012). *A Chronology of the United States Postal Inspection Service.* Available online at https://postalinspectors.uspis.gov/aboutus/History.aspx.
6. Bumgarner, Jeffrey B. (2006). *Federal Agents: The Growth of Federal Law Enforcement in America.* Westport, CT: Praeger.
7. Denniston, Elinore. (1964). *America's Silent Investigators: The Story of the Postal Inspectors Who Protect the United States Mail.* New York: Dodd, Mead & Company.
8. Denniston, *America's Silent Investigators;* USPIS, *A Chronology.*
9. An Act to Revise, Consolidate, and Amend the Statutes Relating to the Post Office Department, ch. 335, 301, 17, Stat. 283, 323 (1872).
10. Bates, Anna Louise. (1995). *Weeder in the Garden of the Lord: Anthony Comstock's Life and Career.* Lanham, MD: University Press of America; Beisel, Nicola Kay. (1997). *Imperiled Innocents: Anthony Comstock and Family Reproduction in Victorian America.* Princeton, NJ: Princeton University Press; Bennett, De Robigne Mortimer. (1971). *Anthony Comstock: His Career of Cruelty and Crime.* New York: De Capo Press; Broun, Heywood & Margaret Leech. (1927). *Anthony Comstock: Roundsman of the Lord.* New York: Albert and Charles Boni.
11. Kahn, E. J. Jr. (1973). *Fraud: The United States Postal Inspection Service and Some of the Fools and Knaves It Has Known.* New York: Harper & Row.
12. United States Postal Inspectors. (2012). *Because the Mail Matters.* Washington, D.C.: U.S. Post Office, p. 6.
13. USPI, *Because the Mail Matters,* p. 7.
14. Officer Down Memorial Page. (2012). *Memorial page for Charles Fitzgerald.* Available online at http://www.odmp.org/officer/4874-postal-inspector-charles-fitzgerald.
15. USPIS, *A Chronology.*
16. Denniston, *America's Silent Investigators;* Kahn, E. J. Jr., *Fraud;* Makris, John N. (1959). *The Silent Investigators: The Great Untold Story of the United States Postal Inspection Service.* New York: E.P. Dutton & Co.
17. Rocha, Guy. (2003). "Myth #95—Staging a Robbery Without a Coach." *Sierra Sage.* Carson City/Carson Valley, Nevada, December 2004.
18. Fattig, Paul. (1998). "D'Autremonts' Bungled Train Robbery in 1923 Left 4 Dead." *Mail Tribune.* Available online at http://www.angelfire.com/wa/andyhiggins/Greattrainrobbery.html.
19. USPI, *Because the Mail Matters,* p. 9.
20. USPI, *Because the Mail Matters,* p. 11.
21. Denniston, *America's Silent Investigators;* Makris, *The Silent Investigators.*
22. USPIS, *A Chronology.*
23. Feldman, Frances Bran. (1984). "Postal Inspection Service." *Postal Inspection Service Bulletin.* Available online at http://www.wifle.org/conference1991/pdf/53-61.pdf.
24. Cole, Leonard A. (2003). *The Anthrax Letters: A Medical Detective Story.* Washington, D.C.: Joseph Henry Press; Cole, Leonard A. (2009). *The Anthrax Letters: A Bioterrorism Expert Investigates the Attacks That Shocked America—Case Closed?* New York: Skyhorse Publishing.
25. USPIS, "Mission Statement."
26. United States Postal Inspection Service, "Jurisdiction and Laws," available at https://postal inspectors.uspis.gov/aboutus/laws.aspx.
27. USPIS, "Mission Statement."
28. United States Postal Inspection Service, "Forensic Laboratory Services," available at https://postalinspectors.uspis.gov/aboutus/lab.aspx.

29. United States Postal Inspection Service, "Distributor and Franchise Fraud," available at https://postalinspectors.uspis.gov/investigations/MailFraud/fraudschemes/employment fraud/Franchise.aspx.

30. United States Postal Inspection Service, "Phony Job Opportunities," available at https://post alinspectors.uspis.gov/investigations/MailFraud/fraudschemes/employmentfraud/ PhonyJob.aspx.

31. United States Postal Inspection Service, "Multi-Level Marketing Jobs (Pyramid Schemes)," available at https://postalinspectors.uspis.gov/investigations/MailFraud/fraudschemes/ employmentfraud/Marketing.aspx.

32. United States Postal Inspection Service, "Six-Cent and Other Short-Paid Postages," available at https://postalinspectors.uspis.gov/investigations/MailFraud/fraudschemes/employment fraud/ShortPaid.aspx.

33. USPIS, "'900' Telephone Number Fraud."

34. United States Postal Inspection Service, "Advance-Fee Loan Schemes," available at https:// postalinspectors.uspis.gov/investigations/MailFraud/fraudschemes/financialfraud/ AdvanceFee.aspx.

35. United States Postal Inspection Service, "Charity Fraud," available at https://postalinspectors. uspis.gov/investigations/MailFraud/fraudschemes/financialfraud/CharityFraud.aspx.

36. United States Postal Inspection Service, "Credit Card Fraud," available at https://postal inspectors.uspis.gov/investigations/MailFraud/fraudschemes/financialfraud/CCfraud.aspx.

37. United States Postal Inspection Service, "Schemes that Charge Money for Free Government Services," available at https://postalinspectors.uspis.gov/investigations/MailFraud/fraud schemes/financialfraud/GovtSchemes.aspx.

38. United States Postal Inspection Service, "Chain Letters," available at https://postalinspectors. uspis.gov/investigations/MailFraud/fraudschemes/sweepstakesfraud/ChainLetters.aspx.

39. United States Postal Inspection Service, "Free-Prize Scheme," available at https://postal inspectors.uspis.gov/investigations/MailFraud/fraudschemes/sweepstakesfraud/FreePrize Fraud.aspx.

40. U.S. Postal Inspection Service (2012) Annual Report FY 2011.

41. U.S. Postal Inspection Service (2012) Annual Report FY 2011.

42. USPIS, "A Chronology."

43. U.S. Postal Inspection Service (2012) Annual Report FY 2011.

44. United States Postal Service, 2013 Annual Report to Congress, available at http://about.usps.com/ publications/annual-report-comprehensive-statement-2013/annual-report-comprehensive- statement-2013_v2.pdf.

45. United States Postal Service, 2013 Annual Report to Congress.

46. U.S. Postal Inspection Service (2012) Annual Report FY 2011.

47. U.S. Postal Inspection Service (2012) Annual Report FY 2011.

4

U.S. Park Police

Created in 1791 by George Washington, the U.S. Park Police is one of the oldest uniformed federal law enforcement agencies in the U.S., being created prior to both the Department of the Interior and the National Park Service. As part of the Department of the Interior, the Park Police has law enforcement jurisdiction in all National Park Service lands (primarily in Washington, D.C., New York City, and San Francisco) as well as in other lands owned by the federal and state governments. They have the responsibility to respond to criminal acts that take place in national parks. Officers patrol the parks, investigate potential crimes, apprehend potential suspects, and protect the nation's monuments and memorials. They also provide escort and protective details for the president of the U.S. and any other foreign and domestic dignitaries who may visit the park system.

The goal of the Park Police is to provide a safe environment in these areas so that visitors can enjoy the surroundings and employees can enjoy a crime-free work environment. At the same time, officers must also ensure that law-abiding citizens are able to exercise their First Amendment rights of free speech and assembly during organized demonstrations and protests.[1]

Simply stated, the mission statement of the organization reads as follows: "We, the United States Park Police, support and further the mission and goals of the Department of the Interior and the National Park Service by providing quality law enforcement to safeguard lives, protect our national treasures and symbols of democracy, and preserve the natural and cultural resources entrusted to us."[2] A value statement for the agency is provided in Figure 4.1.

Figure 4.1: U.S. Park Police Value Statement

"We, the members of the United States Park Police, believe that integrity, honor, and service are the foundation of everything we do. We insist on fairness and responsibility in all facets of our professional and personal conduct and demand the highest standards of ethical behavior. We are dedicated to protecting human life and to providing quality service to the public, the National Park Service, and the Department of the Interior. We meet community needs with sensitivity and professionalism, and we hold ourselves accountable to each other and to the citizens we serve."[3]

The jurisdiction of the Park Police is tied to the state in which an individual park is located. When Mammoth Cave in Kentucky became a national park, it was noted in 16 U.S.C. §404c-10 that:

The Secretary of the Interior shall notify in writing the Governor of the Commonwealth of Kentucky of the passage and approval of this Act, and of the fact that the United States assumes police jurisdiction over the park. Upon the acceptance by the Secretary of the Interior of further cessions of jurisdiction over lands now or hereafter included in the Mammoth Cave National Park, the provisions of sections 2 to 9 inclusive, shall apply to such lands.[4]

In other states, the Park Police have other powers. For example, Park Police officers in Virginia have "Conservator of the Peace" powers. These officers have been appointed certain powers by a Circuit Court to perform any duties authorized and appropriate to secure property and keep the peace. Those Park Police officers in D.C. have been given the same responsibilities as those of the D.C. Metropolitan Police. In New York and New Jersey, the U.S. Park Police have been given the power to arrest law breakers.

The Park Police have also been given the power to enforce regulations concerning boating and other water activities on bodies of water located within the national park system. This is found in 16 U.S.C. §6011, as shown in Figure 4.2.

Figure 4.2: Statutory Authority of U.S. Park Police for Water-Related Activities

In order to facilitate the administration of the national park system, the Secretary of the Interior is authorized, under such terms and conditions as he may deem advisable, to carry out the following activities:

(h) Regulations; promulgation and enforcement

Promulgate and enforce regulations concerning boating and other activities on or relating to waters located within areas of the National Park System, including waters subject to the jurisdiction of the United States: Provided, That any regulations adopted pursuant to this subsection shall be complementary to, and not in derogation of, the authority of the United States Coast Guard to regulate the use of waters subject to the jurisdiction of the United States.

History

The United States Park Police, although formally an early twentieth-century creation, has its roots dating as far back as the creation of Washington, D.C. itself.[5] President George Washington had Pierre Charles L'Enfant and three commissioners create the plans for the nation's Capitol to be built in land encompassing ten square miles, mostly in Maryland along the Potomac River. In 1791, L'Enfant completed his plans and construction on the public grounds began.[6] As construction began, watchmen were employed to protect the buildings and patrol the grounds by night. These early watchmen are in many ways the forerunners to both the United States Secret Service and the U.S. Capitol Police, but they have been more closely associated with what would become the United States Park Police.

When President John Adams and his wife Abigail moved into the White House in 1797, the nation's Capitol was only rudimentarily finished and it would take the next four years to make that building habitable. The U.S. Capitol was built in stages with the Senate wing being completed in 1800 and the House wing in 1811 (although the House moved into the incomplete facility in 1807). At the time, by way of an 1802 act, Prince George's County provided a constable to police the grounds. At the same time, however, the position of superintendent for the buildings and grounds was created. Problems arose with enforcing the law when someone trespassed in the federal buildings or on the grounds. In 1834, Congress passed a law that provided "that the regulations of the city of Washington for the preservation of the public peace and order, be extended to all the public buildings and public grounds belonging to the United States within the city of Washington whenever the application of the same shall be requested by the commissioner of the public buildings."[7] At the time, however, they still relied on the Prince George's Constable to enforce the new federal law for Washington, D.C.

In 1849, with the creation of the Department of the Interior, superintendent became the more commonly used term for commissioner of public buildings. He was to report directly to the secretary of the interior. In 1850, an appropriations act for the newly retitled commissioner allowed for the funding of "two watchmen to be employed in preserving the public grounds around the Capitol."[8] Further appropriations expanded the duties of these watchmen to patrolling the president's garden, the White House, and the public stables. The number of watchmen would increase to five, and all of them served as a night watch.

During the Civil War, from 1861 to 1865, Washington, D.C. had little to worry about in terms of security as the U.S. military largely filled the role of night watchmen, patrolling the city and standing guard at the bridges across the Potomac River in order to protect the city from a Southern invasion. In addition, at the request of President Abraham Lincoln, a Metropolitan Police Department was created in 1861.[9] While the watchmen remained in the employ of the commissioner, their duties were greatly limited during wartime. When the soldiers disbanded and were no longer present, a void was left that simply could not be filled by a mere five night watchmen. In 1866, B. B. French, the commissioner of public buildings, called for a greater force to protect the Capitol and specifically requested 30 Capitol police, 5 Capitol watchmen, 2 White House watchmen, 2 watchmen for the Smithsonian grounds, and 2 on reservations. The two for the Smithsonian grounds were to patrol along the Mall and the grounds of the unfinished Washington Monument.

While these positions were implemented, French would lose his position the following year when Congress abolished the commissioner of public buildings and placed the various police and watchmen under the chief engineer of the army. Congress also mandated that the only individuals allowed to serve as either police or watchmen had to come from the United States military. These watchmen would serve as guards in the park areas, in particular the Smithsonian grounds and Franklin Square.

As the growth of Washington, D.C. led to more public parks, additional watchmen were requested by the chief engineer to provide protection for those areas as well. In fact, in 1879, the chief engineer spelled out the importance of having these additional watchmen and what their duties would entail when he explained to the secretary of war, "the necessity for additional upon the park reservations is rendered more apparent from year to year as these spots become greater resorts for the people . . . each reservation containing either a piece of statuary, a lodge, a fountain, ornamental vases, and drinking fountains, requires a watchman, not only to preserve the property from injury, but to make minor repairs of the walks and sodding, to keep the paths and lawns free of papers and shavings and other rubbish . . . and also to preserve order among and protect those who may chance to visit the squares for their personal pleasure and comfort."[10]

In the following year, 1880, further budgetary allocations allowed for badges, batons, and police whistles to be issued to each of the watchmen. In addition, they were granted the same powers as that of the Metropolitan Police and they began working alongside the Washington, D.C. Police Department. In a letter acknowledging this relationship, the various watchmen were collectively referred to as Park Police, the first time the phrase was used.[11] From that point forward, all of the various police, watchmen, and guards were referred to as the Park Police. Although they still retained many of the duties of maintaining the parks, picking up trash, and other non-police-related duties, they now had full police authority throughout Washington, D.C., and they were recognized as bona fide police.

By 1900, the force had grown to 23 men serving in the various parks throughout Washington, D.C., either by day or night, and 4 more were added that year. In addition, because of problems attracting men to work the night shift, their pay was increased to compensate. One other major change would occur for these Park Police that year and that was the addition of a uniform.[12] Designs were obtained from a number of sources, but the one created by Saks in New York was selected. It was a uniform modeled on the German's Forester uniform, which was dark green in color, featuring a jacket and black striped pants. A dark hat was selected for winter and a tan straw hat for summer months.

Regardless of the season, the uniform was made of wool. The government furnished the cap, along with the badge and billy club, but the officer had to pay for his own uniform, which typically cost $17.75 each year. Despite the best of plans, the uniform had to be switched to a dark blue color by 1903 as the green in the original uniform faded rapidly in the elements. Interestingly, the new uniform featured a collar with ornaments that read "U.S. PP" – United States Park Police. Although still not official, the agency was beginning to refer to itself as such.

The next 20 years would see the force continue to grow, and as new parks were added, new territory existed that they were required to cover. There was a request in 1914 for the Metropolitan Police to cease providing a 28-man detail to the White House and move those duties to the Public Buildings and Grounds of the Army Engineers. It was decided that the current situation was satisfactory, and no changes were made. This did, however, raise the question as to why there was a special police force patrolling the parks. Why not roll these officers into the Metropolitan Police Department and have just one force? The pro-side argued that it would save money in overhead, streamline management costs, and would provide the same services. The con-side argued that the watchmen acting as Park Police performed far more duties than the average police officer and that the environment in which they worked was vastly different from policing the city streets. Although no changes came about over these debates, the Park Police found it to be a perennial debate.

The issue, in some ways, was put to rest when Rock Creek Park was given over to the Public Building and Grounds Police Force to protect. Rock Creek Park had, until 1919, its own governing board, and they had allowed the Metropolitan Police to police the park since its opening in 1894.[13] The governing board decided to dissolve, and responsibility for the park was shifted to the Public Buildings and Grounds. The so-called Park Police now had responsibility for the largest park in Washington, D.C. In recognition of this fact and to acknowledge the name that the officers had been referred to for nearly 20 years, on December 5, 1919, the U.S. Congress passed an act that gave the organization the official title of United States Park Police.[14]

The force now stood at 1 lieutenant, 3 sergeants, and 53 privates. The agency had 7 motorcycles, 45 bicycles, and several horses for patrol. Despite these large numbers, they were not able to keep up with the growing crime resulting from both the Prohibition and the social change of the Roaring Twenties. In 1924, they were granted additional positions and their pay was increased. The following year it was decided that the organization would be removed from the army's chief of engineers and was placed under the newly created Office of Public Buildings and Public Parks of the National Capital. The director of this agency would report directly to the president of the United States. Quite uniquely, the director appointed to this position that year was Major Ulysses S. Grant III, the grandson of the Civil War general and former president of the United States. He would remain as the director until 1933, when the agency itself was folded.

In the meantime, the biggest addition to the U.S. Park Police's responsibilities came in 1932, when the Mount Vernon Memorial Highway was opened on the bicentennial of President George Washington's Birthday. The new highway ran from Washington, D.C. directly to Mount Vernon, connecting the home of the president to the city named for him. It was decided that since the highway itself was declared a park, the United States Park Police would take control of it and be responsible for patrolling and securing its safety.

The following year, after Franklin D. Roosevelt took office as president, he began reorganizing the federal government's bureaucratic structure in the hopes of making it more efficient. By way of presidential executive order he abolished the Office of Public Buildings and Public Parks of the National Capital and assigned those functions to the National Park Service, which had been created in 1916 to supervise the park system created by his cousin Theodore Roosevelt. That same order also gave the National Park System control over the Civil War battlefields. The National Park Service reported to the secretary of the interior, and it is in this organizational framework that the U.S. Park Police still remain today.

Although the movement of the U.S. Park Police under the National Park Service would appear to have ended any controversy over the agency's organizational existence, in many ways it highlighted whether or not the U.S. Park Police were needed at all. Once again, the consideration of abolishing the U.S. Park Police was entertained by many, with most agreeing it could be absorbed by the Metropolitan Police Department. At one point, in a 1939 study, it was recommended by Secretary of the Interior Harold L. Ickes that the traffic duty of the U.S. Park Police be removed but, again, nothing came of it. In 1945, Congress became involved and a bill was put forth that would have returned the Park Police to merely watchmen duty, but President Harry S. Truman vetoed the bill. By the time it was again discussed in 1948 in Congress, the U.S. Park Police patrolled approximately 30,000 acres of parks in and around Washington, D.C., and the realization came that it was probably no longer realistic for the duties to be moved to the Metropolitan Police.

In fact, the one thing that most likely saved the United States Park Police from being abolished this time around was the Mount Vernon Highway itself. If the United States Park Police duties were given over to the Metropolitan Police, that force would not have been able to patrol the highway as the jurisdiction of the highway is located in Virginia, outside the authority of the Washington, D.C. Metropolitan Police. It was considered that the highway could be given to Virginia law enforcement except the highway ran through several jurisdictions and the Virginia State Police, although created in 1932, were not yet a highway patrol agency. By 1950, any discussion of abolishing, absorbing, or structurally moving the United States Park Police was dispelled. The words of Secretary Ickes became the defining quote against any more entertainment of the idea: "The problem of policing the parks is so different from ordinary police work and duties of park policemen are so specialized that it has never proven satisfactory to use city policemen for park duties."[15]

This did not, however, solve other controversies within the United States Park Police. In 1957, Police Chief Donald S. Leonard, a former president of the International Association of Police Chiefs (IACP), was brought in to conduct a review of the U.S. Park Police. Leonard suggested a number of changes: that certain personnel be fired, that the total force should be expanded, and that new recruits should be properly trained. When the Kennedy Administration came to power, Steward L. Udall was appointed as the secretary of the interior, and he wanted to see many of these changes implemented. Udall then tried to oust the current chief, Harold F. Stewart, and have him replaced. Unable to force this change due to civil service rules, Udall reassigned Stewart to Guam. Out of the way, he tried to affect a number of changes, one of which was to change the uniforms to green and make the Park Police more like Park Rangers. A fight of words ensued and Stewart did not disappear quietly, but rather fought back. These battles continued under the Johnson Administration and would eventually lead to congressional hearings on the proper direction of the agency.

Once again, external circumstances prevented changes within the agency. This time it had to do with social change in the 1960s, the rise in crime, and in particular, the rise in crime in the parks. More specifically, it had to do with many of the demonstrations that were taking place in the parks and the fact that the U.S. Park Police were fighting crime more than they were performing any type of duty closely associated with the U.S. Park Rangers. In addition, as the problems of crime were being reported more often by Park Rangers in the United States Parks, U.S. Park Police found themselves being assigned to a number of locations: Big Bend, the Grand Canyon, Rocky Mountain National Park, Yosemite National Park, the Blue Ridge Parkway, and the Nachez Trace Parkway. Their territory thus expanded and their law enforcement duties entrenched, the United States Park Police retained its police duties.

The agency grew to 570 officers by 1977 and its organization began to resemble a more modern police force. The majority of officers were assigned under the Patrol Branch, but a Criminal Investigations Branch was created with 21 investigators and 7 uniformed officers. A Special Operations Force was also created in order to handle all of the unique situations related to park policing, ranging from horse mounted patrols to the K-9 patrols to helicopter patrols. While many of these responsibilities already existed within the United States Park Police—the horses dated back to the nineteenth century, the K-9 patrol was created in 1957, and the helicopter unit was created in 1973—they now fell under the Special Operations Branch to which 97 officers were assigned. In addition, a new team, the Selective Enforcement Unit, was organized to handle major events including protests, visits by dignitaries, and special ceremonies held in park territory. And, in 1975, the U.S. Park Police created its Special Weapons and Tactics Team (SWAT) in order to respond to any high risk encounters.

One more significant change resulted from the 1957 review conducted by Police Chief Donald S. Leonard, and that was his recommendation to enhance new recruit training. This resulted in a police training program being established at Jones Point in Alexandria, Virginia. Then, in 1972, the federal government decided to move all of the federal law enforcement recruit training (except for the FBI and U.S. Military Police) under one training organization—the Federal Law Enforcement Training Center (FLETC) located at the former Glynco Naval Station in Brunswick, Georgia.[16] Captain Charles R. Stebbins had been the head of the United States Park Police Training Branch and he was asked to move to FLETC in order to help establish the new recruit training at Glynco. Thus, the U.S. Park Police had a role in establishing the training that was delivered at Glynco.

Another change that came in the 1970s was the hiring of more women and minorities. The U.S. Park Police had hired women and minorities as early as World War II. The first female park police officer was Beatrice Ball, who was appointed on January 1, 1942, and Grant Wright was the first black officer hired in 1947. These officers tended to be the exception and not the rule, and the women were typically relegated to cases involving women and children. Beginning in 1972, however, females and minorities were hired and became mainstream officers with no distinction. Interestingly, one of the first female officers hired in this new age achieved a scholastic score at FLETC of 971 out of a possible 1,000 points, making her the highest scoring basic trainee at that time.[17]

Thousands of officers have served as United States Park Police, and only 12 have died while serving.[18] Most of them died in accidents. One, Officer Milo John Kennedy, was attacked by a mob and killed while patrolling on August 7, 1932. Another, Officer Ivan Thompson, attempted to make an arrest after a traffic stop in 1940, when the suspect fled. Thompson gave chase, but when he grabbed the suspect, the suspect reached for Thompson's revolver and, having wrested control, fired five shots, killing him. Another, Officer Raymond Leonard Hawkins, died off duty after being shot when he attempted to stop a robbery in progress at a convenience store on February 15, 1972.

Perhaps the most visible act of heroism in the U.S. Park Police's history came on the cold and icy day of January 13, 1982, when Air Florida Flight 90 crashed into the 14th Street Bridge after taking off from Washington National Airport.[19] U.S. Park Police Officer and helicopter pilot, Donald W. Usher, and Paramedic Officer Melvin E. Windsor, were working in the aviation unit that day. Responding after the crash, they risked their lives by lowering the helicopter perilously close to the river in order to rescue survivors caught in the ice-cold river. They saved four lives that day and would receive the U.S. Department of the Interior's Valor Award.

More recently, the United States Park Police came under some controversy regarding its police chief, Teresa Chambers, who accepted the position in February of 2002. Commenting on new requirements made by the U.S. Congress to double the number of stationary guards at Washington, D.C. monuments in the wake of 9/11, Chief Chambers raised the issue that without additional funding, Congress would be putting the safety of park visitors at risk by spreading the officers too thin. This created a controversy, and she was fired in December of 2003. She appealed the decision and, after seven years, was reinstated on January 21, 2011 as Chief of the U.S. Park Police.[20]

Who Gets Hired

In 2010, the Park Police employed 624 sworn officers, 28 security guards, and 87 full-time civilian personnel. In general, the Park Police hire individuals who are highly motivated to protect the nation. Applicants must be willing to work varying hours of the day, seven days of the week, in any National Park in the country. Candidates must be U.S. citizens over the age of 21, but under 37 when they first apply. A valid driver's license with a clean driving record is needed. Applicants should have 20/100 vision or better or correctable vision to 20/20. It is required that applicants have a high school diploma and either a minimum of 60 college credits or at least two years of military service when they receive their appointment. Recruits must also pass a psychological exam, a physical exam, and a medical exam.

New officers complete a basic training program at FLETC in Georgia. It is a 12-week program that gives newly hired agents the knowledge and skills needed to perform the job. After graduating from that program, new officers then attend the Uniformed Police Training Program, a 6-week long course that provides students with 428 hours of training in areas such as criminal and traffic law, firearms, emergency and non-emergency vehicle operations, physical tactics, EMS awareness, and human behavior. Officers must also take courses on accident investigation, criminal investigation, field sobriety testing, crime prevention, and narcotics in order to graduate.[21] New officers remain for an additional five weeks for training that is specifically geared toward the operations, policies, and procedures of the Park Police.[22]

Once the training process is complete, all newly hired agents will be assigned to the Washington area, which houses the largest component of Park Police agents. They must complete a probationary period of one year prior to becoming a full-time agent.[23] The starting salary for an officer is approximately $52,020 a year.[24]

Those interested in becoming dispatchers for the Park Police must be a U.S. citizen at least 18 years of age or older and have either college credits or prior experience in dispatching, law enforcement, the military, or public safety. Those who seek to be dispatchers must pass pre-placement testing and a complete background check.

The Park Police also have a Student Internship Program through which students gain work experience with all units in the Park Police organization. The student interns are not financially compensated for participation in this program but can earn academic credit through their home college or university. To become an intern, a student must be enrolled in a university's law enforcement curriculum and be recommended by the coordinator of the school's internship program. At that point, the Park Police will conduct a background investigation of the applicant. The student must provide the Park Police with an official transcript and a copy of the academic requirements for the internship. The student must also complete an application for federal employment and submit two letters of recommendation.[25]

Table 4.1	U.S. Park Police Budgets, In Billions of Dollars
FY 2011 Enacted	3.003
FY 2012 Enacted	3.013
FY 2014 Requested	3.115

Source: U.S. Department of the Interior, Budget Justification and Performance Information, various years, available at http://www.nps.gov/aboutus/budget.htm.

Budgets

The Budget for the Park Police has remained largely the same over the past three years, hovering somewhere around $3 billion, as shown in Table 4.1.

Organization

The Park Police is headed by a police chief, as described above, and includes agencies as described in Table 4.2.

Table 4.2 **Organization of U.S. Park Police**

Operations Division
    Criminal Investigations Branch
        Major Crimes Unit
        Identification Unit
        Special Investigations Unit
        Narcotics and Vice Unit
        Environmental Crimes Unit
    Patrol Branch
        Horse Mounted Unit
        Traffic Safety Unit
Homeland Security Division
    Icon Protection Branch
        Aviation Unit
        Canine Protection Unit
        Intelligence/Counterterrorism Unit
        Motorcycle Unit
    Special Forces Branch
        Special Weapons and Tactics Team

```
Administrative Division
    Administrative Branch
        Budget and Data Systems Unit
        Information Management Section
        Financial Management Section
    Human Resources Branch
        Human Resources Unit
        Medical Services Section
    Technical Services Branch
        Communications Section
        Transportation and Equipment Section
        Facilities Management Section
    Training Branch
        Washington Metropolitan Area Training Section
        FLETC Specialized
        Federal Law Enforcement Training Center
Community Service Division
    Explorer Post
    Smooth Operator Program
```

Leader

Chief Teresa Chambers is in her fourth decade of law enforcement service. In addition to serving as the chief of the United States Park Police Force, Chief Chambers has served as the chief of the Durham, North Carolina, Police Department and the chief of the Riverdale Park Police Department in Maryland. She also served more than 20 years in the Prince George's County, Maryland, Police Department, retiring at the rank of major to accept the position as chief of police in Durham, North Carolina.

Chief Chambers received her bachelor's degree in law enforcement/criminology from the University of Maryland University College and her master's degree in applied behavioral science with a concentration in community development from Johns Hopkins University. Chief Chambers is also a graduate of the FBI National Academy and the FBI's prestigious National Executive Institute. She currently serves as an adjunct faculty member of Johns Hopkins University.

What They Do

In 2010, Park Police agents responded to 35,957 service incidents. They filed 59,125 incident reports and 3,371 vehicle accident reports.[26] Their 2010 activities are detailed in Table 4.3, and Table 4.4 shows the areas under the jurisdiction of the Park Police.

Table 4.3	U.S. Park Police Activities, 2010

Aviation: Calls for service	1, 041
Communications: Dispatched calls for service	178,595
Criminal Investigations: Assigned investigations	407
Closure rate on assigned cases	52%
Horse Mounted Patrol: Incidents handled	3,782
K-9 Unit (Bomb and Patrol): Incidents handled	15,939
Marine Patrol Unit: Incident responses	1,555
National Icon Protection: Incidents that pose serious potential threats to icons	224
National Icon Protection: Prohibited items confiscated	17,283
National Icon Protection: Incidents documented by camera operator	659
Patrol Unit: Environmental crimes	955
Patrol Unit: Drug cases	1,209
Patrol Unit: DWI/DUI arrests	678
Special Events/Crowd Control: Special events handled by U.S. Park Police	9,296

Source: Department of the Interior, National Park Service, United States Park Police, "2010 Annual Report," available at http://www.nps.gov/inde/parkmgmt/upload/2010-Annual-Report.pdf.

Table 4.4	Sites Protected by the U.S. Park Police

Washington, D.C.
- The National Mall
- The White House
- President's Park
- Rock Creek Park
- George Washington Memorial Parkway
- National Capital Parks—East
- Greenbelt Park
- Baltimore –Washington Memorial Parkway
- C&O Canal National Historical Park
- Wolf Trap National Park

New York City, New York
- Statue of Liberty National Monument and Ellis Island
- Gateway National Recreation Area

San Francisco, California
- Golden Gate National Recreation Area
- The Presidio

Operations Division

The Operations Division oversees the general functions of the Park Police. It includes the Criminal Investigations Branch and the Patrol Branch, as described below.

Criminal Investigations Branch

The Criminal Investigations Branch (CIB) works to prevent, investigate, and detect criminal activity and to apprehend those who violate the law. CIB is made up of detectives, plainclothes investigators, identification technicians, and civilians who are assigned to work in its five units: the Major Crimes Unit, the Identification Unit, the Special Investigation Unit, the Narcotics and Vice Unit, and the Environmental Crimes Unit. The members of the CIB investigate serious incidents that occur within the boundaries of the national parks including deaths, sexual assaults, robberies, assaults, and narcotics violations. In special circumstances, agents may be assigned to assist with local and federal task forces that are created to combat specific types or categories of crime.[27]

Major Crimes Unit

The Major Crimes Unit is comprised of criminal investigators and detectives who are responsible for investigating serious incidents that occur in national parks such as deaths, sexual assaults, robberies, assaults, and violations of federal narcotics laws. In some cases, agents in this unit provide protection of the president and other dignitaries. When needed, the Major Crime Unit participates in situations where it is necessary to make mass arrests.[28]

Identification Unit

The agents in the Identification Unit provide assistance to the detectives and investigators involved in the forensic aspects of various criminal investigations. They collect, preserve, and process any evidence from a crime scene including fingerprints, measurements, sketches, photographs, and videotapes. This unit maintains all drugs seized from crime events.[29]

Special Investigations Unit

The Special Investigations Unit personnel are responsible for the investigation of serious or high-profile crimes or those criminal acts that require specialized training.

Narcotics and Vice Unit

The agents assigned to the Narcotics and Vice Unit of the Park Police focus on street-level drug trafficking activities as well as targeting the heads of street distributors. They also focus on prostitution that may occur on national park land. The unit oversees all assets that are seized by the Park Police within the

Washington D.C. area and processes the evidence for legal action. The majority of officers assigned to this unit are assigned to the District of Columbia and surrounding counties in Maryland and Virginia.[30]

Environmental Crimes Unit

The Environmental Crimes Unit operates primarily in the District of Columbia. The jurisdiction for the unit stems from the Organic Act of 1916, which mandated that the Park Service should strive to conserve the scenery and the natural and historical objects of the parks and the wildlife living there. Thus, the unit enforces criminal laws pertaining to environmental, cultural, and natural resources. The detectives and investigators assigned to this unit work in conjunction with special agents from the FBI, EPA, and others to track down violators. The unit members also train other law enforcement officers from local police agencies about environmental laws. [31]

Patrol Branch

The duties of the officers who are assigned to the Patrol Branch include those revolving around crime reduction and prevention, drug enforcement, public assistance, and traffic duties. They also provide assistance through demonstrations and protection of the president, vice president, and protection of other dignitaries. The Patrol Branch consists of three districts (Central, East, and West) in the Washington metropolitan area.[32] The Patrol Branch is divided into the Horse Mounted Unit and the Traffic Safety Unit.

Horse Mounted Unit

The Horse Mounted Unit was established in 1934 and is now one of America's oldest police equestrian forces across the nation. The horse mounted patrols are used for crowd management and for maintaining order during demonstrations and other special events as needed. The horses are each trained to be comfortable with, and maneuver throughout, large crowds of people so they are not likely to pose a danger to the public, themselves, or their riders.[33]

Traffic Safety Unit

The Traffic Safety Unit (TSU) oversees the speed enforcement program and the alcohol programs in the parks. It also handles all serious collisions and fatal motor vehicle collisions that occur within the force's jurisdiction. The unit oversees the force's radars and lasers as well as intoxilyzers, preliminary breath test (PBT) equipment, and tint meters. TSU provides training to other members of the Park Police as well as other local, state, and federal agencies in the use of radar, laser, PBTs, intoxilyzer, total station, accident investigation, forensic scene mapping, and standardized field sobriety testing. The unit helps to determine the factors that may have caused the accident.[34]

Homeland Security Division

The Homeland Security Division carries out typical law enforcement duties needed to accomplish the goals of the agency. They use cruisers, scooters, foot patrol, bicycles, and plainclothes patrol officers to patrol the park system and respond to incidents as needed.

Icon Protection Branch

An essential part of the Park Police is the protection of our national icons and monuments. Along with the National Park Service, the Park Police are continually evolving to increase the safety and security of the monuments for all visitors. Some of their activities involve providing physical barriers, screening equipment, and improved training for both officers and civilian employees. One new program used by the Park Police is the Community Anti-Terrorism Training Program, otherwise known as "CAT EYES." The program, developed as a way to reduce racism and assist in the fight against domestic terrorism, focuses on training officers to look for characteristics of a terrorist that are not based upon race or religion. The program attempts to increase awareness of terrorism. Within this branch are the Aviation Unit, the Canine Protection Unit, the Intelligence/Counterterrorism Unit, the Motorcycle Unit, the Special Events and Demonstrations Unit, and the Special Weapons and Tactics Unit.

Aviation Unit

The Park Police Aviation Unit was established in April of 1973. They provide aviation support for law enforcement as well as for medivac, search and rescue missions, high-risk prisoner transportation, and presidential and dignitary security.[35]

Canine Protection Unit

The Park Police were the first law enforcement agency in the Washington D.C. area to establish a Canine Unit in 1959. The dogs are trained for many functions. They are trained to detect both drugs and explosives. Beyond that, the dogs are able to provide assistance in search and rescue missions and help agents to secure areas prior to the visits by the president, vice-president, or other visiting foreign heads of state.[36]

Intelligence/Counterterrorism Unit

The Intelligence/Counterterrorism Unit is responsible for collecting, analyzing, and disseminating information related to possible acts of terrorism that may impact the mission of the Park Police. The unit monitors First Amendment activities such as any demonstrations, protests, marches, and gatherings that take place on national park property to ensure that the participants comply with federal laws. To be effective, the unit maintains contact with the Department of

Homeland Security and the FBI Joint Terrorism Task Forces in New York, New Jersey, and San Francisco. They also participate in numerous intelligence-sharing databases and working groups that help to keep track of terrorist acts around the nation and the world.[37] This unit also has detectives that coordinate gang intelligence for the Park Police.

Motorcycle Unit

The Park Police agents assigned to the motorcycle unit receive training in an 80-hour course that focuses on both on-road and off-road driving techniques. Agents must pass courses in high-speed pursuit, short-obstacle maneuvers, and officer safety and survival. The officers who pass the course ride year round and take part in routine traffic control and patrol duties in addition to special events and demonstrations. There are currently approximately 30 officers assigned to the Motorcycle Unit in the Washington, D.C. area and 4 assigned to the Motorcycle Unit in the San Francisco area.[38]

Special Forces Branch

The Park Police maintain responsibility for policing special events and managing crowds attending these events, which can range from just a few people to thousands of individuals. On average, the Park Police issue approximately 4,000 permits a year to groups who seek to assemble. Such large-scale events sometimes present difficult challenges, and the Special Events Forces Branch is responsible for ensuring the safety of these events. When large or high profile events are planned, the Park Police work in conjunction with the National Park Service to create a comprehensive incident action plan. This might involve SWAT, Aviation, the Horse Mounted Patrol Unit, or the Motorcycle Unit. When smaller events are planned, only a small group of agents may be deployed.[39]

Special Weapons and Tactics Unit

The U.S. Park Police Special Weapons and Tactics (SWAT) Team was created in 1975 and is comprised of a select group of officers who are highly trained and proficient with many types of weapons. The SWAT Unit carries out high-risk search warrants. They also provide escorts and motorcade support for the president, vice president, and any visiting dignitaries. During any demonstrations at the capital Mall area, the SWAT team members help to ensure the safety of participants and observers. SWAT agents, along with other organizations, often provide training to other law enforcement, military, and fire personnel from the U.S. and other countries in tactical emergency medicine. They also provide basic SWAT training to outside law enforcement and the military.[40]

Administrative Division

The Administrative Division helps to ensure that the Park Police run effectively each day. The management of budgets and personnel are parts of this division.

Administrative Branch

The Administrative Branch of the U.S. Park Police helps to ensure that the agency functions efficiently on a day-to-day basis. In order to accomplish this, they have a number of offices with different responsibilities. One of those is the Budget and Data Systems Unit. This unit focuses on computer programming, information management, statistical reporting, payroll, purchasing, and financial management. The Information Management Section deals with the classification and maintenance of the police reports filed by officers and any official correspondence to and from the agency, including memorandums and other official documents. Finally, the personnel in the Financial Management Section are responsible for all fiscal activities of the force including payroll, travel, accounts payable, and accounts receivable.

Human Resources Branch

The Human Resources Unit of the U.S. Park Police helps to ensure that personnel are qualified for their positions within the agency. They are responsible for overseeing the recruitment of qualified candidates for both police and civilian positions in a manner that is consistent with hiring policies. They also provide assistance to employees with regards to benefits. The Medical Services Section helps to ensure that all mandated health care programs are effectively administered. In 1990, the Park Police began a new program called CONTOMS to address the need for specialized medical training in its law enforcement special operations and to improve medical procedures of EMTs and paramedics who work with the law enforcement officers. The base of the program is EMT-Tactical (EMT-T), a one-week-long education curriculum for medical personnel.[41]

Technical Services Branch

The U.S. Park Police has developed a Technical Services Branch to oversee its technical needs. The Communications Section maintains communications centers that operate 24-hours a day, 7 days a week. One is in the District of Columbia, one is in San Francisco, and two are in the New York area. The Transportation and Equipment Section is responsible for managing all property owned by the Park Police in the Washington metropolitan area. Finally, the Facilities Management Section coordinates the facility needs of the Park Police with the appropriate officials and other maintenance personnel.

Training Branch

The Training Branch of the U.S. Park Police oversees initial and ongoing training of all of its employees. The Washington Metropolitan Area Training Section has the responsibility for developing, implementing, and maintaining an effective training program for new recruits—both law enforcement officers and civilian personnel. U.S. Park Police all receive basic training from the Federal Law Enforcement Training Center (FLETC). In addition, FLETC Specialized training services provide them with specific training for their duties as Park Police.

In the past, FLETC offered a six-week-long Park Police Citizens' Academy in which agency investigators, trainers, station commanders, and officers explained the Park Police organization, procedures, and daily operations to the area's residents. The program was available to interested residents who were at least 18 years old, who were residents of the national capital region, or were the parents, partners, or spouses of employees of the Park Police. All participants were required to pass a background check to participate in the academy.

Community Service Division

The Park Police designed a program to benefit children and their families who are considered to be underprivileged or at-risk or victims of domestic violence. Officers working in the program, which they call Desire, Knowledge, and Hope (DKH), attempt to help the children develop basic values of integrity, respect, and discipline. Families are given an opportunity to complete group projects such as arts and crafts, household and community cleanup efforts, and relationship-building exercises as a way to foster better communication and self-esteem. They also hold a dance, a coat drive, a toy drive, and a child safety event. DKH also sponsors an Explorer Post and participates with the Make-a-Wish Foundation. Information is provided to participants about physical and mental health care, drug and alcohol abuse, gun safety, and suicide awareness.[42]

Explorer Post

Young people who are interested in a law enforcement career can join the Explorer Post if they are 14 years old (but not older than 21) and have completed eighth grade, are a U.S. citizen or lawful resident alien, and have proof of active enrollment in school with a GPA of at least 2.0. They must also be drug free (including tobacco and alcohol), have good moral character, and have no gang affiliation. They must pass a background check, provide a copy of their birth certificate and a photo ID, and attend mandatory meetings.[43]

Smooth Operator Program

As a public safety initiative, Park Police agents strive to provide education, information, and solutions for the problem of aggressive driving. In the Smooth Operator Program, the Park Police have worked with other law enforcement agencies, trauma experts, and other professionals to teach drivers about risks of aggressive driving.[44]

Conclusion

The Park Police play an essential role in keeping the national parks a safe and enjoyable place for visitors. Agents also work to protect national monuments from harm. The Park Police are an integral part of the federal law enforcement network.

Key Terms

commissioner of public buildings
Teresa Chambers
Uniformed Police Training Program
Student Internship Program
Criminal Investigations Branch
Major Crimes Unit
Narcotics and Vice Unit
Environmental Crimes Unit
Patrol Branch
Horse Mounted Unit
Traffic Safety Unit
Homeland Security

Icon Protection Branch
Community Antiterrorism Training
  Program
Aviation Unit
Canine Protection Unit
Intelligence/Counterterrorism Unit
Motorcycle Unit
Special Forces Branch
Special Weapons and Tactics
Administrative Branch
Desire, Knowledge, and Hope
Smooth Operator Program

Review Questions

1. What is the goal and mission of the U.S. Park Police?

2. Describe the history of the U.S. Park Police.

3. Why was the Mount Vernon Highway critical in the history of the Park Police?

4. What are the qualifications a person must have to be hired as a member of the Park Police?

5. Describe the budgets of the Park Police.

6. How is the Park Police organized?

7. What are some of the responsibilities of the Park Police?

8. What are the sites protected by the Park Police?

Endnotes

1. Department of the Interior, National Park Service, United States Park Police, "2010 Annual Report," available at http://www.nps.gov/inde/parkmgmt/upload/2010-Annual-Report.pdf.
2. Department of the Interior, "2010 Annual Report."
3. Department of the Interior, "2010 Annual Report.
4. U.S.C. §404c-10: Notice of assumption of police jurisdiction by United States.
5. The definitive history of the United States Park Police was written by U.S. Park Police Officer Barry Mackintosh for the National Park Service, U.S. Department of the Interior. This is the primary source used for documenting the history of the U.S. Park Police. *See* Mackintosh, Barry. (1989). *The United States Park Police: A History.* Washington, D.C.: National Park Service, U.S. Department of the Interior. It is also available online at http://www.nps.gov/history/history/online_books/police/.
6. Bordewich, Fergus M. (2008). *Washington: The Making of the American Capital.* New York: Amistad.
7. Mackintosh, *The United States Park Police.*
8. Mackintosh, *The United States Park Police.*
9. Deeben, John P. (2008). "To Protect and to Serve: The Records of the D.C. Metropolitan Police, 1861–1930." *Prologue Magazine,* Vol. 40 No. 1.
10. Chief of Engineers. (1879). *Annual Report of the Chief of Engineers to the Secretary of War.* Washington, D.C.: Department of War, p. 1883.
11. Mackintosh, *The United States Park Police.*
12. Mackintosh, *The United States Park Police.*
13. Mackintosh, Barry. (1985). *Rock Creek Park: An Administrative History.* Washington, D.C.: National Park Service, U.S. Department of the Interior.
14. United States Park Police. (2012). *The United States Park Police.* Available online at http://www.nps.gov/uspp/.
15. As quoted in Mackintosh, *The United States Park Police.*
16. Federal Law Enforcement Training Center. (2012). FLETC History. Available online at http://www.fletc.gov/about-fletc/fletc-history.
17. Mackintosh, *The United States Park Police.*
18. Officer Down. (2012). *Officer Down Memorial Page.* Available online at http://www.odmp.org/.
19. National Transportation Safety Board. (1982). *Aircraft Accident Report.* Available online at http://www.airdisaster.com/reports/ntsb/AAR82-08.pdf.
20. See McArdle, John. (2011). "U.S. Park Police Chief—Fired for Whistle-Blowing in 2004—Is Reinstated." *New York Times.* Available online at http://www.nytimes.com/gwire/2011/01/13/13greenwire-us-park-police-chief-fired-for-whistle-blowing-49802.html; Support Teresa Chambers. (2012). *Support Teresa Chambers: An Honest Police Chief.* Available online at http://www.honestchief.com/nj/.
21. United States Park Police, Services Division, Training Branch, "Federal Law Enforcement Training Center," available at https://www.fletc.gov/.
22. United States Park Police, Services Division, Training Branch, "Federal Law Enforcement Training Center."
23. National Park Service, "U.S. Park Police Officer Career Information," available at criminology-careers.about.com/od/Law-Enforcement-Careers/a/Career-Profile-Park-Police-Officer.htm.
24. Department of the Interior, "2010 Annual Report."
25. United States Park Police, "The United States Park Police Student Internship Program," available at http://www.nps.gov/uspp/.
26. Department of the Interior, "2010 Annual Report."
27. United States Park Police, Operations Division, Patrol Branch, "Criminal Investigations Branch," available at http://www.nps.gov/uspp/.
28. United States Park Police, Operations Division, Patrol Branch, "Major Crimes Unit," available at http://www.nps.gov/uspp/.
29. United States Park Police, Operations Division, Patrol Branch, "Identification Unit," available at http://www.nps.gov/uspp/.

30. United States Park Police, Operations Division, Patrol Branch, "Narcotics and Vice Unit," available at http://www.nps.gov/uspp/.

31. United States Park Police, "The Environmental Crimes Unit," available at http://www.nps.gov/uspp/.

32. United States Park Police, "Homeland Security Division," available at http://www.nps.gov/uspp/.

33. United States Park Police, "Operations Division, Patrol Branch: Horse Mounted Unit," available at http://www.nps.gov/uspp/.

34. United States Park Police, "The United States Park Police Traffic Safety Unit," available at http://www.nps.gov/uspp/.

35. United States Park Police, Homeland Security Division, Icon Protection Branch, "Aviation Unit," available at http://www.nps.gov/uspp/.

36. United States Park Police, Homeland Security Division, Icon protection Branch, "Canine Unit," available at http://www.nps.gov/uspp/.

37. United States Park Police, Homeland Security Division, Icon Protection Branch, "Intelligence/Counter-Terrorism Unit," available at http://www.nps.gov/uspp/.

38. United States Park Police, "Police Motor Units," available at http://www.nps.gov/uspp/.

39. United States Park Police, Homeland Security Division, Icon Protection Branch, "Special Events and Demonstrations," available at http://www.nps.gov/uspp/.

40. United States Park Police, Homeland Security Division, Icon Protection Branch, "Special Weapons and Tactics," available at http://www.nps.gov/uspp/.

41. United States Park Police, "Counter Narcotics and Terrorism Operational Medical Support," available at http://www.nps.gov/uspp/.

42. Department of the Interior, "2010 Annual Report."

43. United States Park Police, Services Division, "Explorer Post," available at http://www.nps.gov/uspp/.

44. United States Park Police, "The United States Park Police Traffic Safety Unit," available at http://www.nps.gov/uspp/.

5

U.S. Secret Service

The U.S. Secret Service is one of the nation's oldest federal law enforcement agencies in the United States, being founded in 1865. Their symbol, a star, represents their mission. Every point of the star represents a core value of the agency: justice, duty, courage, honesty, and loyalty.[1]

Today the mission of the Secret Service is two-fold. First is the protection of current and former national leaders and their families. Secret Service agents strive to minimize the risk of harm to people, property, and events. Protected people include the current president, past presidents, the vice president, presidential candidates, and other visiting heads of state and government officials (i.e., foreign embassies). They are also given the responsibility to protect designated sites and provide protection during national special security events such as the presidential inauguration or State of the Union speech. To do this, agents evaluate information on people, groups, and activities that may pose a threat. They also conduct intelligence "advances" preceding travel.

The second portion of the mission for the Secret Service is to safeguard the country's financial infrastructure and payment systems and preserve the integrity of the economy. To do that, Secret Service agents have the jurisdiction to investigate alleged crimes such as counterfeiting of U.S. currency and treasury bonds, financial and electronic crimes, identity theft, forgery of government-issued checks, money laundering, and cases of major fraud.[2] As such, the Secret Service has concurrent jurisdiction with the FBI over certain violations of federal computer crime laws. They have created 24 electronic crimes task forces around the country that involve not only the FBI but also state and local law enforcement groups, the private sector, and academia in an effort to combat technology-based fraud.

The general statutory authority for the Secret Service is found in 18 U.S.C §3056, as shown in Figure 5.1. The specific duties of the Uniformed Division of the Secret Service are listed in Figure 5.2.

Figure 5.1: Statutory Authority of United States Secret Service

(a) Under the direction of the Secretary of Homeland Security, the United States Secret Service is authorized to protect the following persons:

(1) The President, the Vice President (or other officer next in the order of succession to the Office of President), the President-elect, and the Vice President-elect.

(2) The immediate families of those individuals listed in paragraph (1).

(3) Former Presidents and their spouses for their lifetimes, except that protection of a spouse shall terminate in the event of remarriage.

(4) Children of a former President who are under 16 years of age.

(5) Visiting heads of foreign states or foreign governments.

(6) Other distinguished foreign visitors to the United States and official representatives of the United States performing special missions abroad when the President directs that such protection be provided.

(7) Major Presidential and Vice Presidential candidates and, within 120 days of the general Presidential election, the spouses of such candidates. As used in this paragraph, the term "major Presidential and Vice Presidential candidates" means those individuals identified as such by the Secretary of Homeland Security after consultation with an advisory committee consisting of the Speaker of the House of Representatives, the minority leader of the House of Representatives, the majority and minority leaders of the Senate, and one additional member selected by the other members of the committee. The Committee shall not be subject to the Federal Advisory Committee Act (5 App. U.S.C. 2).

(8) Former Vice Presidents, their spouses, and their children who are under 16 years of age, for a period of not more than six months after the date the former Vice President leaves office. The Secretary of Homeland Security shall have the authority to direct the Secret Service to provide temporary protection for any of these individuals at any time thereafter if the Secretary of Homeland Security or designee determines that information or conditions warrant such protection.

The protection authorized in paragraphs (2) through (8) may be declined.

(b) Under the direction of the Secretary of Homeland Security, the Secret Service is authorized to detect and arrest any person who violates—

(1) section 508, 509, 510, 871, or 879 of this title or, with respect to the Federal Deposit Insurance Corporation, Federal land banks, and Federal land bank associations, section 213, 216, 433, 493, 657, 709, 1006, 1007, 1011, 1013, 1014, 1907, or 1909 of this title;

(2) any of the laws of the United States relating to coins, obligations, and securities of the United States and of foreign governments; or

(3) any of the laws of the United States relating to electronic fund transfer frauds, access device frauds, false identification documents or devices, and any fraud or other criminal or unlawful activity in or against any federally insured financial institution; except that the authority conferred by this paragraph shall be exercised subject to the agreement of the Attorney General and the Secretary of Homeland Security and shall not affect the authority of any other Federal law enforcement agency with respect to those laws.

(c)

(1) Under the direction of the Secretary of Homeland Security, officers and agents of the Secret Service are authorized to—

(A) execute warrants issued under the laws of the United States;

(B) carry firearms;

(C) make arrests without warrant for any offense against the United States committed in their presence, or for any felony cognizable under the laws of the United States if they have reasonable grounds to believe that the person to be arrested has committed or is committing such felony;

(D) offer and pay rewards for services and information leading to the apprehension of persons involved in the violation or potential violation of those provisions of law which the Secret Service is authorized to enforce;

(E) pay expenses for unforeseen emergencies of a confidential nature under the direction of the Secretary of Homeland Security and accounted for solely on the Secretary's certificate; and

(F) perform such other functions and duties as are authorized by law.

(2) Funds expended from appropriations available to the Secret Service for the purchase of counterfeits and subsequently recovered shall be reimbursed to the appropriations available to the Secret Service at the time of the reimbursement.

(d) Whoever knowingly and willfully obstructs, resists, or interferes with a Federal law enforcement agent engaged in the performance of the protective functions authorized by this section or by section 1752 of this title shall be fined not more than $1,000 or imprisoned not more than one year, or both.

(e)

(1) When directed by the President, the United States Secret Service is authorized to participate, under the direction of the Secretary of Homeland Security, in the planning, coordination, and implementation of security operations at special events of national significance, as determined by the President.

(2) At the end of each fiscal year, the President through such agency or office as the President may designate, shall report to the Congress—

(A) what events, if any, were designated special events of national significance for security purposes under paragraph (1); and

(B) the criteria and information used in making each designation.

(f) Under the direction of the Secretary of Homeland Security, the Secret Service is authorized, at the request of any State or local law enforcement agency, or at the request of the National Center for Missing and Exploited Children, to provide forensic and investigative assistance in support of any investigation involving missing or exploited children.

(g) The United States Secret Service shall be maintained as a distinct entity within the Department of Homeland Security and shall not be merged with any other Department function. No personnel and operational elements of the United States Secret Service shall report to an individual other than the Director of the United States Secret Service, who shall report directly to the Secretary of Homeland Security without being required to report through any other official of the Department.

Figure 5.2: 18 U.S.C. §3056A: Powers, Authorities, and Duties of United States Secret Service Uniform Division

(a) There is hereby created and established a permanent police force, to be known as the "United States Secret Service Uniformed Division." Subject to the supervision of the Secretary of Homeland Security, the United States Secret Service Uniformed Division shall perform such duties as the Director, United States Secret Service, may prescribe in connection with the protection of the following:

(1) The White House in the District of Columbia.

(2) Any building in which Presidential offices are located.

(3) The Treasury Building and grounds.

(4) The President, the Vice President (or other officer next in the order of succession to the Office of President), the President-elect, the Vice President-elect, and their immediate families.

(5) Foreign diplomatic missions located in the metropolitan area of the District of Columbia.

(6) The temporary official residence of the Vice President and grounds in the District of Columbia.

(7) Foreign diplomatic missions located in metropolitan areas (other than the District of Columbia) in the United States where there are located twenty or more such missions headed by full-time officers, except that such protection shall be provided only—

(A) on the basis of extraordinary protective need;

(B) upon request of an affected metropolitan area; and

(C) when the extraordinary protective need arises at or in association with a visit to—

(i) a permanent mission to, or an observer mission invited to participate in the work of, an international organization of which the United States is a member; or

(ii) an international organization of which the United States is a member;

except that such protection may also be provided for motorcades and at other places associated with any such visit and may be extended at places of temporary domicile in connection with any such visit.

(8) Foreign consular and diplomatic missions located in such areas in the United States, its territories and possessions, as the President, on a case-by-case basis, may direct.

(9) Visits of foreign government officials to metropolitan areas (other than the District of Columbia) where there are located twenty or more consular or diplomatic missions staffed by accredited personnel, including protection for motorcades and at other places associated with such visits when such officials are in the United States to conduct official business with the United States Government.

(10) Former Presidents and their spouses, as provided in section 3056 (a)(3) of title 18.

(11) An event designated under section 3056 (e) of title 18 as a special event of national significance.

(12) Major Presidential and Vice Presidential candidates and, within 120 days of the general Presidential election, the spouses of such candidates, as provided in section 3056 (a)(7) of title 18.

(13) Visiting heads of foreign states or foreign governments.

(b)

(1) Under the direction of the Director of the Secret Service, members of the United States Secret Service Uniformed Division are authorized to—

(A) carry firearms;

(B) make arrests without warrant for any offense against the United States committed in their presence, or for any felony cognizable under the laws of the United States if they have reasonable grounds to believe that the person to be arrested has committed or is committing such felony; and

(C) perform such other functions and duties as are authorized by law.

(2) Members of the United States Secret Service Uniformed Division shall possess privileges and powers similar to those of the members of the Metropolitan Police of the District of Columbia.

(c) Members of the United States Secret Service Uniformed Division shall be furnished with uniforms and other necessary equipment.

(d) In carrying out the functions pursuant to paragraphs (7) and (9) of subsection (a), the Secretary of Homeland Security may utilize, with their consent, on a reimbursable basis, the services, personnel, equipment, and facilities of State and local governments, and is authorized to reimburse such State and local governments for the utilization of such services, personnel, equipment, and facilities. The Secretary of Homeland Security may carry out the functions pursuant to paragraphs (7) and (9) of subsection (a) by contract. The authority of this subsection may be transferred by the President to the Secretary of State. In carrying out any duty under paragraphs (7) and (9) of subsection (a), the Secretary of State is authorized to utilize any authority available to the Secretary under title II of the State Department Basic Authorities Act of 1956.

History

The origins of the United States Secret Service are often not very clear because like many of the other federal law enforcement agencies, it has antecedents that date back to earlier times. In the case of the United States Secret Service, however, there was even an agency that had the same name but carried out a very different function. The nightwatchmen that would eventually develop into the United States Park Police (see Chapter 4) also had the duty of protecting the White House Gardens, so they acted as a form of security for the president. In addition, the U.S. Metropolitan Police Department had a special detail of being assigned to the White House to provide security prior to and during the Civil War. There is also evidence that after the assassination attempt on President Andrew Jackson's life by the deranged painter Richard Lawrence, a sentry box was established at the front entrance to the White House, staffed by a lone sentry.[3]

During the Civil War, two needs arose that would see two organizations draw upon the name Secret Service. The first issue was the devaluing of the federal currency by counterfeit dollars being produced in the South and transported to the North. This flooding of the currency system with bogus dollars undercut the value of the American dollar and necessitated an organization to pursue counterfeiters. Another need, due to the use of either Southern agents against the North or for the fact many Southern sympathizers already lived in the Northern states, intelligence gathering against this potential threat became critical to the survival of the Union. The private detective Allan Pinkerton was employed in this capacity, and after his services were diverted for other purposes, Lafayette C. Baker, a rather colorful individual, took over as the lead investigator into Southern espionage.[4] Part of Baker's intelligence-oriented agency was also dedicated to fighting counterfeiters. When the war ended, by all accounts the organization known as the Secret Service as a wartime expediency was also going to end.

It became clear, however, that the issue of counterfeiting U.S. dollars was not going to end and in order to gain control of the economy, enforcement of counterfeiting was still necessary. President Abraham Lincoln actually created the Secret Service Division on April 14, 1865, but his assassination that evening slowed the implementation of his plans. It was not until July 5, 1865, that Treasury Secretary Hugh McCulloch officially created the United States Secret Service Division of the U.S. Treasury Department. Its mission, and its only mission, was to investigate the crime of counterfeiting. Although the organization was created within the administrative element of the United States government, the fact the U.S. Constitution explicitly states that Congress has the power "to provide for the Punishment of counterfeiting the Securities and current Coin of the United States,"[5] the creation of the agency was considered to be fully acceptable within the Constitutional framework.

The first chief appointed to head the new Secret Service Division was William P. Wood, the man who already had experience with the agency's predecessor that dealt with the issue of counterfeiting. In their early years, it has been said that "business was brisk," for "during its first four years of operation, 1865–1869, the Service's so-called 'operatives' stalked and nabbed over two hundred counterfeiters."[6] Mid-way through these four years, the Secret Service would gain further investigatory powers and responsibilities when Congress expanded their duties to "detecting persons perpetrating frauds against the government."[7] With additional appropriations in hand, the U.S. Secret Service began to target smugglers, mail robbers, land frauds, illegal distillers, and perhaps most successfully, the Ku Klux Klan.

In light of those first four years where the majority of the Secret Service's work was taking place in New York City, because the primary location for the printing of U.S. currency was there and it was considered the financial capital of the United States, the Secret Service Division decided to move its headquarters to New York City in 1870. Several things worked to undercut this move. The first being that the resources for the agency were derived solely from appropriations by Congress and the secretary of the Treasury—both located in Washington, D.C. Still further, Congress was in the process of establishing the Bureau of Engraving and Printing in Washington, D.C., meaning that all U.S. currency would be produced in the capital. Thus, after five years of diminishing ability administratively, the Secret Service Division returned its headquarters to Washington, D.C., where it has remained ever since.

The Secret Service's responsibilities in regard to counterfeiting continued to grow in the late 1800s, with the passage of an act in 1877 prohibiting the counterfeiting of any coin, gold, or silver bar, and in 1895, with the added responsibility for investigating counterfeit stamps. In addition, in 1883, they would become officially recognized by Congress as a distinct organization within the U.S. Department of the Treasury. What was slow to develop, however, was the duty of protecting the president of the United States. In fact, it would end up taking the assassinations of three U.S. presidents before it was deemed to be a full-time duty of the Secret Service.

In the wake of the assassination of President Abraham Lincoln, additional guards were posted at the White House, but little else was done to protect the next several presidents. Once again, in 1881, after the assassination of President Garfield by Charles Guiteau, additional guards were provided to the president as was deemed necessary.[8] Yet, even in 1894, the protection of President Grover Cleveland was only a part-time and informal duty of the U.S. Secret Service. And why the U.S. Secret Service? The primary reason was for the fact that there were few federal law enforcement agencies at the time (actually only the four previous agencies reviewed in this book), and that if you look outside of the White House, the Treasury Department is located right next door. It was more a matter of convenience than anything else.

Not until the assassination of President McKinley by anarchist Leon Czolgosz, however, would full-time protection of the president be considered.[9] Although there had been a U.S. Secret Service agent with President McKinley in the receiving line of the Pan-American Exposition in Buffalo, New York, on September 6, 1901, Czolgosz managed to use a bandage dressing wrapped around his hand to conceal a gun.[10] After McKinley died, Theodore Roosevelt became president of the United States and two operatives were assigned to him full time. Oddly enough, there were no permanent appropriations for this duty, so Congress passed a Sundry Civil Expense Act in 1907 and provided funds for the protection of the president, but this expense had to be renewed annually in the United States budget.[11]

Under Roosevelt the agents would take on a variety of expanded duties. As there were a number of fraud cases involving western lands owned by the U.S. government, Secret Service agents were often sent to investigate. Another interesting duty came of Roosevelt's desire to have an investigatory agency within the federal bureaucracy, one that could serve to investigate crimes against (and potentially by) members of the federal government. Roosevelt began the practice of "borrowing" agents from the United States Secret Service to be investigators in this Bureau of Investigation under the Department of Justice. Congress balked at the idea and passed a law that prevented the use of agents or funds from agencies for other than directed purposes, thus ending the "borrowing" of Secret Service agents. However, never one to be outdone, Roosevelt passed an executive order creating the Bureau of Investigation, which would ultimately become the Federal Bureau of Investigation (see Chapter 6). Also in 1908, an election year in which Roosevelt decided not to run for reelection, Secret Service protection was extended to the president-elect, in this case William Howard Taft. Under Taft, in 1913, the United States Secret Service would be authorized permanent protection duty of the president and president-elect under statutory law.

During World War I, President Wilson directed the Secretary of the Treasury to use the Secret Service to investigate espionage against the United States. The Bureau of Investigation was still too young an agency and the earlier embryonic Secret Service had held this same responsibility during the Civil War. In addition, Congress expanded the protection of the president to include his immediate family, and any threat made against the president of the United States was made a violation of federal law. This gave the Secret Service more power to investigate threats made against the president's life and to take preventive action by arresting those making threats before they attempted to carry out those threats.

From the end of World War I through World War II, for the most part, the Secret Service entered a quiet period of existence. Threats against the president ebbed after the war, rose during Prohibition, ebbed again, then rose with the deleterious effects of the Great Depression. Although there was an attempt on Franklin D. Roosevelt's life in Florida when he was running for president, no other major attempts arose during this time frame. It was also during this time period that the White House Police Force was created at the request of President Warren G. Harding. Effective October 1, 1922, the responsibility of protecting the White House was removed from the Washington, D.C. Metropolitan Police and placed under the protection of a police force solely dedicated to the White House itself. As a result of the close relationship between this new uniformed police force and the Secret Service, in 1930, the White House Police were placed under the supervision of the U.S. Secret Service.[12]

A major shift in duties and responsibilities came as a result of the assassination attempt on President Harry S. Truman by two Puerto Rican separatists.[13] As the White House was undergoing the first major repairs since it was built, Truman had moved across the street to the Blair House. On November 1, 1950, Griselio Torresola and Oscar Collazo, two members of a group demanding independence for Puerto Rico, walked up to the Blair House and opened fire. Although Truman was upstairs taking a nap when the event occurred, he was not harmed. Both Secret Service agents and White House Police were on duty that day and shot and killed one of the suspects (Torresola) and arrested the other (Collazo). In the exchange of gunfire, Officer Leslie Coffelt was shot and killed.[14]

Congress immediately took action in response to the assassination attempt on Truman's life. They enacted legislation that permanently authorized Secret Service protection for the president, his immediate family, the president-elect, and the vice-president (if he so wished). In addition, fixed funds were now budgeted for the Secret Service so that monetary costs for protecting the president did not have to be renewed on an annual basis. The United States Secret Service was now a fixed part of the Treasury Department and a permanent fixture within the Office of the Presidency. Ten years later, in 1961, protection of former presidents was added, thus in place for the retirement of President Eisenhower; and in 1962, protection was extended to the vice president and the vice president-elect (whether they wanted it or not now).[15]

The next significant change to the United States Secret Service came in the wake of the assassination of President John F. Kennedy.[16] Although the Secret Service had become a more professional organization up to that point, its capacity for dealing with the more modern American presidency (i.e., more mobile) had not kept pace. The agency was spread thin. On November 22, 1963, with the assassination of Kennedy, the Secret Service had to rethink what it was doing and how it was doing it. A major investigation into the policies, practices, and procedures created both internal and external changes. In the immediate aftermath, Congress passed legislation to continue the protection of Mrs. Kennedy and her children for two years. There was no provision for protecting the family after a president was no longer president. In 1965, Congress would make this permanent by extending protection to former presidents and their spouses during their lifetime and protecting their children up to age 16. A second Kennedy assassination, this time Senator Robert Kennedy, who was running for president in 1968, caused Congress to authorize the protection of major presidential and vice presidential candidates and nominees, the widows of presidents until death or remarriage, and their children, until age 16.[17]

Other administrative changes began to take hold in the 1970s. During this time frame, the White House Police Force was renamed the Executive Protective Service, and they were given the increased responsibility of protecting major diplomatic missions in the Washington, D.C. area, which usually meant protecting dignitaries and heads-of-state visiting the president at the White House. This was eventually expanded to cover the entire United States and its territories. In 1977, the Executive Protective Service was again renamed to what it is now referred to as today—the Secret Service Uniformed Division. In 1986, the Uniformed Division would absorb its next door neighbor, the Treasury Police Force, taking over their duties of protecting the U.S. Treasury.

The United States Secret Service once again came to the forefront of America's attention on March 30, 1981 and, in reviewing the films of that day, it is very clear the internal changes to the United States Secret Service paid off.[18] On that day, President Ronald Reagan, who had only been in office two months, gave a speech at the Washington Hilton Hotel. Upon exiting to his waiting limousine, John Hinckley, Jr. pulled a pistol and fired in close proximity to President Reagan. The Secret Service agent closest to Reagan, Jerry Parr, reacted instinctively from his training and pushed Reagan into the limousine. Secret Service Agent Timothy

McCarthy turned toward the gunfire, making himself a target, and subsequently was shot in the stomach. White House Press Secretary and Washington D.C. Metropolitan Police Officer Thomas Delahanty were also shot by the would-be assassin's bullets. Although at first it was not believed Reagan had been shot, it turned out he had been struck by a bullet deflected off the car door, but it was very clearly the fast reaction of the Secret Service that saved the president's life that day in March of 1981.

As the United States Secret Service reached the end of the twentieth century, it maintained the split duties of counterfeiting investigation and presidential security. From time to time a debate would arise as to whether or not these duties should be split into two separate agencies. It has been argued that the duties are so vastly different that each would be improved if a sole agency was dedicated to its own specific mission rather than trying to accomplish the two missions so ingrained within the United States Secret Service. Although tradition was part of the counterargument, in reality it was only a minor part. The true argument that typically arises is the fact that the presidential detail is so time consuming and stressful that the ability to rotate agents back and forth between the two different missions provides for a better-prepared agency. Most recently, this debate surfaced in 2009 in Congress, but once again the agency was left unaltered.[19]

A number of additional laws passed by Congress in the late twentieth century would continue to expand the roles and responsibilities of the United States Secret Service. One issue that continued to surface in regard to both presidential protection and counterfeiting operations was the overlap with investigations that were deemed to be under the purview of the Federal Bureau of Investigation. In 1990, the Secret Service was given concurrent jurisdiction with the FBI to alleviate this particular issue. When it came to counterfeiting, the Secret Service would see their role expand under the 1994 Crime Bill when Congress made it a crime to manufacture, traffic, or possess counterfeit U.S. currency overseas, meaning the U.S. Secret Service could investigate counterfeiting around the world and prosecute it as if the crime had occurred in the United States. In addition, the 1998 Telemarketing Fraud Prevention Act and the Identity Theft and Assumption Deterrence Act expanded the crimes they could investigate under the category of frauds committed against the United States.

There was one law that actually contracted the responsibilities of the U.S. Secret Service. Congress passed a law that was part of the Crime Bill, which went into effect in 1997, limiting the protection of former presidents to ten years. This was an acknowledgement to the fact that presidents truly do return to being just citizens and that protection detail for a lifetime is unnecessary.

One additional presidential protection duty came with the Presidential Threat Protection Act of 2000. This act was primarily a bill that clarified and amended the federal code to clearly state the scope of duties that the Secret Service had in investigating threats against the president. One additional aspect of the bill authorized the Secret Service to participate in the planning, coordination, and implementation of security operations for special events of national significance. As the Secret Service was already highly trained in the planning, coordination, and implementation of security for the president every time he moved and at the hundreds of special events he attended on an annual basis, it was determined that this capability could be beneficial to those events that might be targeted due to the chance that the president might attend. Examples include major sporting events, such as the Superbowl or the Olympics, or the visits of important dignitaries such as Pope John Paul II or Benedict XVI.

Like so many of the other federal law enforcement agencies, the United States Secret Service would be profoundly impacted by the events of September 11, 2001. The USA PATRIOT Act was passed, both increasing the number and type of investigatory tools the Secret Service would have to fight fraud against the government and greatly expanding their duties and responsibilities. The following year, with the passage of the Homeland Security Act of 2002, the federal law enforcement bureaucracy was restructured and the United States Department of Homeland Security was created. The United States Secret Service was transferred from underneath the Treasury Department and was placed in the Department of Homeland Security as an independent agency, meaning that the agency was not broken apart but moved intact, and the Director of the Secret Service was ordered to report directly to the Secretary of Homeland Security. The United States Secret Service remains there today, continuing to perform its two critical missions—protecting America's currency and its commander-in-chief.

Who Gets Hired

There are approximately 3,543 special agents working at the Secret Service today. This includes 1,389 in the Uniformed Division and 1,872 administrative, professional, and technical staff.[20]

To be an agent, a candidate must be a citizen of the U.S., be between 21 and 37 years old, possess a current valid driver's license, and have visual acuity no worse than 20/60 uncorrected but correctable to 20/20 in each eye. A four-year academic degree from a college or university or a combination of education and law enforcement experience is required. The applicant should be in good physical condition and must be able to pass a complete background check and a polygraph.

New agents attend training at the Federal Law Enforcement Training Center (FLETC) in Glynco, Georgia, where they enroll in the Criminal Investigator Training Program (CITP) for a ten-week session. Here the recruits are trained in areas such as criminal law and investigative techniques. Upon completing this training, recruits are then sent to the James J. Rowley Training Center. Here the curriculum is geared toward teaching new recruits the specifics needed to become an effective Secret Service agent. They receive training in protection of officials and sites, firearms, use of force/control, emergency medical situations, detection of financial crimes, and water survival.[21]

The Secret Service also takes advantage of the James J. Rowley Training Center. This center has facilities for classrooms, labs, physical training, and tactical training along with indoor and outdoor firearm ranges. In FY 2013, 12,709 agents received training in over 400 courses. Additionally, over 100,000 courses were completed in a variety of topics such as emergency preparedness and leadership through the Center.[22]

New special agents spend their first six to eight years in the agency assigned to a field office. After this, they can transfer to a protective detail for a three- to five-year period. Upon completion of this detail, many agents choose to return to the field. Some choose to work overseas. Some agents opt to receive additional training in the Electronic Crimes Special Agent Program. This was established to provide Secret Service agents with the advanced computer forensic training needed to conduct computer forensic investigations and gather electronic evidence from computers and other electronic media devices.

The Secret Service employs interns in three ways. First is the Secret Service Student Temporary Education Employment Program (STEP). This program provides a federal employment opportunity to those students who are enrolled or accepted for enrollment at least on a half-time basis at an academic, technical, or vocational program in an accredited high school, technical, vocational, two-or four-year college or university, graduate, or professional school. The second internship program is the Student Career Experience Program. This program combines classroom training along with a participatory work environment. Interns in this program participate in a two-year work-study program that is in line with their chosen field of study. Finally, the Student Volunteer Service Program provides an unpaid work assignment for students who seek to explore career options with the Secret Service while developing personal and professional skills.

Budgets

The budget allocation given to the Secret Service from Congress is usually between $1.7 and $1.9 billion each year, as shown in Table 5.1.

Table 5.1	Budget Authority (In Billions of Dollars)
FY 2010 enacted	$1.719
FY 2011 enacted	$1.722
FY 2012 enacted	$1.914
FY 2013 enacted	$1.806
FY 2014 enacted	$1.839
FY 2015 presidential budget	$1.896

Source: U.S. Department of Homeland Security, "FY 2014 Budget in Brief," available at http://www.dhs.gov/sites/default/files/publications/MGMT/FY%20 2014%20BIB%20-%20FINAL%20-508%20Formatted%20%20%284%29.pdf; U.S. Department of Homeland Security, "FY 2015 Budget in Brief," available at http:// www.dhs.gov/sites/default/files/publications/FY15BIB.pdf.

Organization

The Secret Service is part of the Department of Homeland Security. The agency is headquartered in Washington, D.C. but also operates 136 field offices throughout the U.S. and abroad. The agency is headed by a director, as described below.

Leader

The interim director of the Secret Service is Joe Clancy, who was appointed to oversee the agency after the resignation of Julia Pierson, who stepped down after security breaches at the White House. Before being named as the interim director in October, 2014, Clancy served as head of the Presidential Protective Division, acting as the lead agent on President Obama's security detail until his retirement in 2011. At that time, Clancy took a job as the executive director of cable security at Comcast Corporation.

Before joining the Secret Service, Clancy attended the U.S. Military Academy at West Point. He graduated from Villanova University, earning a B.A. degree in political science/criminal justice. As part of the Philadelphia Archdiocese, Clancy was a high school teacher and coach for football and baseball. Clancy first became a Secret Service agent in May, 1984, and was assigned to the Philadelphia field office. He was transferred to the Presidential Protective Division in 1989, where he served for eight years. In the year following this assignment, Clancy worked in the New York Field Office until he returned to the Presidential Protective Division, this time as the assistant to the special agent in charge. He became a staff assistant in the Office of Congressional Affairs two years later, working for the Commerce, Justice, and State Senate Appropriations Subcommittee. Throughout this time, Clancy also worked for the Internal Affairs Division of the Secret Service (the Office of Inspection).

Following the 9/11 attacks, Clancy was chosen to be a staff assistant in the newly created Office of Homeland Security. Here, he was appointed to be the director for national special security events. He served in this position until March of 2003, when he returned to the Presidential Protective Division. At first, Clancy was an assistant special agent in charge, but he was soon promoted to deputy special agent in charge. In June, 2005, he was chosen to be part of the Senior Executive Service, where he served until his promotion to special agent in charge of the Presidential Protective Division. Clancy has been described by coworkers as disciplined, levelheaded, and willing to take on a challenge—such as leading the Secret Service.

What They Do

As noted earlier, the Secret Service has both special agents and uniformed division agents. The duties of special agents include both investigations and protection. The Uniformed Division provides protection and security for the White House complex, the main Treasury building and other protected facilities, the official residence of the vice-president, and foreign diplomatic missions in the D.C. area. There are three branches within the Unformed Division: the White House Branch, the Foreign Missions Branch, and the Naval Observatory Branch.

The White House Branch is responsible for protecting the president. The White House is guarded by 500 uniformed division officers who continually patrol the perimeters of the White House. The president is given protection while in the Oval Office and on trips domestically and abroad. The agents arrange for all security while the president is at home or away. When the president travels, the Uniformed Division officers coordinate the security details with the FBI and local law enforcement agencies.

There are five basic components to the activities of the Secret Service. They include a protective mission, investigation of financial crimes, forensic and investigative support, technical development, and strategic intelligence.

Protective Mission

After President William McKinley was assassinated in 1901, Congress directed the Secret Service to provide protection for the president of the United States. Since then, the role of the Secret Service has expanded to include other top government officials. The Secret Service is authorized by Title 18 of the U.S.C. §3056 to protect:

> a. The president, vice-president (or other individuals next in order of succession to the Office of the President), the president-elect and vice president-elect;
> b. The immediate families of the above individuals;
> c. Former presidents and their spouses for their lifetimes, except when the spouse remarries. A new law passed by Congress in 1997 limited Secret Service protection to former presidents for a maximum period of ten years from the date the president leaves office;
> d. Children of former presidents (until they reach the age of 16);
> e. Visiting heads of foreign governments and their spouses traveling with them; other distinguished foreign visitors to the U.S.; and official representatives of the U.S. performing special missions abroad;
> f. Major presidential and vice-presidential candidates, and their spouses, within 120 days of a general presidential election;
> g. Other individuals as designated by the president;
> h. National Special Security Events, when designated as such by the secretary of the Department of Homeland Security.[23]

Each of these individuals can decline protection except president, vice-president, the president-elect and vice-president elect.

Secret Service agents do not discuss the techniques they typically use to protect these officials. However, it is known that the president and other family members have agents permanently assigned to them. Those who are given temporary protective services, such as candidates, are assigned special agents on an interim basis from field offices and from the Dignitary Protective Division.[24] Each year, agents investigate thousands of threats made against the president or other officials. The Office of Protective Research conducts background checks on each individual who makes a threat against an official.

The Secret Service also provides protection at events of national significance. For example, the United States hosted the Asia Pacific Economic Cooperation Summit in 2011, in Hawaii. In 2012, the G-8 Economic Summit was held in the United States. In these (and other) situations, Secret Service agents take the lead in the planning, coordination, and implementation of security plans.[25] They work with other federal agencies and local police to ensure the event goes smoothly. In some cases, the protective role is assisted by the Division's Airspace Security Branch, Counter Sniper Team, Emergency Response Team, Canine Explosive Detection Unit, Counter Assault Team, Counter Surveillance Unit, Hazardous Agent Mitigation and Medical Emergency Response Team, and the Magnetometer Operations Units.[26]

Investigation of Financial Crimes

The original mandate for the Secret Service was to investigate and prevent counterfeiting of currency in the U.S. Today, the agency's primary investigative role is based upon safeguarding the financial systems of the U.S. Over the years, their mission has evolved from enforcing counterfeiting laws that protect the integrity of U.S. currency, coin, and financial obligations to now include investigation of financial and computer-based crimes.[27] Today, agents continually implement new measures geared toward deterring electronic crimes and other computer-related fraud.[28] Currently, Secret Service agents typically investigate identity crimes (credit card/access device fraud, check fraud, bank fraud, false identification fraud, passport fraud, identity theft, forgery, money laundering, electronic benefits transfer fraud [i.e., food stamps], asset forfeiture, and advance fee fraud).[29] Often, the investigations can be international in scope.

Counterfeiting

Counterfeiting of currency has changed in recent years due to advances in computer-based technology and digital printing technology.[30] The Secret Service works with both domestic and international law enforcement agencies to conduct investigations to identify those who are counterfeiting currency.[31] Agents often work with the Bureau of Engraving and Printing and the Federal Reserve System to ensure the integrity of the nation's currency. One such investigation was named Project Colombia. Created in 2001, the program was an effort to support Vetted Anti-Counterfeiting Forces (VACF) in Colombia, one of the largest producers of counterfeit U.S. currency. Through the program, the Secret Service provides assistance to Colombian law enforcement groups in targeting groups producing counterfeit money.

Financial Crimes

The Secret Service has the primary role in investigating financial crimes such as credit and debit card fraud and identity theft. The Secret Service also has the primary authority to investigate fraud as it relates to computers and, along with the

Department of Justice, financial institution fraud.[32] Secret Service agents are part of the Financial Crimes Task Forces in which they have formed partnerships with state, local, and other federal law enforcement agencies to investigate financial crimes. These task forces utilize the resources of both the private sector and other law enforcement agencies to create an organized effort to combat financial crimes. There are currently 37 FCTFs nationwide and one in San Juan, Puerto Rico.

The Secret Service investigates mortgage fraud through the Mortgage Fraud Section of the Criminal Investigative Division (CID). They participate in 36 mortgage fraud task forces around the country alongside Housing and Urban Development, the Department of Justice, the Department of the Treasury, and financial institutions. They also work with the attorney general's Financial Fraud Enforcement Task Force (FFETF) Mortgage Fraud Working Group, which works both with criminal and civil enforcement of laws. They often inform financial institutions and members of the law enforcement community about the most current mortgage fraud trends and schemes.

In 2010, the FFETF Mortgage Fraud Working Group supervised a national mortgage fraud investigation they nicknamed "Operation Stolen Dreams," to target mortgage fraud. The operation included officials from the Department of Justice as well as various federal, state, and local law enforcement agencies.[33]

Cybercrimes

The focus of the work done by investigators in the Secret Service has evolved as technology has advanced and the globalization of the Internet has emerged. Their investigations must now concentrate on transnational cybercrime as records show that the amount of cybercrimes aimed at U.S. financial institutions and critical infrastructures are on the increase. There are more cases of phishing emails, malicious software, and hacking attacks. The Secret Service uses many techniques to protect the nation's financial infrastructure from financial crimes. They provide agents with enhanced computer-based training through their Electronic Crimes Special Agent Program (ECSAP). They have also created 31 Electronic Crimes Task Forces (ECTS) that utilize the resources of academia, the private sector, and local, state, and federal law enforcement agencies in an effort to combat computer-based threats. They work to identify and locate international cyber criminals who are involved in cyber-attacks, identity theft, credit card fraud, bank fraud, and other computer-related crimes. Moreover, Secret Service agents provide computer-based training and investigative tools to state and local law enforcement groups through the National Computer Forensics Institute.

The USA PATRIOT Act mandated the Secret Service establish Electronic Crimes Task Forces (ECTFs) that would bring together federal, state, and local law enforcement personnel, prosecutors, and representatives from private industry and academia to investigate and prevent attacks on the nation's financial and critical infrastructure. The task forces provide support and resources to field investigations. Recently, two ECTFs were established in Kansas City and St. Louis to fight computer-based crimes.[34]

The Secret Service created a European Electronic Crimes Task Force in Italy in 2009 and one in the United Kingdom in 2010. Both task force groups investigate computer-based criminal activity such as network intrusions, hacking, and identity theft.

The National Computer Forensics Institute is a cooperative partnership with the Department of Homeland Security and officials from the state of Alabama that provides a national standard of training for a the investigation of electronic crimes. The Institute provides law enforcement officers from state and local departments the training needed to conduct basic computer forensic examinations and to respond to network intrusion incidents. The Institute will allow the Secret Service to have additional highly trained officers who can investigate electronic crimes when needed.[35]

In recent years, the Secret Service has reported an increase in cyber-related criminal activity from Eurasian groups who target U.S. citizens and financial institutions. They have also reported an increase in transnational criminal groups in South America, specifically Peru, that target U.S. banking and other related financial interests. To investigate these activities, the International Programs Division (IPD) of the Secret Service provides administrative support, procedures, and guidelines to the 23 foreign field offices in those regions. The Division oversees annual budgets and serves as the central liaison point between the international offices and the Office of Investigations. IPD also oversees the international training given to officers that will enable them to effectively fight cybercrimes.

Forensic and Investigative Support

The Secret Service provides both forensic and investigative support to law enforcement. The Forensic Services Division (FSD) houses an advanced forensic laboratory that in turn houses the world's largest ink library, the largest known forensic collection of writing inks in the world. The database contains nearly 10,000 samples that can be used by forensic analysts when examining documents, looking for fingerprints, analyzing handwriting samples, and other related forensic science areas.[36]

The Investigative Support Division houses the Criminal Research Specialist Program, which was originally established to support the investigative needs of Secret Service personnel. Agents assigned to the program provide investigators with financial analyses, link analyses, event flow, and geospatial and telephone analyses. They carry out research for cases of possible mortgage fraud, cybercrimes, bank fraud, money laundering, identity theft, wire fraud, and counterfeiting. They can provide assistance to agents who must execute search warrants and testify in court. They currently provide analytical support to about 300 criminal investigations on a monthly basis.[37]

In the 1994 Crime Bill, the Secret Service was given the responsibility to provide forensic/technical assistance in cases of missing and exploited children. Later, when President George W. Bush signed the PROTECT Act of 2003, otherwise known as the "Amber Alert Bill," the Secret Service was given full authorization in this area.[38]

Technical Development

The Secret Service continues to work with other agencies to develop technology that will allow for greater information sharing. This, in turn, will potentially allow agents to detect crimes before they happen or to solve them more quickly. Through their eInformation Network, information is shared between agencies at no cost to law enforcement officers, financial institution investigators, academics, and commercial partners. The Internet site also contains the eLibrary and the U.S. Dollars Counterfeit Note Search to help track criminal activity between jurisdictions.

Strategic Intelligence

Some agents from the Secret Service are assigned temporarily to positions with other government agencies as a way to enhance relationships and share information about criminal intelligence or new crime trends. In the past, Secret Service agents have been assigned to the Department of the Treasury, the Financial Crimes Enforcement Network, the National Cyber Investigative Joint Task Force, the United States–Computer Emergency Readiness Team (U.S.–CERT), the Homeland Security Council, the Department of Homeland Security National Cyber Security Division, the DHS Office of Infrastructure Protection, Interpol, and even Europol. Moreover, Secret Service agents are part of every Joint Terrorism Task Force located in field offices across the country.[39]

Conclusion

The functions of the Secret Service are central to protecting the country's national leaders and visiting officials from harm. Their services also help to protect the nation's financial systems from those who might seek to commit acts of financial fraud. The Secret Service remains a key agency in federal law enforcement today.

Key Terms

William P. Wood

Presidential Threat Protection Act of 2000

special agents

Secret Service Student Temporary Education Employment Program

Student Career Experience Program

Student Volunteer Service Program

Mark Sullivan

Uniformed Division

White House Branch

Foreign Missions Branch

Naval Observatory Branch

Protective Division

Electronic Crimes Task Forces

Forensic and Investigative Support Division

Review Questions

1. What are the two primary functions or roles of the Secret Service?

2. Who are the people protected by the Secret Service?

3. Describe the history of the Secret Service.

4. How did the events of 9/11 impact the Secret Service?

5. What are the qualifications needed to be hired by the Secret Service?

6. Summarize the budgetary allocations of the Secret Service.

7. How is the Secret Service organized?

8. Describe the role that the Secret Service plays in investigating counterfeiting.

Endnotes

1. U.S. Department of Homeland Security, United States Secret Service, "Fiscal Year 2010 Annual Report," available at http://www.secretservice.gov/USSS2010AYweb.pdf.
2. U.S. Department of Homeland Security, "Fiscal Year 2010 Annual Report."
3. Oliver, Willard M. & Nancy E. Marion. (2010). *Killing the President: Assassinations, Attempts, and Rumored Attempts on U.S. Commanders-in-Chief.* Santa Barbara, CA: Praeger Publishers.
4. Baker, L.C. (1867). *United States Secret Service.* Philadelphia, PA: L. C. Baker.
5. United States Constitution, Article 1, Section 8.
6. Melanson, Philip H. & Peter F. Stevens. (2002). *The Secret Service: The Hidden History of an Enigmatic Agency.* New York: Carroll & Graff Publishers, p. 12.
7. United States Secret Service. (2012). Secret Service History. Available online at http://www.secretservice.gov/history.shtml.
8. Millard, Candice. (2011). *Destiny of the Republic: A Tale of Madness, Medicine, and the Murder of a President.* New York: Doubleday.
9. Oliver, *Killing the President.*
10. Miller, Scott. (2011). *The President and the Assassin.* New York: Random House.
11. Melanson, *The Secret Service.*
12. United States Secret Service, Secret Service History.
13. Hunter, Stephen & John Bainbridge, Jr. (2005). *American Gunfight: The Plot to Kill Harry Truman and the Shoot-Out That Stopped It.* New York: Simon & Schuster.
14. Oliver, *Killing the President.*
15. United States Secret Service, Secret Service History.
16. Blaine, Gerald with Lisa McCubbin. (2010). *The Kennedy Detail.* New York: Gallery Books.
17. United States Secret Service, Secret Service History.
18. Wilber, Del Quentin. (2011). *Rawhide Down: The Near Assassination of Ronald Reagan.* New York: Henry Holt and Company.
19. Reese, Shawn. (2009). *The U.S. Secret Service: An Examination and Analysis of Its Evolving Mission.* Washington, D.C.: Congressional Research Service.
20. U.S. Department of Homeland Security, "Fiscal Year 2010 Annual Report."
21. U.S. Department of Homeland Security, "Fiscal Year 2010 Annual Report"; also United States Secret Service, "James J. Rowley Training Center," available at http://www.secretservice.gov/about_rtc.shtml.
22. United States Secret Service, "2013 Annual Report," available at http://www.secretservice.gov/USSS_FY13AR.pdf.
23. United States Secret Service, "Protective Mission," available at http://www.secretservice.gov/protection.shtml.
24. U.S. Department of Homeland Security, "Fiscal Year 2010 Annual Report."
25. U.S. Department of Homeland Security, "Fiscal Year 2010 Annual Report."
26. U.S. Department of Homeland Security, "Fiscal Year 2010 Annual Report
27. U.S. Department of Homeland Security, "Fiscal Year 2010 Annual Report."
28. United States Secret Service, "Criminal Investigations," available at http://www.secretservice.gov/criminal.shtml.
29. United States Secret Service, "Criminal Investigations."
30. U.S. Department of Homeland Security, "Fiscal Year 2010 Annual Report."
31. U.S. Department of Homeland Security, "Fiscal Year 2010 Annual Report."
32. U.S. Department of Homeland Security, "Fiscal Year 2010 Annual Report."
33. U.S. Department of Homeland Security, "Fiscal Year 2010 Annual Report."
34. U.S. Department of Homeland Security, "Fiscal Year 2010 Annual Report."
35. U.S. Department of Homeland Security, "Fiscal Year 2010 Annual Report."
36. United States Secret Service, "Forensic Services," available at http://www.secretservice.gov/forensics.shtml.
37. U.S. Department of Homeland Security, "Fiscal Year 2010 Annual Report," available at http://www.secretservice.gov/USSS2010AYweb.pdf.
38. United States Secret Service, "Forensic Services."
39. U.S. Department of Homeland Security, "Fiscal Year 2010 Annual Report."

6

Federal Bureau of Investigation

Since it was first organized, the Federal Bureau of Investigation (FBI) has sought to protect the American public from a variety of criminals, beginning with gangsters and corrupt public officials and expanding into cyber criminals and white collar offenders. After the terrorist attacks of September 11, 2011, the FBI again evolved to focus on those who pose a risk of terrorism to the U.S., whose crimes are made all the more serious by globalization and advanced technologies. As the principal investigative arm of the U.S. Department of Justice, the FBI is a domestic intelligence agency with the motto, "Fidelity, Bravery and Integrity."[1] It is a member of the U.S. Intelligence Community.

Today, the FBI's primary responsibility is to protect the United States and its citizens from domestic and international terrorism and foreign intelligence threats by upholding and enforcing the nation's criminal laws. Agents also work to protect the U.S. from any foreign intelligence operations and espionage geared toward revealing secrets that could put the country in harm's way. The agents work to deter those criminals who seek to use cyber-based attacks and other high-technology crimes and to combat public corruption at all levels of government. They also fight emerging threats such as international criminal organizations.[2] Agents clearly recognized the dangers of transnational and national criminal organizations and enterprises and seek to end them. They work to combat major white-collar crime and significant violent crime that occurs across the nation.[3] At the same time, the FBI works to protect the civil rights of citizens.

103

Figure 6.1: FBI Core Values

1. Rigorous obedience to the Constitution of the United States;
2. Respect for the dignity of all those we protect;
3. Compassion;
4. Fairness;
5. Uncompromising personal integrity and institutional integrity;
6. Accountability by accepting responsibility for our actions and decisions and the consequences of our actions and decisions; and
7. Leadership, both personal and professional

Source: Federal Bureau of Investigation, "Quick Facts," available at http://www.fbi.gov/about-us/quick-facts.

The FBI is the lead federal agency responsible for investigating and preventing attacks that might involve any weapons of mass destruction: chemical, radiological or biological agents, or even nuclear weapons. The FBI also has jurisdiction over specific terrorism-related offenses, such as violence at airports, money laundering, or attacks on U.S. officials. The FBI constantly works with other U.S. intelligence agencies to collect and analyze any intelligence related to possible terrorism and security threats.[4] The FBI has been more predictive when analyzing possible criminal activity than ever before.[5]

The FBI also provides leadership and criminal justice services to other federal, state, local, and international law enforcement agencies. This can include assistance with fingerprint identification, laboratory examinations, and training of officers. The FBI helps other agencies when threats are made against American society or when the crime is too large or complex for local or state authorities to handle by on their own.

There are many parts of the U.S. Code that help to define responsibilities of the FBI. According to 28 U.S.C. §532, the attorney general may appoint a director of the Federal Bureau of Investigation. According to this code, the director of the Federal Bureau of Investigation is the head of the Federal Bureau of Investigation. Further responsibilities of the FBI are found in 18 U.S.C. §3052, which states:

> The Director, Associate Director, Assistant to the Director, Assistant Directors, inspectors, and agents of the Federal Bureau of Investigation of the Department of Justice may carry firearms, serve warrants and subpoenas issued under the authority of the United States and make arrests without warrant for any offense against the United States committed in their presence, or for any felony cognizable under the laws of the United States if they have reasonable grounds to believe that the person to be arrested has committed or is committing such felony.

More general duties of the agencies are found in 28 Code of Federal Regulations 0.85. These are presented in Figure 6.2.

Figure 6.2: General Functions of the FBI

The Director of the Federal Bureau of Investigation shall:

(a) Investigate violations of the laws, including the criminal drug laws, of the United States and collect evidence in cases in which the United States is or may be a party in interest, except in cases in which such responsibility is by statute or otherwise exclusively assigned to another investigative agency. The Director's authority to investigate violations of and collect evidence in cases involving the criminal drug laws of the United States is concurrent with such authority of the Administrator of the Drug Enforcement Administration under § 0.100 of this part. In investigating violations of such laws and in collecting evidence in such cases, the Director may exercise so much of the authority vested in the Attorney General by sections 1 and 2 of Reorganization Plan No. 1 of 1968, section 1 of Reorganization Plan No. 2 of 1973 and the Comprehensive Drug Abuse Prevention and Control Act of 1970, as amended, as he determines is necessary. He may also release FBI information on the same terms and for the same purposes that the Administrator of the Drug Enforcement Administration may disclose DEA information under § 0.103 of this part. The Director and his authorized delegates may seize, forfeit and remit or mitigate the forfeiture of property in accordance with 21 U.S.C. 881, 21 CFR 1316.71 through 1316.81, and 28 CFR 9.1 through 9.7.

(b) Conduct the acquisition, collection, exchange, classification and preservation of fingerprints and identification records from criminal justice and other governmental agencies, including fingerprints voluntarily submitted by individuals for personal identification purposes; provide expert testimony in Federal, State and local courts as to fingerprint examinations; and provide fingerprint training and provide identification assistance in disasters and for other humanitarian purposes.

(c) Conduct personnel investigations requisite to the work of the Department of Justice and whenever required by statute or otherwise.

(d) Carry out the Presidential directive of September 6, 1939, as reaffirmed by Presidential directives of January 8, 1943, July 24, 1950, and December 15, 1953, designating the Federal Bureau of Investigation to take charge of investigative work in matters relating to espionage, sabotage, subversive activities, and related matters, including investigating any potential violations of the Arms Export Control Act, the Export Administration Act, the Trading with the Enemy Act, or the International Emergency Economic Powers Act, relating to any foreign counterintelligence matter.

(e) Establish and conduct law enforcement training programs to provide training for State and local law enforcement personnel; operate the Federal Bureau of Investigation National Academy; develop new approaches, techniques, systems, equipment, and devices to improve and strengthen law enforcement and assist in conducting State and local training programs, pursuant to section 404 of the Omnibus Crime Control and Safe Streets Act of 1968, 82 Stat. 204.

(f) Operate a central clearinghouse for police statistics under the Uniform Crime Reporting Program, and a computerized nationwide index of law enforcement information under the National Crime Information Center.

(g) Operate the Federal Bureau of Investigation Laboratory to serve not only the Federal Bureau of Investigation, but also to provide, without cost, technical and scientific assistance, including expert testimony in Federal or local courts, for all duly constituted law enforcement agencies, other organizational units of the Department of Justice, and other Federal agencies, which may desire to avail themselves of the service. As provided for in procedures agreed upon between the Secretary of State and the Attorney General, the services of the Federal Bureau of Investigation Laboratory may also be made available to foreign law enforcement agencies and courts.

(h) Make recommendations to the Office of Personnel Management in connection with applications for retirement under 5 U.S.C. 8336(c).

(i) Investigate alleged fraudulent conduct in connection with operations of the Department of Housing and Urban Development and other alleged violations of the criminal provisions of the National Housing Act, including 18 U.S.C. 1010.

(j) Exercise the power and authority vested in the Attorney General to approve and conduct the exchanges of identification records enumerated at § 50.12(a) of this chapter.

(k) Payment of awards (including those over $10,000) under 28 U.S.C. 524(c)(2), and purchase of evidence (including the authority to pay more than $100,000) under 28 U.S.C. 524(c)(1)(F).

(l) Exercise Lead Agency responsibility in investigating all crimes for which it has primary or concurrent jurisdiction and which involve terrorist activities or acts in preparation of terrorist activities within the statutory jurisdiction of the United States. Within the United States, this would include the collection, coordination, analysis, management and dissemination of intelligence and criminal information as appropriate. If another Federal agency identifies an individual who is engaged in terrorist activities or in acts in preparation of terrorist activities, that agency is requested to promptly notify the FBI. Terrorism includes the unlawful use of force and violence against persons or property to intimidate or coerce a government, the civilian population, or any segment thereof, in furtherance of political or social objectives.

(m) Carry out the Department's responsibilities under the Hate Crime Statistics Act.

(n) Exercise the authority vested in the Attorney General under section 528(a), Public Law 101-509, to accept from federal departments and agencies the services of law enforcement personnel to assist the Department of Justice in the investigation and prosecution of fraud or other criminal or unlawful activity in or against any federally insured financial institution or the Resolution Trust Corporation, and to coordinate the activities of such law enforcement personnel in the conduct of such investigations and prosecutions.

(o) Carry out the responsibilities conferred upon the Attorney General under the Communications Assistance for Law Enforcement Act, Title I of Pub. L. 103-414 (108 Stat. 4279), subject to the general supervision and direction of the Attorney General.

History

The FBI originated from a force of special agents created in 1908 by Attorney General Charles Bonaparte during the presidency of Theodore Roosevelt.[6] Roosevelt and Bonaparte both were "Progressives" and they shared the conviction that efficiency and expertise, not political connections, should determine who could best serve in government. Theodore Roosevelt became president of the United States in 1901; four years later, he appointed Bonaparte to be attorney general. In 1908, Bonaparte applied that Progressive philosophy to the Department of Justice by creating a corps of special agents. It had neither a name nor an officially designated leader other than the attorney general. Yet, these former detectives and Secret Service men were the forerunners of the Federal Bureau of Investigation.[7]

By 1907, the Department of Justice most frequently called upon Secret Service "operatives" to conduct investigations.[8] These men were well-trained, dedicated—and expensive. Moreover, they reported not to the attorney general, but to the chief of the Secret Service. This situation frustrated Bonaparte, who wanted complete control of investigations under his jurisdiction. Congress provided the impetus for Bonaparte to acquire his own force. On May 27, 1908, it enacted a law preventing the Department of Justice from engaging Secret Service operatives.

The following month, Attorney General Bonaparte appointed a force of special agents within the Department of Justice.[9] Accordingly, ten former Secret Service employees and a number of Department of Justice peonage (i.e., compulsory servitude) investigators became special agents of the Department of Justice. On July 26, 1908, Bonaparte ordered them to report to Chief Examiner Stanley W. Finch. This action is celebrated as the beginning of the FBI.

Both Attorney General Bonaparte and President Theodore Roosevelt, who completed their terms in March 1909, recommended that the force of 34 agents become a permanent part of the Department of Justice. Attorney General George Wickersham, Bonaparte's successor, named the force the Bureau of Investigation on March 16, 1909. At that time, the title of chief examiner was changed to chief of the Bureau of Investigation.

When the Bureau was established, there were few federal crimes. The Bureau of Investigation primarily investigated violations of laws involving national banking, bankruptcy, naturalization, antitrust, peonage, and land fraud. Because the early Bureau provided no formal training, previous law enforcement experience or a background in the law was considered desirable.

The first major expansion in Bureau jurisdiction came in June 1910 when the Mann Act (also known as the White Slave Traffic Act) was passed, making it a crime to transport women over state lines for immoral purposes. It also provided a tool by which the federal government could investigate criminals who evaded state laws but had no other federal violations. Finch became commissioner of White Slavery Act violations in 1912, and former Special Examiner A. Bruce Bielaski became the new Bureau of Investigation chief.

Over the next few years, the number of special agents grew to more than 300, and these individuals were complemented by another 300 support employees. Field offices existed from the Bureau's inception. Each field operation was controlled by a special agent in charge who was responsible to Washington. Most field offices were located in major cities. However, several were located near the Mexican border where they concentrated on smuggling, neutrality violations, and intelligence collection, often in connection with the Mexican revolution.

With the April 1917 entry of the U.S. into World War I during Woodrow Wilson's administration, the Bureau's work was increased again. As a result of the war, the Bureau acquired responsibility for the Espionage, Selective Service, and Sabotage Acts and assisted the Department of Labor by investigating enemy aliens. During these years, special agents with general investigative experience and facility in certain languages augmented the Bureau.

William J. Flynn, former head of the Secret Service, became director of the Bureau of Investigation in July 1919 and was the first to use that title. In October 1919, passage of the National Motor Vehicle Theft Act gave the Bureau of Investigation another tool by which to prosecute criminals who previously evaded the law by crossing state lines. With the return of the country to "normalcy" under President Warren G. Harding in 1921, the Bureau of Investigation returned to its pre-war role of fighting the few federal crimes.

The years from 1921 to 1933 were sometimes called the "lawless years" because of the growth of organized crime and the public disregard for Prohibition, which made it illegal to sell or import intoxicating beverages. Prohibition created a new federal medium for fighting crime, but the Department of the Treasury, not the Department of Justice, had jurisdiction for these violations.[10]

Attacking crimes that were federal in scope but local in jurisdiction called for creative solutions. The Bureau of Investigation had limited success using its narrow jurisdiction to investigate some of the criminals of "the gangster era." For example, it investigated Al Capone as a "fugitive federal witness." Federal investigation of a resurgent white supremacy movement also required creativity. The Ku Klux Klan (KKK), dormant since the late 1800s, was revived in part to counteract the economic gains made by African Americans during World War I. The Bureau of Investigation used the Mann Act to bring Louisiana's philandering KKK "Imperial Kleagle" to justice.

Through these investigations and more traditional investigations of neutrality violations and antitrust violations, the Bureau of Investigation gained stature. Although the Harding Administration suffered from unqualified and sometimes corrupt officials, the Progressive Era reform tradition continued among the professional Department of Justice special agents. The new Bureau of Investigation director, William J. Burns, who had previously run his own detective agency, appointed 26-year-old J. Edgar Hoover as assistant director. Hoover, a graduate of George Washington University Law School, had worked for the Department of Justice since 1917, where he headed the enemy alien operations during World War I and assisted in the General Intelligence Division under Attorney General A. Mitchell Palmer, investigating suspected anarchists and communists.

After Harding died in 1923, his successor, Calvin Coolidge, appointed replacements for Harding's cronies in the Cabinet. For the new attorney general, Coolidge appointed Attorney Harlan Fiske Stone. On May 10, 1924, Stone then selected Hoover to head the Bureau of Investigation. By inclination and training, Hoover embodied the Progressive tradition. His appointment ensured that the Bureau of Investigation would keep that tradition alive.[11]

When Hoover took over, the Bureau of Investigation had approximately 650 employees, including 441 special agents who worked in field offices in nine cities.[12] By the end of the decade, there were approximately 30 field offices, with divisional headquarters in New York, Baltimore, Atlanta, Cincinnati, Chicago, Kansas City, San Antonio, San Francisco, and Portland. He immediately fired those agents he considered unqualified and proceeded to professionalize the organization. For example, Hoover abolished the seniority rule of promotion and introduced uniform performance appraisals. At the beginning of the decade, the Bureau of Investigation established field offices in nine cities. He also scheduled regular inspections of the operations in all field offices. Then, in January 1928, Hoover established a formal training course for new agents, including the requirement that new agents had to be in the 25-35 year range to apply. He also returned to the earlier preference for special agents with law or accounting experience.[13]

The new director was also keenly aware that the Bureau of Investigation could not fight crime without public support. In remarks prepared for the attorney general in 1925, he wrote, "The agents of the Bureau of Investigation have been impressed with the fact that the real problem of law enforcement is in trying to obtain the cooperation and sympathy of the public and that they cannot hope to get such cooperation until they themselves merit the respect of the public."[14] Also in 1925, Agent Edwin C. Shanahan became the first agent to be killed in the line of duty when he was murdered by a car thief.

During the early and mid-1930s, several crucial decisions solidified the Bureau's position as the nation's premier law enforcement agency. Responding to the kidnapping of the Lindbergh baby in 1932, Congress passed a federal kidnapping statute.[15] Then, in May and June 1934, with gangsters like John Dillinger evading capture by crossing over state lines, Congress passed a number of federal crime laws that significantly enhanced the Bureau's jurisdiction. In the wake of the Kansas City Massacre, Congress also gave Bureau agents statutory authority to carry guns and make arrests.[16]

The Bureau of Investigation was renamed the United States Bureau of Investigation on July 1, 1932. Then, beginning July 1, 1933, the Department of Justice experimented for almost two years with a Division of Investigation that included the Bureau of Prohibition. Public confusion between Bureau of Investigation special agents and Prohibition agents led to a permanent name change in 1935 for the agency composed of Department of Justice investigators; the Federal Bureau of Investigation was thus born.

Contributing to its forensic expertise, the Bureau established its Technical Laboratory in 1932. Then, in 1935, the FBI National Academy was established to train police officers in modern investigative methods, since at that time only a few states and localities provided formal training to their peace officers. The legal tools given to the FBI by Congress, as well as Bureau initiatives to upgrade its own professionalism and that of law enforcement resulted in the arrest or demise of the most visible gangsters by 1936. By that time, however, fascism in Adolph Hitler's Germany and Benito Mussolini's Italy and communism in Josef Stalin's Soviet Union threatened American democratic principles. With war on the horizon, a new set of challenges faced the FBI.[17]

The FBI was alert to these fascist and communist groups as threats to American security. Authority to investigate these organizations came in 1936 with President Roosevelt's authorization through Secretary of State Cordell Hull.[18] A 1939 Presidential Directive further strengthened the FBI's authority to investigate subversives in the U.S., and Congress reinforced it by passing the Smith Act in 1940, outlawing advocacy of violent overthrow of the government.

With the actual outbreak of war in 1939, the responsibilities of the FBI escalated. Subversion, sabotage, and espionage became major concerns. In addition to agents trained in general intelligence work, at least one agent trained in defense plant protection was placed in each of the FBI's 42 field offices. The FBI also developed a network of informational sources, often using members of fraternal or veterans' organizations. With leads developed by these intelligence networks and through their own work, special agents investigated potential threats to national security.[19]

Despite the threats to the U.S. of subversion and espionage, the FBI's extended jurisdiction, and the time-consuming nature of background investigations, the Bureau did not surpass the number of agents it had during World War II—or its yearly wartime budget—until the Korean War in the early 1950s. After the Korean War ended, the number of agents stabilized at about 6,200, while the budget began a steady climb in 1957. At the same time, Congress gave the FBI new federal laws with which to fight civil rights violations, racketeering, and gambling. These new laws included the Civil Rights Acts of 1960 and 1964; the 1961 Crimes Abroad Aircraft Act; an expanded Federal Fugitive Act; and the Sports Bribery Act of 1964.

Up to this time, the interpretation of federal civil rights statutes by the Supreme Court was so narrow that few crimes, however heinous, qualified to be investigated by federal agents.[20]

The turning point in federal civil rights actions occurred in the summer of 1964 with the murder of voting registration workers Michael Schwerner, Andrew Goodman, and James Chaney near Philadelphia, Mississippi.[21] At the Department of Justice's request, the FBI conducted the investigation as it had in previous, less-publicized racial incidents. The case against the perpetrators took years to go through the courts. Only after 1966, when the Supreme Court made it clear that federal law could be used to prosecute civil rights violations, were seven men found guilty. By the late 1960s, the confluence of unambiguous federal authority and local support for civil rights prosecutions allowed the FBI to play an influential role in enabling African Americans to vote, serve on juries, and use public accommodations on an equal basis. Other civil rights investigations included the assassination of Martin Luther King, Jr., with the arrest of James Earl

Ray, and the murder of Medgar Evers, Mississippi field secretary of the NAACP, with the arrest of Byron De La Beckwith who, after two acquittals, was finally found guilty in 1994.[22]

FBI Director J. Edgar Hoover died on May 2, 1972, just shy of 48 years as the FBI Director. He was 77. The next day his body lay in state in the Rotunda of the Capitol, an honor accorded only 21 other Americans. Hoover's successor would have to contend with the complex turmoil of that troubled time. In 1972, unlike 1924 when Attorney General Harlan Fiske Stone selected Hoover, the president appointed the FBI director with confirmation by the Senate. President Nixon appointed L. Patrick Gray as acting director the day after Hoover's death. After retiring from a distinguished naval career, Gray had continued in public service as the Department of Justice's assistant attorney general for the Civil Division. As acting director, Gray appointed the first women as special agents since the 1920s.

Shortly after Gray became acting director, five men were arrested photo-graphing documents at the Democratic National Headquarters in the Watergate Office Building in Washington, D.C. The break-in had been authorized by Republican Party officials. Within hours, the White House began its effort to cover up its role, and the new acting FBI director was inadvertently drawn into it. FBI agents undertook a thorough investigation of the break-in and related events. However, when Gray's questionable personal role was revealed, he withdrew his name from the Senate's consideration to be director. He was replaced hours after he resigned on April 27, 1973, by William Ruckleshaus, a former congress-man and the first head of the Environmental Protection Agency, who remained until Clarence Kelley's appointment as director on July 9, 1973. Kelley, who was Kansas City police chief when he received the appointment, had been an FBI agent from 1940 to 1961.[23]

Director Kelley sought to restore public trust in the FBI and in law enforce-ment. He instituted numerous policy changes that targeted the training and selection of FBI and law enforcement leaders, the procedures of investigative intelligence collection, and the prioritizing of criminal programs. During Kelley's tenure as director, the FBI made a strong effort to develop an agent force with more women and one that was more reflective of the ethnic composition of the United States. By the late 1970s, nearly 8,000 special agents and 11,000 support employees worked in 59 field offices and 13 legal attaché offices.

In 1978, Director Kelley resigned and was replaced by former federal Judge William H. Webster. At the time of his appointment, Webster was serving as judge of the U.S. Court of Appeals for the Eighth Circuit. He had previously been a judge of the U.S. District Court for the Eastern District of Missouri. In 1982, following an explosion of terrorist incidents worldwide, Webster made coun-terterrorism a fourth national priority. He also expanded FBI efforts in the three others: foreign counterintelligence, organized crime, and white-collar crime. Part of this expansion was the creation of the National Center for the Analysis of Violent Crime.

The FBI solved so many espionage cases during the mid-1980s that the press dubbed 1985 "the year of the spy." The most serious espionage damage uncov-ered by the FBI was perpetrated by the John Walker spy ring and by former

National Security Agency employee William Pelton. In 1986, Congress had expanded FBI jurisdiction to cover terrorist acts against U.S. citizens outside the U.S. boundaries. Later, in 1989, the Department of Justice authorized the FBI to arrest terrorists, drug traffickers, and other fugitives abroad without the consent of the foreign country in which they resided.

On May 26, 1987, Judge Webster left the FBI to become director of the Central Intelligence Agency. On November 2, 1987, former federal Judge William Steele Sessions was sworn in as FBI director. Prior to his appointment as FBI director, Sessions served as the chief judge of the U.S. District Court for the Western District of Texas. Under Director Sessions, crime prevention efforts, in place since Director Kelley's tenure, were expanded to include a drug demand reduction program. FBI offices nationwide began working closely with local school and civic groups to educate young people to the dangers of drugs. Subsequent nationwide community outreach efforts under that program evolved and expanded through such initiatives as the Adopt-A-School/Junior G-Man Program. The expansion in initiatives required a larger workforce and, by 1988, the FBI employed 9,663 special agents and 13,651 support employees in 58 field offices and 15 legal attachés.

Two events occurred in late 1992 and early 1993 that were to have a major impact on FBI policies and operations.[24] In August 1992, the FBI responded to the shooting death of Deputy U.S. Marshal William Degan, who was killed at Ruby Ridge, Idaho, while participating in a surveillance of federal fugitive Randall Weaver. In the course of the standoff, Weaver's wife was accidentally shot and killed by an FBI sniper. Eight months later, at a remote compound outside Waco, Texas, FBI agents sought to end a 51-day standoff with members of a heavily armed religious sect who had killed four officers of the Bureau of Alcohol, Tobacco, and Firearms. Instead, as agents watched in horror, the compound burned to the ground from fires lit by members of the sect. Eighty people, including children, died in the blaze. These two events set the stage for public and congressional inquiries into the FBI's ability to respond to crisis situations.

On July 19, 1993, following allegations of ethics violations committed by director Sessions, President Clinton removed him from office and appointed Deputy Director Floyd I. Clarke as acting FBI director. Louis J. Freeh was sworn in as director of the FBI on September 1, 1993. Freeh had served as an FBI agent from 1975 to 1981. He was appointed U.S. District Court judge for the Southern District of New York in 1991 and served on that court until he was nominated to be director of the FBI during the summer of 1993.

Director Freeh began his tenure with a clearly articulated agenda to respond to deepening and evolving crime problems both at home and abroad.[25] Subsequently, the Bureau sharpened joint efforts against organized crime, drug-trafficking, and terrorism, and it expanded standardized training of international police in investigative processes, ethics, leadership, and professionalism, including, in April 1995, the opening of the first International Law Enforcement Academy (ILEA) in Budapest, Hungary. The Bureau also expanded its international presence by opening 21 new legal attaché offices overseas. Between 1993 and 2001, the FBI's mission and resources expanded to address the increasingly international nature of crime in U.S. localities. The FBI's budget grew by more than $1.27 billion as the Bureau hired 5,029 new agents and more than 4,000 new support personnel.

On September 4, 2001, former U.S. Attorney Robert S. Mueller, III was sworn in as FBI director with a specific mandate to upgrade the Bureau's information technology infrastructure, to address records management issues, and to enhance FBI foreign counterintelligence analysis and security in the wake of the damage done by former special agent and convicted spy Robert Hanssen.[26]

Within days of his entering on duty, however, the September 11 terrorist attacks were launched against New York and Washington. Director Mueller led the FBI's massive investigative efforts in partnership with all U.S. law enforcement, the federal government, and allies overseas. On October 26, 2001, President George W. Bush signed into law the USA PATRIOT Act, which granted new provisions to address the threat of terrorism, and Director Mueller accordingly accepted on behalf of the Bureau responsibility for protecting the American people against future terrorist attacks. To support the Bureau's change in mission and to meet newly articulated strategic priorities, Director Mueller called for a reengineering of FBI structure and operations to closely focus the Bureau on prevention of terrorist attacks, countering foreign intelligence operations against the U.S., and addressing cybercrime-based attacks and other high-technology crimes. Although his ten-year term expired in 2011, Mueller was asked to continue in his position as director of the FBI by President Obama.

Who Gets Hired

There are many types of employees at the FBI. Special agents gather evidence of criminal activity, make arrests of those thought to be guilty of criminal acts, execute search warrants, and testify in court. To become an FBI special agent, a candidate must be a U.S. citizen, at least 23 years of age but younger than 37 at the time of appointment, and must possess a 4-year degree from an accredited college or university. A successful recruit will have a valid driver's license and be available for assignment anywhere in the country. Every candidate must have at least 20/20 vision in one eye and not worse than 20/40 vision in the other eye, pass a background check and a polygraph exam, and be in top physical condition. A previous felony conviction, some illegal drug use, the default of a student loan, failure to pass a drug test, or, for males, failure to register with the Selective Service System will disqualify a potential candidate from eligibility.[27] Newly hired agents receive training at the FBI national training academy in Quantico, Virginia, for 20 weeks. There they will receive instruction in physical fitness, defensive tactics, practical application exercises, and the use of firearms.[28]

In addition to the special agents, the FBI employs others as specialists. For example, someone could be hired as a linguist, who could play a key role in the translation, transcription, reporting, and analysis of materials. There are also many options for professional staff throughout the FBI. The agency also hires college interns through their internship program, called FBI4U.

On October 31, 2013, a total of 35,344 people worked for the FBI, including 13,598 special agents and 21,746 professional staff.[29] About one quarter of the employees are considered to belong to a minority population, and almost half of the employees are female. The employees come from a variety of backgrounds, such as banking, law, law enforcement, accounting, and other professions.[30]

Budgets

As Table 6.1 shows, Congress has allocated around $8 billion to fund the FBI in recent years.

Organization

The main headquarters of the FBI is in Washington, D.C. There are also 56 field offices located in major cities throughout the U.S. and approximately 400 smaller offices, referred to as "resident agencies," located in smaller cities and towns. There are more than 60 international offices called "legal attachés" in U.S. embassies worldwide.[31] The FBI is overseen by the Directorate of Intelligence, who ensures that the FBI is working to gather the intelligence necessary to protect the nation. The Directorate manages all FBI intelligence-related activities.[32]

Leader

The seventh and current director of the FBI is James B. Comey, who was sworn in on September 4, 2013. Comey grew up in Yonkers, New York, and attended the College of William and Mary, followed by law school at the University of Chicago. Upon graduation, he returned to New York and started a job as an assistant U.S. attorney at the U.S. Attorney's Office for the Southern District of New York. In that position, Comey fought against members of organized crime, as in the case of *United States v. John Gambino, et al.* When this case ended, Comey served as an assistant U.S. attorney in the Eastern District of Virginia. In this office, he was

Table 6.1	Budget Authority for the FBI (In Billions of Dollars)
2011 Enacted	7.926
2012 Enacted	8.117
2013 Request	8.443

Source: United States Department of Justice, Fiscal Year 2013 Budget and Performance Summary, available at http://www.justice.gov/jmd/2014summary/pdf/fbi.pdf.

involved with prosecuting the defendants in the 1996 terrorist attack on the U.S. military's Khobar Towers in Khobar, Saudi Arabia.

Not long after the terrorist attacks of 9/11, Comey returned to New York after being appointed U.S. attorney for the Southern District of New York. In 2003, he was then asked to serve as the deputy attorney general at the U.S. Department of Justice (DOJ) under Attorney General John Ashcroft in Washington, D.C.

In 2005, Comey left public service to become the general counsel and senior vice president at Lockheed Martin, a defense contractor. A few years later, he began as the general counsel for Bridgewater Associates, an investment fund based in Connecticut.

In addition to these positions, Comey also served as a lecturer in law, a senior research scholar, and Hertog Fellow in National Security Law at Columbia Law School.

What They Do

FBI agents investigate possible criminal offenses. Upon completion of FBI investigations, collected evidence is given to the U.S. attorney or an official in the Department of Justice who must then determine if prosecution or other action is warranted. FBI investigations fall into two main priorities: national security and criminal.

National Security Priorities

The National Security Branch of the FBI was created in 2005 when different offices that were responsible for some aspects of national security were combined into a single unit. The National Security Branch includes personnel who are active in areas of counterterrorism, counterintelligence (terrorism, counterespionage, counter-proliferation, economic espionage), weapons of mass destruction and intelligence, cybercrime (computer intrusions, online predators, piracy/intellectual property theft, Internet fraud, identity theft), and other Internet crime.

The National Counterterrorism Center was created to serve as the government's "knowledge bank" on international terrorism activities and trends. The Center publishes reports based on incidents of terrorism as reported in open source information. The information collected by the Center is the most complete collection of this information in the world. Moreover, they post information on terror attacks and track and analyze terrorist incidents.

The FBI seeks to reduce Internet crime through the Internet Crime Complaint Center (iC3), an organization founded in 2000 to provide law enforcement with a resource for victims of online crime as well as for law enforcement officers who are investigating and prosecuting all categories of cybercrime offenders. It allows law enforcement to share their findings with others who may be pursuing similar cases. IC3 was founded by the National White Collar Crime Center/Bureau of Justice Assistance and the Federal Bureau of Investigation.[33]

The IC3 has a public awareness program that spends time to teach children how to protect themselves when working online. They also help senior citizens know how to avoid becoming the victim of identity theft. They often provide presentations to local, national, and international law enforcement and to key industrial leaders. IC3 has also created the Internet Crime Working Group (ICWG), a collaboration with IC3 analysts and the National Cyber-Forensics and Training Alliance (NCFTA) that uses email to exchange critical unclassified data related to cyber intelligence to enhance case and intelligence reports. The FBI also has the Terrorist Screening Center, which collects intelligence on terrorism trends for state and local law enforcement.[34]

Criminal Priorities

The FBI's focus on investigating criminal acts and preventing further crime is enhanced by the FBI Laboratory Services. The FBI uses the most advanced techniques to solve crimes. Their first lab, created in 1932, has evolved into a modern facility with 300 scientific experts and special agents who travel around the world to provide technical support, expert witness testimony, and advanced training to both Bureau personnel and other law enforcement agencies.[35]

Some other offices that comprise the FBI include:

- **Public Corruption:** Dealing with government fraud, election fraud, foreign corrupt practices
- **Civil Rights:** Dealing with hate crime, human trafficking, color of law, freedom of access to clinics
- **Organized Crime:** Dealing with sports bribery; Italian Mafia; and Eurasian, Balkan, Middle Eastern, Asian, and African organized crime groups
- **White Collar Crime:** Dealing with antitrust, bankruptcy fraud, corporate/securities fraud, health care fraud, insurance fraud, mass marketing fraud, money laundering, mortgage fraud, other white-collar frauds

Financial Crimes

The mission of the Financial Crimes section is to investigate all types of financial fraud and to facilitate the forfeiture of assets from those who profit from these crimes. FBI agents investigate and try to deter fraud or embezzlement occurring within or against the national and international financial community or against individual businesses.[36] The Financial Fraud section oversees several offenses in particular. These include corporate fraud, securities and commodities fraud, health care fraud, insurance fraud, and mass marketing fraud.

Corporate Fraud

The FBI is the lead agency to investigate incidents of corporate fraud by corporate executives. Corporate fraud has the potential to cause significant financial losses to investors but, if severe enough, can also damage the U.S. economy.[37]

Securities and Commodities Fraud

The FBI works closely with both governmental and private groups to investigate possible fraudulent activity in the securities markets. Often this requires that FBI agents cooperate with other agencies including the Securities and Exchange Commission, the U.S. Attorney's Office, the U.S. Commodity Futures Trading Commission, the Financial Industry Regulatory Authority, the U.S. Postal Inspection Service, and the Internal Revenue Service.[38]

Health Care Fraud

The FBI investigates individuals and organizations that are accused of defrauding the public and private health care systems. To do this, FBI agents must work with the Centers for Medicare and Medicaid Services (CMS) and other government and privately sponsored programs.[39]

Mortgage Fraud

The FBI investigates mortgage fraud in two areas: fraud for profit and fraud for housing. Mortgage fraud for profit is usually carried out by industry insiders who rely on their expertise to carry out the crime, whereas fraud for housing is usually carried out by a borrower who may lie on a loan application as a way to acquire ownership of a house.[40]

Insurance Fraud

The FBI works continuously to prevent fraud against insurance companies.

The FBI works with many insurance groups and state fraud bureaus and state insurance regulators in their quest to combat insurance fraud.[41]

Mass Marketing Fraud

This type of offense occurs when offenders take advantage of mass-communication media such as telemarketing, mass mailings, or the Internet. In these crimes, offenders use false or deceptive language that entices victims to make payments for which they receive no goods or services.[42]

Violent Crime and Major Thefts

Agents in the FBI focus their attention on major national and international crimes such as art theft, bank robbery, cargo theft, crimes against children, crimes that occur on cruise ships, gang-related crimes, crimes that take place in Indian country, the theft of jewelry and gems, retail theft, and vehicle theft.[43]

Online Child Pornography/Child Sexual Exploitation Investigations

Computer technology is the easiest way pedophiles have to manufacture and share photographic images of minors and to lure children into illicit sexual relationships.[44] The FBI has created the Innocent Images National Initiative (IINI), an intelligence-driven, multi-agency investigative unit that is geared toward combating the growth of child pornography and exploitation that is easily manufactured with the use of a computer. The IINI provides for analysis of evidence and coordinates the investigation. This sometimes requires cooperation between state, local, and international organizations, as well as FBI field offices and legal attachés.[45] The IINI seeks to reduce the number of children who are sexually exploited or abused through the use of computers. They seek to identify and rescue child victims of pornography and at the same time investigate and prosecute predators who prey on children through the Internet or other online services.[46]

National Gang Threat Assessment 2011

Gang activity is a serious threat to the community's safety in many areas of the country. The FBI continues to track gang-related membership and activity. The FBI estimates that there are currently about 1.4 million gang members in the United States. This includes active gang members, prison gang members, and outlaw motorcycle gang (OMG) members. Membership in these gangs has increased significantly across the United States in recent years. Ethnic-based gangs are expanding in many communities. These gangs are responsible for a large portion of the violent crime in many areas of the country. They are involved in nontraditional crimes including alien smuggling and human trafficking but also in white-collar crimes such as counterfeiting, identity theft, and mortgage fraud.

The FBI has also discovered that many of the gangs in the U.S. have developed strong working relationships with Mexican drug trafficking organizations (MDTO) and organized crime groups in the United States. They also continue their gang behaviors if sentenced to prison. Most gangs have access to high-powered, military-style weapons that pose serious threats to others.[47]

Conclusion

The FBI is probably the most well-known federal law enforcement agency. The agents working for the FBI work to enforce the nation's laws, especially those related to homeland security and civil rights of citizens. There is no doubt that the agency will continue to protect the country from both violent and white collar crime across the nation in the years to come.

Key Terms

Federal Bureau of Investigation

Mann Act

J. Edgar Hoover

field agents

Field Offices

L. Patrick Gray

Ruby Ridge

legal attachés

Directorate of Intelligence

James Comey

National Security Branch

National Counterterrorism Center

Internet Crime Complaint Center (IC3)

Online Child Pornography/Child
     Sexual Exploitation Investigations

National Gang Threat Assessment

Review Questions

1. What is the primary responsibility of the FBI?

2. What are the core values of the FBI?

3. Describe the history of the FBI.

4. What are the general functions of the FBI?

5. Why is the "Mann Act" a pivotal part of the history of the FBI?

6. Who were some of the directors of the FBI?

7. If you were interested in becoming an FBI agent, what qualifications would you need to possess?

8. What are the budget allocations that have been provided by Congress to fund the FBI?

9. How is the FBI organized?

10. What kinds of financial crime does the FBI investigate?

Endnotes

1. Federal Bureau of Investigation, "Quick Facts," available at http://www.fbi.gov/about-us/quick-facts.
2. Federal Bureau of Investigation, "Quick Facts."
3. Federal Bureau of Investigation, "Careers," available at http://www.fbijobs.gov/61.asp; Federal Bureau of Investigation, "Quick Facts."
4. Federal Bureau of Investigation, "Frequently Asked Questions," available at http://www.fbi.gov/about-us/faqs.
5. Mueller, Robert S. III, "Facts and Figures," available at http://www.fbi.gov/stats-services/publications/todays-fbi-facts-figures/facts-and-figures-031413.pdf/view.
6. The following history section is based in large part on "A Brief History of the FBI," provided by the Federal Bureau of Investigation. See Federal Bureau of Investigation. (2012). *A Brief History of the FBI.* Available online at http://www.fbi.gov/about-us/history/brief-history/brief-history.
7. Holden, Henry M. (2008). *FBI: 100 Years.* Minneapolis, MN: Zenith Press.
8. Bumgarner, Jeffrey B. (2006). *Federal Agents: The Growth of Federal Law Enforcement in America.* Westport, CT: Praeger.
9. Jeffreys-Jones, Rhodri. (2007). *The FBI: A History.* New Haven, CT: Yale University Press.
10. Holden, *FBI: 100 Years.*
11. Ackerman, Kenneth D. (2007). *Young J. Edgar: Hoover, The Red Scare, and the Assault on Civil Liberties.* New York: Carroll & Graf Publishers.
12. Bumgarner, *Federal Agents.*
13. Ackerman, *Young J. Edgar.*
14. Federal Bureau of Investigation, *A Brief History of the FBI.*
15. Bumgarner, *Federal Agents.*
16. Burroughs, Bryan. (2009). *Public Enemies: America's Greatest Crime Wave and the Birth of the FBI, 1933-34.* New York: Penguin.
17. Jeffreys-Jones, *The FBI: A History.*
18. Jeffreys-Jones, *The FBI: A History.*
19. Lamphere, Robert J. & Tom Shachtman. (1986). *The FBI-KGB War: A Special Agent's Story.* New York: Random House.
20. Jeffreys-Jones, *The FBI: A History.*
21. Cagin, Seth & Philip Dray. (2006). *We Are Not Afraid: The Story of Goodman, Schwerner, and Chaney and the Civil Rights Campaign for Mississippi.* New York: Nation Book.
22. Jeffreys-Jones, *The FBI: A History.*
23. Holden, *FBI: 100 Years.*
24. Moore, James. (2001). *Very Special Agents: The Inside Story of America's Most Controversial Law Enforcement Agency – The Bureau of Alcohol, Tobacco, and Firearms.* Champaign, IL: University of Illinois Press; Vizzard, William J. (1997). *In the Cross Fire: A Political History of the Bureau of Alcohol, Tobacco and Firearms.* Boulder, CO: Lynne Rienner Publishers.
25. Holden, *FBI: 100 Years.*
26. Holden, *FBI: 100 Years.*
27. Federal Bureau of Investigation, "Careers."
28. Federal Bureau of Investigation, "The FBI Academy," available at http://www.fbi.gov/about-us/training.
29. Federal Bureau of Investigation, "Frequently Asked Questions."
30. Federal Bureau of Investigation, "Careers."
31. Federal Bureau of Investigation, "Quick Facts."
32. Federal Bureau of Investigation, "Directorate of Intelligence," available at http://www.fbi.gov/about-us/intelligence.
33. Internet Crime Complaint Center, "2010 Internet Crime Report," available at http://www.ic3.gov/media/2011/110224.aspx.

34. Federal Bureau of Investigation, "National Security Branch," available at http://www.fbi.gov/about-us/nsb.

35. Federal Bureau of Investigation, "Laboratory Services," available at http://www.fbi.gov/about-us/lab.

36. Federal Bureau of Investigation, "2009 Financial Crimes Report," available at http://www.fbi.gov/stats-services/publications/financial-crimes-report-2009.

37. Federal Bureau of Investigation, "2009 Financial Crimes Report."

38. Federal Bureau of Investigation, "2009 Financial Crimes Report."

39. Federal Bureau of Investigation, "2009 Financial Crimes Report."

40. Federal Bureau of Investigation, "2009 Financial Crimes Report."

41. Federal Bureau of Investigation, "2009 Financial Crimes Report."

42. Federal Bureau of Investigation, "2009 Financial Crimes Report."

43. Federal Bureau of Investigation, "What We Investigate," available at http://www.fbi.gov/about-us/investigate/what_we_investigate.

44. Federal Bureau of Investigation, "Innocent Images," available at http://www.fbi.gov/news/stories/2006/february/innocent_images022406.

45. Federal Bureau of Investigation, "Innocent Images."

46. Federal Bureau of Investigation, "Innocent Images."

47. Federal Bureau of Investigation, "2011 National Gang Threat Assessment—Emerging Trends." National Gang Intelligence Center. Available at http://www.fbi.gov/stats-services/publications/2011-national-gang-threat-assessment.

7

Drug Enforcement Administration

Established in 1973, the Drug Enforcement Administration (DEA) provides for the enforcement of federal drug laws across the country and around the world. The DEA is the primary agency dedicated to drug enforcement, and it is the only single-mission federal drug law enforcement agency.

As the lead agency for domestic enforcement of the Controlled Substances Act, the primary mission of the DEA is to enforce the federal laws concerning controlled substances. Given the task of combating drug smuggling, DEA agents work to investigate, disrupt, and then dismantle networks that grow, manufacture, or traffic in illicit drugs and bring them to the attention of the criminal and civil justice system. Of particular importance to the DEA is to attack the drug organizations that use the profits from trafficking in illicit drugs to fund terrorism. By dismantling their financial structures, the organizations can be weakened.

The DEA also supports non-enforcement programs that are aimed at reducing the availability of illicit substances on both the domestic and international markets. They support initiatives that are geared toward drug demand reduction found in communities. The DEA has jurisdiction, along with the Federal Bureau of Investigation and Immigration and Customs Enforcement, to coordinate and pursue U.S. drug investigations overseas. They have developed partnerships with both domestic and foreign law enforcement agencies in the war against drugs. In recent years, the DEA has also become involved in the fight against the diversion of licit or pharmaceutical substances into the illicit market, which often occurs via the Internet.[1]

The general functions of the DEA administrator are listed in Figure 7.1. These can be found in 28 CFR 0.100. The specific duties are described in Figure 7.2 and are found in 28 CFR 0.101.

Figure 7.1: General Functions of the DEA Administrator

The following-described matters are assigned to, and shall be conducted, handled, or supervised by, the Administrator of the Drug Enforcement Administration:

(a) Functions vested in the Attorney General by sections 1 and 2 of Reorganization Plan No. 1 of 1968.

(b) Except where the Attorney General has delegated authority to another Department of Justice official to exercise such functions, and except where functions under 21 U.S.C. 878(a)(5) do not relate to, arise from, or supplement investigations of matters concerning drugs, functions vested in the Attorney General by the Comprehensive Drug Abuse Prevention and Control Act of 1970, as amended. This will include functions which may be vested in the Attorney General in subsequent amendments to the Comprehensive Drug Abuse Prevention and Control Act of 1970, and not otherwise specifically assigned or reserved by him.

(c) Functions vested in the Attorney General by section 1 of Reorganization Plan No. 2 of 1973 and not otherwise specifically assigned.

Figure 7.2: Specific Functions of the DEA Administrator

The Administrator of the Drug Enforcement Administration shall be responsible for:

(a) The development and implementation of a concentrated program throughout the Federal Government for the enforcement of Federal drug laws and for cooperation with State and local governments in the enforcement of their drug abuse laws.

(b) The development and maintenance of a National Narcotics Intelligence System in cooperation with Federal, State, and local officials, and the provision of narcotics intelligence to any Federal, State, or local official that the Administrator determines has a legitimate official need to have access to such intelligence.

(c) The development and implementation of a procedure to release property seized under section 511 of the Controlled Substances Act (21 U.S.C. 881) to any innocent party having an immediate right to possession of the property, when the Administrator, in his discretion, determines it is not in the interests of justice to initiate forfeiture proceedings against the property.

(d) Payment of awards (including those over $10,000) under 28 U.S.C. 524(c)(2) and purchase of evidence (including the authority to pay more than $100,000) under 28 U.S.C. 524(c)(1)(F).

History

The Drug Enforcement Administration (DEA) officially came into being in 1973 under the Nixon Administration. However, like so many other federal law enforcement agencies, the DEA has a genealogy that traces its roots back to a number of other agencies. In fact, the DEA traces itself back to the 1915 establishment of the Bureau of Internal Revenue under the Department of the Treasury.[2] In 1927, the responsibilities for drug tax enforcement under the Harrison Narcotics Tax Act of 1914, which the Bureau of Internal Revenue had been responsible for, were transferred to the Bureau of Prohibition within the U.S. Department of the Treasury. This lasted until the creation of the Bureau of Narcotics within the Department of the Treasury in 1930, and it would remain their duty and responsibility until 1968.[3]

As the prevalence of drugs increased dramatically in the 1960s, and the mechanisms of tax enforcement were no longer an effective means of dealing with the problem (if they ever were), a new emphasis on, first, drug treatment, and second, drug enforcement, arose. In 1966, the Bureau of Drug Abuse Control (BDAC) was created within the Food and Drug Administration under the Department of Health, Education, and Welfare, to try and deal with the problem of drug addiction.[4] In 1968, President Johnson proposed combining this agency with the Federal Bureau of Narcotics to create a new agency that he believed would be better equipped to deal with the problem of drugs.[5] The result was that BDAC and FBN merged and was placed in the U.S. Department of Justice as the newly created Bureau of Narcotics and Dangerous Drugs (BNDD).[6]

The BNDD became the primary drug law enforcement agency in the country and it concentrated its efforts on both international and interstate activities. By 1970, the BNDD had nine foreign offices in Italy, Turkey, Panama, Hong Kong, Vietnam, Thailand, Mexico, France, and Columbia to respond to the dynamics of the drug trade. Domestically, the agency initiated a task force approach involving federal, state, and local officers. The first such task force was established in New York City.[7]

By the early 1970s, although drug use had not yet reached its all-time peak (that came in 1979), the problem was sufficiently serious to warrant a more elevated response.[8] In response to America's growing drug problem, Congress passed the Controlled Substance Act (CSA), Title II of the Comprehensive Drug Abuse Prevention and Control Act of 1970. It replaced more than 50 pieces of drug legislation, went into effect on May 1, 1971, and was enforced by the BNDD.[9] The problem was, the BNDD was still not the only existing agency that dealt with the problems of drug-related crime.

At that time, there were not only the organizations that shared a direct lineage to the DEA, but there were at least four other bureaucratic agencies responsible for dealing with the myriad problems of drugs. One was the U.S. Customs Service Drug Investigation Unit under the Department of the Treasury. Under the U.S. Department of Justice, in addition to the BNDD, there was the Office of National Narcotics Intelligence (ONNI) and the Office of Drug Abuse Law Enforcement (ODALE).[10] Finally, even President Nixon, realizing the pervasiveness of drugs, had created an office within the White House dubbed the Narcotics Advance Research Management Team. The idea behind this team was to try and coordinate all of the other federal bureaucratic agencies dealing with the problems of drugs, but it quickly became clear that the team was ineffective and the various bureaucratic elements needed to work together.[11]

In the spring of 1973, President Nixon announced his Reorganization Plan No. 2 (President Johnson had issued the first such plan) calling for "an all-out global war on the drug menace."[12] He explained the reasoning for calling for the reorganization of the drug enforcement structure when he said, "the federal government is fighting the war on drug abuse under a distinct handicap, for its efforts are those of a loosely confederated alliance facing a resourceful, elusive, worldwide enemy. Certainly, the cold-blooded underworld networks that funnel narcotics from suppliers all over the world are not respecters of the bureaucratic dividing lines that now complicate our anti-drug efforts."[13] Then, on July 10, 1973, President Nixon issued Executive Order #11727, which clarified some aspects of the July 1, 1973 reorganization plan that Congress had passed, stating "that all functions of the Office for Drug Abuse Law Enforcement and the Office of National Narcotics Intelligence would, together with other related functions be merged into the new Drug Enforcement Administration."[14] Thus, through the reorganization plan and the Executive Order, the U.S. Drug Enforcement Administration (DEA) was officially created on July 1, 1973.

The benefits of this reorganization were debated by Congress, but that fall, the Senate issued its report anticipating the benefits that a "super agency" focused on the problems of drugs would have. They believed it would end the interagency rivalries amongst all of the federal drug law enforcement agencies and that it would give the FBI a significant role in assisting in the drug war. There was hope that it would also provide a focal point for all federal drug enforcement resources, consolidate those resources for more effective deployment, and hold the drug law enforcement community more accountable by appointing a single administrator over the new agency.

On September 12, 1973, the White House selected John R. Bartels, Jr. to be that Drug Enforcement Administration administrator. Bartels was a former federal prosecutor and was, at the time, deputy director of ODALE. When he was confirmed on October 4, 1973, he set two goals for the new agency: 1) to integrate narcotics agents and U.S. Customs agents into one effective force and 2) to restore public confidence in narcotics law enforcement. Both of these were lofty goals that would encompass his two years as the DEA's administrator.

As the agency was relatively new, a number of agency mechanisms had to be built from scratch, while others were modified from previous agency components. The creation of the DEA Intelligence Program is but one example.[15] The agency needed to create an intelligence analysis unit, which meant they also had to create an intelligence analyst school, as well as a system that could effectively deal with the vast amounts of intelligence that would be gathered over time. Even the training of the DEA special agents required the creation of a new school. In addition, any relationships previously built with foreign governments, such as the nine foreign field offices of the BNDD, had to be reworked for the new DEA administration.

There were a number of highs and lows during these early years. The DEA touted its ability to bring down the French Connection, but the majority of the work had actually been done by the BNDD and New York Police Department, creating some confusion.[16] They were proud to be one of the earliest agencies to hire female DEA special agents, and Ms. Mary Turner became the first graduate from the DEA training program. By 1974, they had 23 female special agents working in field offices throughout the United States. Perhaps the greatest tragedy for the new agency, however, was a mere accident, when on August 5, 1974, at 10:24 a.m., the roof of the Miami Office came crashing down, killing seven and injuring dozens. One of those killed that morning was special agent Nickolas Fragos. It was his first day at work as a DEA special agent.[17]

In 1975, DEA Administrator Bartels resigned and Henry Dogin became the acting administrator until February of 1976, when Peter S. Bensinger was appointed. Bensinger had made a career in Illinois in criminal justice with his last post being director of the Illinois Department of Corrections. Bensinger was hired primarily to implement the White House White Paper on drug abuse in the United States. President Ford had created a Domestic Council Drug Abuse Task Force that had been chaired by Vice President Nelson Rockefeller, himself a tough crusader against illicit drugs when he was governor of New York. The White House White Paper encouraged the DEA to shift its focus from low level marijuana and cocaine smuggling to focus more attention on major international drug dealing, especially that of heroin. Bensinger's DEA began focusing worldwide on a number of drug cartels, including the infamous Medellin Cartel. This type of enforcement made the DEA a far more visible agency internationally and the job became far more dangerous. A number of agents lost their lives in the line of duty during this time period, including DEA Special Agent Octavio Gonzalez, who was shot and killed by an informant in Bogota, Columbia.[18]

In 1981, with the newly inaugurated Reagan Administration, Bensinger stepped down and Francis M. Mullen, Jr. was appointed as the DEA administrator, serving until 1985. Unlike Besinger, who had no background in federal investigations, Mullen came over from a career in the FBI and brought with him an extensive investigatory background. In light of the fact he was from the FBI, Mullen stressed multi-agency cooperation. In addition, in 1982, Attorney General William French Smith, in a federal law enforcement reorganization move, authorized the FBI to have concurrent jurisdiction in drug interdiction, although the DEA would remain the lead agency. Mullen's replacement in 1985, John C. Lawn, also came over from the FBI and had a similar focus as well during the late 1980s.

While the DEA had been combating the Medellin Cartel in the late 1970s, as that organization's structure and reach grew, so did the DEA's concentration on bringing that cartel down.[19] Columbia became a hotbed for marijuana and cocaine drug interdiction. In addition, the heroin being trafficked out of Southwest Asia also became a focus of the DEA during the 1980s. In addition to focusing on South America and Southwest Asia, the DEA also began working with Mexico to try to stem the tide of drugs coming into the United States through that country. One case that again highlighted the dangerousness of working international drug trafficking cases, even in America's own backyard, came in February of 1985 when DEA Special Agent Enrique "Kiki" Camarena was abducted, tortured, and murdered for his role in trying to assist Mexican authorities operating against a Mexican marijuana trafficking organization.[20]

By the mid-1980s, however, one drug that began creating enormous political attention at home was crack cocaine. The DEA began to focus heavily in the late 1980s on cocaine in order to try and curtail the spread of crack cocaine. Whether it was the increase in drug usage, drug availability, or simply drug war politics, the issue of drugs was taking center stage in America by the late 1980s.[21]

The result was a flurry of bills coming out of Congress, each giving the DEA more authority and more investigative powers to target illicit drugs. The Crime Control Act of 1984, the 1984 Amendment to the Controlled Substances Act, the Drug Free Workplace Program via Executive Order in 1986, the Anti-Drug Abuse Act of 1986, and another in 1988 all showed that the Reagan and Bush Administrations resolved to make the illegal drug trade a center piece of their emphasis in federal law enforcement.[22] In fact, once again, the issue of tighter control over the various agencies that were becoming involved in the war on drugs found its way into the last act, the Anti-Drug Abuse Act of 1988. This act allowed for the creation of the Office of National Drug Control Policy (ONDCP) allowing for one person within the White House to oversee all of the drug law enforcement in America.[23] This individual became known as the "Drug Czar," and would conflict with the DEA administrator on many occasions in the coming years, for since 1973 it had been the DEA administrator who had held this particular oversight role.

In 1989, the DEA moved its headquarters from Washington, D.C. across the Potomac River to Arlington, Virginia in a new, high-rise facility. That same year, the DEA made the highly visible arrest of former Panamanian dictator Manuel Noriega, who was taken to Miami and placed on trial for his involvement in international drug trafficking. The following year, the DEA appointed its first career agent to serve as the DEA administrator, and Robert C. Bonner continued implementing many of the Reagan and Bush policies before he stepped down.

In 1994, Thomas A. Constantine was sworn in as the new DEA administrator, coming from his position as superintendent of the New York State Police. Although the Clinton Administration focused more on street crime, operations against international drug trafficking continued all over the world. Operations with such names as Tiger Trap, Green Ice II, Global Sea, and Zorro II were used to target specific cartels such as the Cali Cartel and the Juan Garcia-Abrego Organization.[24] More funding continued to be channeled to the DEA, and in 1997 their budget exceeded $1 billion for the first time in their history. In addition, Congress authorized new legislation to allow the DEA to combat new problems, such as the growth in production and usage of methamphetamines, which spawned the Comprehensive Methamphetamine Control Act of 1996.

Two new creations in 1999 helped to highlight the fact that the DEA had truly become a fixed federal law enforcement agency in America. The first was the creation of a new Justice Training Center (JTC) in Quantico, Virginia at the

FBI Academy, used primarily for the training of DEA special agents. The second creation was the DEA Museum. Opening on May 11, 1999, and located at the DEA headquarters in Arlington, Virginia, the museum gave gravitas to the fact that the DEA, by 1999, did in fact have a history of its own. In addition, the museum highlights the history of illegal drugs in the United States and throughout the world.[25]

As the DEA entered the twenty-first century, the number of drug trafficking operations would continue to increase. Numerous operations, such as Juno (1999), Impunity I (1999) and II (2000), New Generation (2000), Tar Pit (2000), Red Tide (2001), and White Horse (2001), all proved highly successful in making mass arrests and seizing millions of dollars in illicit narcotics.[26] In addition, the DEA established Regional Enforcement Teams and Mobile Enforcement Teams, as a rapid deployment force for many of the final arrests and dismantling of drug organizations at the end of the extensive investigations carried out by special agents in the field.

In 2001, with the newly inaugurated President George W. Bush's Administration coming into office, a new administrator was appointed in August of 2001, Asa Hutchinson. Although Hutchinson was in his third term as a U.S. Congressman, he had an extensive background as a U.S. attorney. The following month, America was attacked by Al Qaeda terrorists, and DEA agents were some of the first federal law enforcement agents to respond in both Washington, D.C. and New York City due to the proximity of their headquarters and field offices. In light of the many changes brought on by these terrorist attacks, the DEA would quickly witness a change in its focus. The pursuit of drug traffickers was not just limited to cartels and organizations dealing in drugs; the focus on narco-terrorism or narcotics being used to fund terrorism now became their number one priority.[27] One such pursuit was Operation Containment, which focused on the vast amounts of drugs being produced in Afghanistan and trafficked through that country.

In July 2003, Hutchinson stepped down and Karen P. Tandy, a career Department of Justice attorney took over as the DEA administrator.[28] A number of concerns marked her tenure from 2003 to 2007. As the amount of drugs being trafficked into the U.S. through Mexico was greatly increasing, that country became the focus of many of the DEA's operations. Organizations were targeted, joint programs with Mexican authorities were created, and drug tunnels coming into the United States were being exposed on a seemingly regular basis. International drug trafficking operations continued, especially those centered upon possible terrorist organizations or terrorist connections.

At home, two major issues seemed most prevalent during this time period. The first was the rise in methamphetamines, with their highly addictive and destructive nature. A number of programs, many in coordination with Mexico, were aimed at targeting the production, transport, and sale of this illicit drug. The second issue seemed to be the rise in marijuana production and the fact that many of the strains of the drug were being produced with higher levels of THC, the chemical that causes the effects of cannabis. In addition, as cities (such as San Francisco) and states (such as California) legalized marijuana for medicinal purposes, it made the DEA's enforcement of federal law versus the states' laws a very controversial federalist issue. When the DEA made a number of raids on some of the establishments selling the medical marijuana, it created much controversy, and the raids and pressure would not cease until the next presidential administration came into office.

In 2008, with a new administration came a new DEA administrator. Confirmed by the U.S. Senate with a unanimous vote, Michele M. Leonhart, a career DEA special agent, became the tenth administrator of the DEA. The DEA continues to focus on narco-terrorism, but in many ways it has returned to the broader approach prior to the events of September 11. In addition, as new drug problems arise, it continues to shift its focus. While methamphetamines continue to be a problem, new synthetic drugs (designer drugs) and club drugs have become a focus of the DEA in recent years.

Who Gets Hired

Almost 10,000 men and women are employed by the DEA. This includes approximately 4,700 special agents, 600 diversion investigators, 800 intelligence research specialists, and 300 chemists.[29]

Special agents in the DEA are trained to be the foremost authorities on federal drug laws. They spend many hours in the field fighting drug trafficking. Diversion investigators have the duty to carry out investigations into the distribution and abuse of controlled substances. They investigate the diversion of pharmaceutical substances to the illegal market. To do so, these investigators gather evidence, analyze data, and try to develop solutions to the problems.

Forensic chemists are responsible for investigating those who manufacture illicit substances. They must rely on their knowledge of chemistry to identify new compounds that are produced and sold in the illicit drug market. These agents must determine if new chemical compounds fall under DEA regulations and the Controlled Substances Act. To become a forensic chemist, a candidate must have earned a four-year college degree in either the physical or life sciences or engineering with at least 30 semester hours in chemistry and mathematics and an additional six semester hours in physics.[30]

A fingerprint specialist within the DEA is trained to use the most recent techniques in the effort to develop latent prints and otherwise assist in crime scene investigations. To be eligible for this position, a candidate must have earned a four-year degree in a science and complete the DEA training program for fingerprint specialists.[31]

Forensic computer examiners in the DEA collect and analyze digital evidence. They work to recover and analyze digital evidence associated with drug offenses. Similarly, intelligence research specialists in the DEA research trends in drug cultivation and production, as well as patterns in modes of transportation, such as new trafficking routes and changes in the structure of organizations that traffic in drugs. Candidates for this position must have prior administrative experience and pass the DEA training program, Basic Intelligence Research Specialist Training Course.[32]

There are also many other opportunities for employment in the DEA as professionals and administrators. This can include attorneys, facilities management personnel, or financial personnel, among many others.

Those who want to work for the DEA must pass a polygraph test, a background check, and a mandatory drug test. All male applicants must be registered with the Selective Service System. The DEA has its own training academy (the DEA Academy) located on the U.S. Marine Corps base at Quantico, VA along with the FBI Academy. All recruits must pass a 16-week training program that includes firearms training and physical training. All students must maintain an average of 80%on all examinations and demonstrate strong leadership skills.

Budget

The DEA's budget has remained fairly consistent, hovering around $2.3 billion. These figures are detailed in Table 7.1.

Organization

The DEA is housed within the Department of Justice. It is headed by the administrator of drug enforcement, who is appointed by the president and then must pass confirmation hearings in the Senate. The administrator reports to the attorney general. The DEA administrator is assisted by a deputy administrator and others, including the chief of operations, the chief inspector, and three assistant administrators (in Operations Support, Intelligence, and Human Resources).

Headquartered in Arlington, VA, the DEA has 222 offices in 21 domestic field divisions located throughout the U.S. They also have 86 foreign offices in 67 countries.[33]

Leader

Michele M. Leonhart was unanimously confirmed as the administrator of the Drug Enforcement Administration by the U.S. Senate on December 22, 2010, following her nomination by President Obama in February 2010. In this capacity, Ms. Leonhart, a career DEA special agent, directs the $2.02 billion agency and is

Table 7.1	Budget Authority for DEA (In Billions of Dollars)
2011 Enacted	$2.306
2012 Enacted	$2.035
2013 Request	$2.051

Source: United States Department of Justice, Fiscal Year 2013 Budget and Performance Summary, available at http://www.justice.gov/jmd/2013summary/pdf/fy13-dea-bud-summary.pdf.

responsible for over 10,000 employees in domestic offices throughout the U.S. and in 83 foreign offices in 63 countries. Ms. Leonhart had been the acting administrator since November 2007 and served as DEA's deputy administrator since 2004.

Prior to becoming DEA administrator and deputy administrator, Ms. Leonhart held several positions within the DEA's Senior Executive Service (SES). She was the special agent in charge of the DEA's Los Angeles Field Division from 1998-2003. In that capacity, she commanded one of the DEA's largest field divisions and was responsible for all enforcement and administrative operations in the Los Angeles area as well as in Nevada, Hawaii, Guam, and Saipan. She previously held the position of special agent in charge of the DEA's San Francisco Field Division from 1997-1998, becoming the DEA's first female ever to be promoted to the position of special agent in charge. Ms. Leonhart's first appointment within the SES was in 1996, when she spearheaded the DEA's special agent recruitment efforts at DEA Headquarters.

As a career DEA special agent, Ms. Leonhart held several key positions as she moved through the ranks of the DEA. In 1995 she was promoted to the position of assistant special agent in Charge of the Los Angeles Field Division, responsible for Southwest border enforcement operations and division administrative functions. Between 1993 and 1995, Ms. Leonhart held management positions within the DEA Headquarters to include career board executive secretary, office of professional responsibility (OPR) inspector, and staff coordinator in the Operations Division. Ms. Leonhart's first supervisory position was in the DEA's San Diego Field Division. Prior to that, Ms. Leonhart initiated major drug investigations and conspiracy cases in Minneapolis and St. Louis and served as a DEA special agent recruiter.

While at the DEA, she attended Boston University's Leadership Institute. She is the recipient of numerous awards and commendations in recognition of her leadership, performance, and commitment to public service. She was awarded the rank of Distinguished Executive by President Bush in 2004, the Presidential Rank Award for Meritorious Service from President Bush in 2005, and the Presidential Rank Award for Meritorious Service from President Clinton in 2000. Additionally, Administrator Leonhart received the Law Enforcement Exploring William H. Spurgeon Award in 2006, the Women in Federal Law Enforcement Outstanding Federal Law Enforcement Employee Award in 2005, and the DEA Administrator's Award in 1993.

Ms. Leonhart has more than 30 years in law enforcement, beginning her law enforcement career as a Baltimore City Police Officer after graduating from college in Minnesota with a B.S. degree in criminal justice in 1978. She joined the ranks of DEA as a special agent in 1980. A native of Minnesota, Ms. Leonhart is married and has two sons.

What They Do

In 2013, DEA agents made 30,688 arrests, seized 22,512 kgs of cocaine, 965 kgs of heroin, 267,957 kgs of marijuana, 3,990 kgs of methamphetamines, and 116,215 dosage units of hallucinogens.[34]

To carry out its mission, the DEA has many responsibilities. One is to investigate offenses related to violations of the Controlled Substances Act at the national and international levels. Agents must also enforce laws pertaining to the manufacture, distribution, and dispensation of legally produced drugs. Other investigations revolve around those offenders (and gangs) who rely on violence, fear, and intimidation of citizens while trafficking drugs. The DEA is responsible for managing the seizure of any assets that were derived from profits from illegal drug trafficking.

In addition to investing drug-related offenses, the DEA manages a national intelligence program in which they collect, analyze, and disseminate information on drug use patterns and trends to other federal, state, local, and foreign law enforcement officials.

The DEA works in cooperation with federal, state, and local law enforcement officials on enforcement efforts as well as with international officials to both enforce laws and design programs geared toward reducing the availability of illicit drugs. This includes the United Nations, Interpol, and other international organizations.[35]

In order to carry out the above responsibilities, the DEA has developed numerous different divisions. Some are described below.

Asset Forfeiture

Under federal law, any profits from drug-related activities and the items that were used to carry out drug-related crimes can be seized by the government. This policy has become an effective tool against drug organizations as it eliminates any potential profit from the crimes. Since international drug groups use their profits to purchase state-of-the-art-technology to further their sales, asset seizures can financially disable groups who traffic in drugs, rendering them unable to commit further crimes. A portion of the money seized by the government is transferred to the Asset Forfeiture Fund, which is then given to crime victims. Some of the money is directed to fund law enforcement programs that are geared toward anti-drug abuse programs or other crime prevention programs.[36]

Aviation

Established in 1971, the mission of the DEA's Aviation Division is to provide aviation support to help agents detect, locate, identify, and assess illicit drug trafficking activities. They use aerial surveillance and photographic reconnaissance to track drug activity. They also use the Aviation Division to transport DEA personnel and transport fugitives and prisoners. The division trains special agent/pilots to fly both airplanes and helicopters. The Agency operates approximately 100 aircraft out of the Aviation Operations Center in Fort Worth, Texas, but there are other personnel based in other locations throughout the U.S., the Caribbean, Central and South America, and Afghanistan.[37]

Cannabis Eradication

The DEA works to stop the spread of marijuana cultivation across the U.S. through their Domestic Cannabis Eradication/Suppression Program. This is the only national law enforcement program that exclusively focuses on Drug Trafficking Organizations that are involved in growing marijuana. The program began eradication programs in Hawaii and California in 1979 and since then has expanded to all 50 states.[38]

Clandestine Drug Laboratory Cleanup

In 1990 the DEA, along with the EPA and the U.S. Coast Guard, published new guidelines for the cleanup of clandestine drug laboratories. This provides state and local law enforcement officials, environmental protection groups, and public health agencies with standards for the safe clean-up of illegal drug laboratories.[39]

Drug Prevention (Demand Reduction)

Special agents from the DEA work in communities around the nation as demand reduction coordinators. They provide expertise and intelligence to individuals and community groups on drug prevention techniques. Through the program, formally created in 1985, the DEA has been able to form partnerships with federal, state, local, and private groups who also want to reduce the demand for illicit drugs. In some states, DEA agents work with representatives from the governor's office and legislature to identify trends, priorities, and issues which could impact drug prevention programs on the state level. By working with community leaders and government officials, effective programs to reduce drug use have been implemented. Agents also work with members of the general public as a means to increase support for drug enforcement activities. They discuss issues relevant to the drug problem so that they have a better understanding of the damage that drugs can cause. DEA agents also work directly with schools to provide them with knowledge of the dangers of using drugs.[40]

Diversion Control/Prescription Drug Abuse

There are many legitimately manufactured controlled substances that are being diverted from their lawful purpose into the illicit drug traffic. The DEA's Office of Diversion Control attempts to detect this movement and prevent it. In recent years, a market for purely synthetic drugs has opened. These drugs are often created in clandestine laboratories that can pose significant public health and safety issues to others. The DEA monitors these new drugs to prevent harm to users.[41]

Foreign Cooperative Investigations

Since drug traffickers do not operate only within the U.S., the DEA regularly cooperates with foreign law enforcement agencies in the war against drug trafficking and abuse. DEA special agents assist foreign law enforcement agents by gathering evidence through interviewing witnesses, carrying out surveillance, checking shipping and passport records, or conducting laboratory analysis on drugs. The DEA participates in international forums geared toward advancing international cooperation and provides training to foreign police agencies.[42]

Forensic Sciences

The Forensic Sciences Division provides assistance to DEA agents through the analysis of suspected controlled substances, crime scene evidence, or processing of cleanups at clandestine laboratories. The DEA's Computer Forensics Program processes digital evidence collected from computers and other devices.[43]

High Intensity Drug Trafficking Areas

The High Intensity Drug Trafficking Areas (HIDTA) Program, carried out by the Office of National Drug Control Policy, is intended to reduce drug trafficking in critical areas around the country. If an area is identified as being a major center of illegal drug production, manufacturing, importation, or distribution; already has state and local law enforcement agencies present; has a harmful impact on other areas of the country; and is in need of a significant increase in federal resources, it could be designated as an HIDTA. Currently, 31 areas of the country have been identified as HIDTAs, including 5 along the Southwest border with Mexico.[44]

Intelligence

The DEA is responsible for collecting, analyzing, and disseminating information about drug trafficking and use. They coordinate this responsibility with other federal, state, local, and foreign law enforcement organizations. Over the years, the Intelligence Program has helped to initiate new investigations of major drug groups while strengthening ongoing investigations. They have collected information that has led to seizures and arrests. They often provide trend information to policy makers who may be reviewing narcotics policies.[45]

Money Laundering

The Money Laundering Division of the DEA is focused on tracing money used in drug operations to the international sources of supply. Since the reason people sell drugs is the money, the DEA seeks to attack the financial infrastructure of drug trafficking organizations. The DEA seeks to stop the organizations from using the profits from drug sales to finance their continued operations. It is thought that eliminating the sources of revenue from the organization will halt their ability to either acquire or produce additional drugs. The DEA has 24 Financial Investigation Teams (FITs) in each of its 21 domestic field divisions and offices in Bogota and Bangkok. The FITs conduct multi-agency financial investigations into the profits.[46]

Office of the Administrative Law Judges

The DEA's Office of Administrative Law Judges is responsible for conducting legal hearings in cases brought by the DEA under the Controlled Substances Act. U.S. administrative law judges are appointed through a process administered by the Office of Personnel Management. The government is represented at all hearings by the DEA's Office of Chief Counsel. Recommended decisions issued by the judges are forwarded to the DEA deputy administrator, who issues final Agency decisions.[47]

Organized Crime and Drug Enforcement Task Force

The Organized Crime and Drug Enforcement Task Force (OCDETF) Program was established in 1982 and conducts investigations on drug trafficking and money laundering organizations. The OCDETF works in conjunction with federal agencies such as the FBI; Bureau of Immigration and Customs Enforcement; the Bureau of Alcohol, Tobacco, Firearms, and Explosives; the U.S. Marshals Service; the IRS; the U.S. Coast Guard; and state and local law enforcement agencies to identify, disrupt, and dismantle drug trafficking and money laundering groups that are largely responsible for the drug supply in the U.S.[48]

Southwest Border Initiative

The Southwest Border Initiative (SWBI) is a cooperative effort by federal law enforcement to address the threat posed by groups based in Mexico and operating along the Southwest border. The initiative, established in 1994, focuses on groups that are trafficking in heroin, methamphetamine, and marijuana. The agents working for the SWBI target the communication systems of the groups. The agents on the SWBI work with other law enforcement groups such as the FBI, U.S. Customs Service, and U.S. Attorney's Offices.[49]

State and Local Task Forces

As drug trafficking increased nationwide, the DEA recognized the need for cooperation and coordination of drug enforcement efforts with their state and local counterparts. The Task Force Program provides a federal presence in areas where the DEA would not otherwise be seen. With these efforts, the federal expertise is combined with state and local officers' investigative knowledge of their individual jurisdictions to create a highly effective drug law enforcement investigation. In 2009, the DEA State and Local Task Force Program managed 381 state and local task forces. The task forces are staffed by over 1,890 DEA special agents and over 2,200 state and local officers.[50]

Victim-Witness Assistance Program

The DEA Victim Witness Assistance Program provides for victim witness training, guidance, and assistance to victims of crimes and those serving as government witnesses during court hearings. They work alongside state and local law enforcement as well as victim organizations.

Under the program, a crime victim can request assistance, such as information regarding an investigation, such as when charges are filed, when an arrest is made, or the date of an upcoming trial. A crime victim may also request a referral for services they may need, including referrals for counseling, medical assistance, emergency shelter, transportation, and/or the State Crime Compensation Program, if available. [51]

Foreign-Deployed Advisory and Support Teams

Otherwise known as FAST, the Foreign-Deployed Advisory and Support Teams conduct missions related to counternarcotics and counterterrorism. There are five teams. One team is located in Afghanistan, and the other four are located at the Marine Corps Base in Quantico, Virginia. FAST originally was created to conduct missions only in Afghanistan but has evolved into a global action arm for the U.S. Department of Justice and the DEA.

Conclusion

The DEA exists because of a reorganization of agencies during the 1970s that had the intent of bringing together those who played a role in fighting illicit drug use in the U.S. Today, agents work in the U.S. and internationally to reduce the flow of drugs and their use. They often work with other agencies in this battle, both on the federal and state levels. The DEA is an essential part of federal law enforcement in the U.S.

Key Terms

Controlled Substances Act

Bureau of Drug Abuse Control

Federal Bureau of Narcotics

Bureau of Narcotics and Dangerous Drugs

Reorganization Plan No. 2

Executive Order 11727

John R. Bartels

Enrique "Kiki" Camarena

Crime Control Act of 1988

Office of National Drug Control Policy

Drug Czar

Michele M. Leonhart

asset forfeiture

Aviation Division

cannabis eradication

Clandestine Drug Laboratory Cleanup

drug prevention (demand reduction)

diversion control/prescription drug abuse

foreign cooperative investigations

forensic sciences

high intensity drug trafficking areas

intelligence

money laundering

Office of Administrative Law Judges

Organized Crime and Drug Enforcement Task Force

Southwest Border Initiative

state and local task forces

Victim-Witness Assistance Program

foreign-deployed advisory and support teams

Review Questions

1. What is the primary function of the DEA?

2. What are the general and specific functions of the DEA administrator?

3. Provide an overview of the history of the DEA.

4. What was the Reorganization Plan No. 2 and why was it important to the DEA?

5. Who were some of the Directors of the DEA?

6. What qualifications must a person hold in order to become an agent with the DEA?

7. Describe the different employment opportunities available in the DEA.

8. How has Congress funded the DEA over the past few years?

9. How is the DEA organized?

Endnotes

1. "DEA Mission Statement," available at http://www.justice.gov/dea/about/mission.shtml.

2. Drug Enforcement Administration. (2012). "DEA History." Available online at http://www.justice.gov/dea/about/history.shtml.

3. Drug Enforcement Administration, "U.S. Drug Enforcement Administration Genealogy."

4. Bumgarner, Jeffrey B. (2006). *Federal Agents: The Growth of Federal Law Enforcement in America.* Westport, CT: Praeger.

5. Marion, Nancy E. (2011). *Federal Government and Criminal Justice.* New York: Palgrave Macmillan.

6. Drug Enforcement Administration. (2003). *Drug Enforcement Administration History.* Available online at http://www.justice.gov/dea/about/history.shtml.

7. Drug Enforcement Administration, *Drug Enforcement Administration History.*

8. The primary source for the history of the Drug Enforcement Administration comes from the following publication: Drug Enforcement Administration, *Drug Enforcement Administration History.*

9. Bumgarner, *Federal Agents.*

10. Bertham, Eva, Morris Blachman, Kenneth Sharpe, and Peter Andreas. (1996). *Drug War Politics.* Berkeley, CA: University of California Press.

11. Bertham, *Drug War Politics.*

12. Drug Enforcement Administration, *Drug Enforcement Administration History.*

13. Drug Enforcement Administration, *Drug Enforcement Administration History.*

14. Nixon, Richard. (1973). Executive Order No. 11727, Drug Law Enforcement." *Federal Register.* Available online at http://www.archives.gov/federal-register/codification/executive-order/11727.html.

15. Drug Enforcement Administration, *Drug Enforcement Administration History.*

16. Moore, Robin. (2003). *The French Connection: A True Account of Cops, Narcotics, and International Conspiracy.* Guildford, CT: Lyons Press.

17. Drug Enforcement Administration, *Drug Enforcement Administration History.*

18. Drug Enforcement Administration, *Drug Enforcement Administration History.*

19. Bowden, Mark. (2002). *Killing Pablo: The Hunt for the World's Greatest Outlaw.* New York: Penguin.

20. Andreas, Peter. (2009). *Border Games: Policing the U.S. – Mexico Divide.* Second Edition. Ithaca, NY: Cornell University Press.

21. Bertham, *Drug War Politics.*

22. Marion, *Federal Government and Criminal Justice.*

23. Bertham, *Drug War Politics.*

24. Drug Enforcement Administration, *Drug Enforcement Administration History.*

25. For more information on the DEA Museum see the Drug Enforcement Administration Museum and Visitors Center Web site at http://www.deamuseum.org/.

26. Drug Enforcement Administration, *Drug Enforcement Administration History.*

27. Bumgarner, *Federal Agents.*

28. Drug Enforcement Administration, *Drug Enforcement Administration History.*

29. Drug Enforcement Administration, "DEA Fact Sheet," available at http://www.justice.gov/dea/docs/factsheet.pdf.

30. "Finding Drug Enforcement Careers in DEA," available at http://criminal.laws.com/controlled-substances/dea/drug-enforcement-careers-in-dea.

31. "Finding Drug Enforcement Careers in DEA."

32. "Finding Drug Enforcement Careers in DEA."

33. Drug Enforcement Administration, "Office Locations," available at http://www.justice.gov/dea/about/Domesticoffices.shtml.

34. "Statistics and Facts," available at http://www.dea.gov/resource-center/statistics.shtml#arrests; "DEA Mission Statement."

35. "DEA Mission Statement."

36. "Asset Forfeiture," available at http://www.justice.gov/dea/ops/af.shtml.

37. "Aviation Division," available at http://www.justice.gov/dea/ops/aviation.shtml.

38. "Domestic Cannabis Eradication/Suppression Program," available at http://www.justice.gov/dea/ops/cannabis.shtml.
39. "Clandestine Lab Cleanup," available at http://www.justice.gov/dea/ops/clandestine.shtml.
40. "Drug Prevention/Demand Reduction," available at http://www.justice.gov/dea/ops/drugprevention.shtml.
41. "Diversion Control/Prescription Drug Abuse," available at http://www.justice.gov/dea/ops/diversion.shtml.
42. "Foreign Cooperative Investigations," available at http://www.justice.gov/dea/ops/fci.shtml.
43. "DEA Forensic Sciences," available at http://www.justice.gov/dea/ops/forensic.shtml.
44. "High Intensity Drug Trafficking Areas (HIDTAs)," available at http://www.justice.gov/dea/ops/hidta.shtml.
45. "National Drug Pointer Index," available at http://www.justice.gov/dea/FOIA/pia_docs/ndpix_signed_pia_032907.pdf.
46. "Money Laundering," available at http://www.justice.gov/dea/ops/money.shtml.
47. "Office of the Administrative Law Judges," available at http://www.justice.gov/dea/ops/oalj.shtml.
48. "Organized Crime and Drug Enforcement Task Force (OCDETF)," available at http://www.justice.gov/dea/ops/ocdetf.shtml.
49. "Southwest Border Initiative," available at http://www.justice.gov/dea/ops/sbi.shtml.
50. "State and Local Task Forces," available at http://www.justice.gov/dea/ops/taskforces.shtml.
51. "Victim Witness Assistance," available at http://www.justice.gov/dea/ops/vwap.shtml.

8

U.S. Customs and Border Protection

Customs and Border Protection (CBP) is the federal law enforcement agency that protects the U.S. borders and ports from terrorists and illegal immigrants, illegal trade, and other harmful elements. According to the agency, their mission is to protect the nation's borders and keep terrorists and their weapons, including weapons of mass destruction, from entering the U.S. To carry out their mission, agents from CBP watch nearly 7,000 miles of land that borders Canada and Mexico as well as 2,000 miles of coastal waters around Florida and off the coast of Southern California. The agency also protects 95,000 miles of maritime border in conjunction with the U.S. Coast Guard.[1] CBP Officers ensure the nation's safety by screening passengers and cargo at over 300 ports of entry.

Agents work to protect the security of the U.S. in many ways. They seek to stop immigrants from coming into the U.S. through illegal means and arrest those with outstanding criminal warrants. They also prevent those who seek to bring illegal drugs and other contraband into the country from crossing the borders. They inspect inbound as well as outbound cargo for illegal or dangerous materials. Agents at CBP protect agricultural and economic interests from pests and diseases that could harm crops and affect the country's food supply. CBP also prevents smuggled goods from entering the country.[2]

At the same time, CBP must protect and maintain the nation's economic security through maintaining legitimate international trade and safe travel.[3] To do this, agents regulate international trade by collecting import duties.[4]

The core values of CBP are listed in Figure 8.1.

Figure 8.1: Core Values of Customs and Border Protection

Vigilance: is how we ensure the safety of all Americans. We are continuously watchful and alert to deter, detect and prevent threats to our Nation. We demonstrate courage and valor in the protection of our Nation.

Service to Country: is embodied in the work we do. We are dedicated to defending and upholding the Constitution of the United States. The American people have entrusted us to protect the homeland and defend liberty.

Integrity: is our cornerstone. We are guided by the highest ethical and moral principles. Our actions bring honor to ourselves and our agency.[5]

The authority of Customs and Border Protection and its responsibilities are found in 22 Code of Federal Regulations 127.4, shown in Figure 8.2.

Figure 8.2: Statutory Authority of Customs and Border Protection

Authority of U.S. Immigration and Customs Enforcement and U.S. Customs and Border Protection officers:

(a) U.S. Immigration and Customs Enforcement and U.S. Customs and Border Protection officers may take appropriate action to ensure observance of this subchapter as to the export or the attempted export or the temporary import of any defense article or technical data, including the inspection of loading or unloading of any vessel, vehicle, or aircraft. This applies whether the export is authorized by license or by written approval issued under this subchapter or by exemption.

(b) U.S. Immigration and Customs Enforcement and U.S. Customs and Border Protection officers have the authority to investigate, detain or seize any export or attempted export of defense articles or technical data contrary to this subchapter.

(c) Upon the presentation to a U.S. Customs and Border Protection Officer of a license or written approval authorizing the export of any defense article, the customs officer may require the production of other relevant documents and information relating to the proposed export. This includes an invoice, order, packing list, shipping document, correspondence, instructions, and the documents otherwise required by the U.S. Customs and Border Protection or U.S. Immigration and Customs Enforcement.

(d) If an exemption under this subchapter is used or claimed to export, transfer, reexport or retransfer, furnish, or obtain a defense article, technical data, or defense service, law enforcement officers may rely upon the authorities noted, additional authority identified in the language of the exemption, and any other lawful means or authorities to investigate such a matter.

History

In the wake of the September 11, 2011 terrorist attacks on America, a major reorganization of federal law enforcement was undertaken. Developed by the Bush Administration, the Homeland Security Act of 2002 was passed by Congress and signed into law on November 25 of that year.[6] Thus was born the U.S. Department of Homeland Security (DHS). In 2003, as the plan was set into motion and the new DHS was formed, various federal law enforcement agencies were brought into DHS either whole or in part. They were then assigned to a particular directorate within DHS. In the case of (CBP), elements of the former U.S. Customs Agency (Department of the Treasury), the Immigration and Naturalization Service (Department of Justice), the Animal and Plant Health Inspectors (Department of Agriculture), the U.S. Coast Guard (Department of Transportation), and the Border Patrol (Department of Justice), were brought into the fold.[7] As a result, the historical lineage of CBP is more difficult to trace than most other federal law enforcement agencies. The key historical antecedents of CBP, however, are the former U.S. Customs Service, the Immigration and Naturalization Service, and the U.S. Border Patrol.[8]

Shortly after the inauguration of George Washington, his newly formed cabinet developed a plan for dealing with the issues of a country about to go bankrupt. Secretary of the Treasury Alexander Hamilton had developed a well-received plan to take up the states' debt from the American Revolution in exchange for certain trade-offs, but then the national government needed to find some means for raising funds to pay off these debts. On July 4, 1789, President Washington signed into law the Tariff Act, which was dubbed the "Second Declaration of Independence" at the time. In order to collect these tariffs, however, an agency was necessary to enforce the new laws. On July 31, 1789, Congress established the Bureau of Customs and designated ports of entry.[9] Because the agency was largely a tax collection agency, it was housed in the U.S. Department of the Treasury. These agents were some of the first federal law enforcement agents in United States history.[10]

In addition to the Bureau of Customs, there was also the development of the Revenue Cutter Service, which consisted of boats patrolling American shores, assisting stranded vessels, and enforcing the law against violators seeking to avoid the tariffs. This service would eventually evolve into the U.S. Coast Guard. By and large, the late eighteenth century and early nineteenth century Bureau of Customs was oriented on tax collection and it was not until the late nineteenth century that the focus began to shift more toward law enforcement. In 1870, Congress passed a law that created a Special Service Agency within the Bureau of Customs that operated as an office of investigation, thus enhancing their focus on law enforcement.[11] It was World War I and events thereafter, however, that would fundamentally change much of the focus of the Bureau of Customs.

During World War I, the fear of infiltrators, smugglers, and saboteurs ran high, and the Bureau of Customs and Coast Guard began to focus their attention on the enforcement of laws to catch these types of criminals. After the Great War, in 1918, one change that was implemented to gain a more visible presence was the introduction of police-like uniforms. Then came the era of Prohibition, which created the greatest change in the mission of the Bureau of Customs. It transformed the agency from tax collectors to law enforcers.[12] In order to reflect this change and to train its agents properly, in 1935, the Bureau of Customs developed its own academy, and while revenue collecting was one aspect of the training, law enforcement was the primary focus.

Once again, with America's entry into a World War, in 1941 the Bureau of Customs became focused on counter-espionage and embargo violations. After the war, the new emphasis was on drug law enforcement, in particular interdiction. As the Bureau of Customs reached the 1970s, it changed its name to the U.S. Customs Service and began to take on a wider role in enforcing the laws along the borders through the development of both air and marine assets in order to interdict violators. The scope of their mission would continue to grow and, until 2003 when the U.S. Customs Service became part of the Department of Homeland Security, it was the second largest federal law enforcement agency with 12,000 employees, second only to the Immigration and Naturalization Service. In 2003, the entire U.S. Customs Service was moved into the Department of Homeland Security. The majority of the law enforcement agents (investigation and intelligence), however, were moved into U.S. Immigration and Customs Enforcement (ICE) (see Chapter 9), but the rest were moved into U.S. Customs and Border Protection (CBP).

The largest federal law enforcement agency before the creation of the Department of Homeland Security was the Immigration and Naturalization Service (INS), which also, in part, was absorbed into U.S. Customs and Border Protection.[13] Although immigration had been addressed in the U.S. Constitution, there was little concern in America about immigrants coming to America until the post-Civil War time frame. As the number of immigrants rose dramatically in the 1870s and 1880s, there was a clear need for a response. Many states, especially the border states, began enacting their own immigrant legislation, which raised a number of legal challenges that eventually found their way to the United States Supreme Court. The Court determined that the U.S. Constitution was clear on the issue: Immigration law fell under the purview of the national government, not the states.

In light of the U.S. Supreme Court decision, it became clear that what was needed was a federal agency that could deal with the immigration influx. In 1891, Congress passed an Immigration Act that created the Office of the Superintendent of Immigration within the U.S. Department of the Treasury. The office was responsible for processing the paperwork for those seeking admission into the United States, for conducting immigrant inspections at the ports of entry, and enforcing the immigrant laws. They were also responsible for collecting a "head tax" of 50 cents from each immigrant, hence the reason the agency was placed under the Department of the Treasury. The task became so overwhelming so quickly that the agency became a bureau, the Bureau of Immigration, and the superintendent became known as the commissioner-general of immigration.

The original idea behind placing the Office of the Superintendent of Immigration under the Department of the Treasury was because there was a revenue-generating aspect to the immigration laws. Congress, however, wrote the laws to emphasize the protection of American workers and their wages. As these laws were much more oriented on issues of commerce than revenue, in 1903 the Bureau of Immigration was transferred to the Department of Commerce and Labor. Three years later, Congress would retitle the agency the Bureau of Immigration and Naturalization in order to emphasize the federal role of naturalizing immigrants. This was done by way of the Basic Naturalization Act of 1906.

In 1913, the Department of Commerce and Labor split into two departments, the Department of Commerce and the Department of Labor. The decision over what to do with the Bureau of Immigration and Naturalization followed suit. It was decided that the Bureau would also split into two: the Bureau of Immigration and the Bureau of Naturalization. Then, as the issue of immigration, both legal and illegal, heated up in the 1920s, more laws were passed and the lines between immigration and naturalization began to blur. In addition, with a depressed economy arising from the Stock Market Crash of 1929, the Hoover Administration was looking for ways to save money. So, President Hoover, by way of an executive order, merged the two Bureaus back into one entity, the Immigration and Naturalization Service (INS). It was then placed under the Department of Labor. It would not remain there for long.

In 1940, with war imminent, President Franklin Roosevelt foresaw the issue of immigration as a matter of national security, so he ordered the service transferred from the Department of Labor to the Department of Justice. No longer was the immigration issue about protecting America's jobs, it was about protecting its borders. Roosevelt proved to be prescient, for the demands on the service rose during the war and it doubled in size, going from 4,000 employees to over 8,000 by war's end. Although immigration overall declined after the war, there were still displaced persons and refugees to deal with and the enforcement of two acts related to these issues (the Displaced Persons Act of 1948 and the Refugee Relief Act of 1953) became the focus of the service.

The INS continued to enforce a wide array of immigration laws passed by Congress, but most of these laws were oriented on documentation, visas, and naturalization. Although enforcement of illegal aliens was one task, it was not a primary focus of the INS. That changed under the Reagan Administration with the passage of the Immigration Reform and Control Act of 1986. This act charged the INS to enforce the laws against employers who hired illegal aliens, to deport the aliens and levy fines on the employers. These additional laws had the agency handling not only the administrative aspects of immigration but the law enforcement aspects as well, causing the agency to balloon to over 30,000 employees by 2000.

In 2003, with the creation of the U.S. Department of Homeland Security, it was determined that the various elements of immigration administration and enforcement would be divided into three areas. Those focused on the administration and naturalization would fall under the newly created U.S. Citizenship and Immigration Service. Those that enforced the immigration violation laws would fall under U.S. Immigration and Customs Enforcement (see Chapter 9), and those who handled entry into the U.S., focusing on tourists, business travelers, and those with temporary visas, would fall under U.S. Customs and Border Protection. Thus, elements of the INS became part of the CBP.

One aspect of immigration enforcement that is such a fixture of today's federal law enforcement is the border patrol.[14] Yet in the first 100 years of the United States, most border protection was handled by state officials, such as the Texas Rangers along the Texas–Mexico border. In 1904, the Bureau of Immigration assigned some agents along the border who served primarily as inspectors, but even they were few and far between. In March of 1915, the U.S. Congress authorized a new group of inspectors to serve along the Mexican border as mounted guards. They patrolled the Mexican–American border not for illegal Mexicans coming across the border but rather for Chinese immigrants who came across in an attempt to avoid the Chinese Exclusion Laws. Finally, twice in the nineteen-teens, the U.S. Military was placed along the Mexican–American border; the first time because of the Mexican Revolution and incursion into the United States by Pancho Villa and the second time because of World War I.

Despite all of these various scenarios, it was not until the early 1920s, when the Immigration Acts of 1921 and 1924 placed quotas on the number of immigrants allowed to enter the United States, that the issue of illegal border crossings became a major issue.[15] As a result, on May 28, 1924, Congress passed the Labor Appropriations Act of 1924 and established a new agency under the Bureau of Immigration, the United States Border Patrol. The patrol area extended from the California–Mexico border to the Texas–Mexico border and across the entire gulf coast and Florida seacoast. By the early 1930s, the U.S. Border Patrol was assigned border duties along the U.S.–Canada border as well. There were two directors, one for the northern border and one for the southern. Their headquarters were located in Detroit, Michigan, and El Paso, Texas, respectively.

During World War II, the duties of the U.S. Border Patrol expanded greatly, as would their numbers. The Border Patrol was responsible for manning alien detention camps, guarding diplomats, and assisting the U.S. Coast Guard in searching for saboteurs. The service added over 700 agents during the war, bringing their total to 1,531 by war's end. Then, beginning in the early 1950s, illegal immigration into the United States along the American–Mexican border rose and many of the agents along the northern border were sent south. Additional agents were added to the service but, once again, new issues surfaced. Aircraft hijackings, drug smuggling, and illegal entry by air all became new threats to national security, and the border patrol was called upon to increase its presence and enforcement. By the 1990s, potential terrorist threats were added to list of concerns and responsibilities, and the U.S. Border Patrol was again overextended.

In the wake of the September 11 attacks and the reorganization of the federal homeland security structure, the U.S. Border Patrol was looking at being absorbed into the newly formed U.S. Department of Homeland Security. As the plans developed through 2002, it became clear that the U.S. Border Patrol would not lose its institutional identity for it would be moved whole into the new department. Placed as a largely independent agency under U.S. Customs and Border Protection, the U.S. Border Patrol became one of the two key agencies absorbed to create the CBP.

One last bureaucratic element that was absorbed into U.S. Customs and Border Protection was the Animal and Plant Health Inspection Service (APHIS) of the United States Department of Agriculture. APHIS was created in 1972, during the Nixon Administration, by way of a memorandum by the secretary of agriculture (Memorandum No. 1769). Like the CBP itself, APHIS was not created from whole cloth, but rather was the merger of a number of related entities that were part of the Department of Agriculture. The first of these pre-existing offices was created in 1854, when the Office of Entomology under the Agricultural Section of the U.S. Patent Office was created. The second, the Cattle Commission, created under the U.S. Department of the Treasury, came in 1881. Three years later it was transferred to the U.S. Department of Agriculture (USDA). The third element was created in 1912, when the Federal Horticultural Board, under the USDA, was created to deal with plant quarantines. These three entities would eventually evolve into their own bureaus, the Bureau of Entomology, the Bureau of Animal Industry, and the Bureau of Plant Quarantine.

In 1953, under an Agricultural Department reconstruction, the three Bureaus were combined into one entity, the Agricultural Research Service. In 1971, the animal and plant regulatory functions were removed from the Agricultural Research Service and placed under a newly created service, the Animal and Plant Health Services. The following year, two divisions from the Consumer Marketing Service, the meat and poultry inspection divisions, were added to the Animal and Plant Health Services, and became the Animal and Plant Health Inspection Service (APHIS). As this service dealt with aspects of customs and border protection, when the CBP was created, the APHIS agricultural border inspectors were transferred from the U.S. Department of Agriculture and placed under the U.S. Department of Homeland Security.

As a result of the Homeland Security Act of 2002, all of these elements were brought into the newly created U.S. Department of Homeland Security. The secretary of Homeland Security established a number of directorates to separate out the functions of Homeland Security, and one of those was the Directorate of Border and Transportation Security. This Directorate serves as the parent agency for U.S. Customs and Border Protection (CBP). It also serves as the parent agency for U.S. Immigration and Customs Enforcement (ICE), the Transportation Security Administration (TSA), and the U.S. Coast Guard.

The newly combined agency, CBP, essentially provides the front line responders to immigrations and customs violations and serves as the law enforcement arm of DHS (ICE serves as its investigative branch—see Chapter 9).[16] CBP's mission is to prevent terrorists and terrorist weapons from entering the country, provide security at U.S. borders and ports of entry, apprehend illegal immigrants, stem the flow of illegal drugs, and protect American agricultural and economic interests from harmful pests and disease. Its duties have focused on law enforcement between ports of entry as well as at ports of entry. In order to carry out their mission and duties, CBP employs the largest number of federal employees within DHS. This has led to a number of difficulties for the agency since its creation.

The wide array of the agencies absorbed into CBP and the vast scale of its employees left CBP with perhaps the most difficult job of leadership, management, and organization.[17] In 2006, the Office of Personnel Management conducted a job satisfaction survey and found CBP was either last or close to last in nearly every category. A follow up assessment by the U.S. Government Accountability Office found that low staffing, lack of training, and overwork was plaguing the agency, and the turnover rate at CBP was high.[18] Plans have been developed to deal with the issues, but they have been slow to be implemented, and calls for new organizational restructuring have been made in the wake of these allegations.

Who Gets Hired

Those who wish to be hired to serve as an agent in CBP (as a CBP officer) must pass a written test that includes logical and quantitative reasoning skills, writing skills, and an assessment of experience and achievement. There are also medical and fitness requirements for candidates, including an EKG, a vision test, a hearing test, a physical exam, and a background investigation. Applicants must be under the age of 40, unless they have previous federal law enforcement experience or are eligible for a qualified Veterans' Preference. A candidate must be a U.S. citizen and resident of the U.S., be fluent in Spanish or be able to learn the Spanish language, and possess a valid state driver's license.[19]

A candidate must also pass a video-based test (VBT) and a structured interview (SI). The video-based test consists of four scenarios to which the applicant must respond as if he were in that particular situation. The interview is a face-to-face meeting in which the candidate is asked about past experience, among other things. A candidate may be disqualified if he has had prior arrests or convictions for certain offenses such as a misdemeanor domestic violence charge. If a candidate has been fired from a previous job, has large debt or other financial issues, has a pattern of excessive alcohol use, or has used or distributed illegal drugs, he may also be disqualified.[20]

Those who pass the tests will then receive training through an 18-week program at the Federal Law Enforcement Training Center. They will be trained in basic law enforcement skills including anti-terrorism skills, detection of contraband, interviewing suspects, cross-cultural communications, firearms handling, immigration and naturalization laws, U.S. customs export and import laws, defensive tactics, arrest techniques, and baton techniques. They will also be trained in the examination of cargo, bags, and merchandise, border search inspection, entry and control procedures, passenger processing, and officer safety and survival. Recruits may also receive an additional six weeks of Spanish language training.

Student interns are hired through the Student Educational Employment Program (SEEP) for either paid or unpaid employment. Candidates must be accepted for enrollment or enrolled in and taking at least a half-time course load at either an accredited high school, technical school, vocational school, two-or four-year college or university, graduate school, or professional school. This includes students pursuing their education through correspondence, videotaped lecture/instruction, the Internet, or telecom and video telecom media.

Once hired, there are different types of positions available in CBP. The most well-known and most visible positions are operational and mission support positions, which are the frontline occupations of CBP. Those agents hired to serve as air and marine interdiction agents receive specialized training to prevent people, weapons, or narcotics from being brought into the U.S. illegally by air and water transportation modes. CBP agriculture specialists focus on preventing the spread of harmful pests and diseases that may harm farms and the food supply and averting bio-and agro-terrorism.

CBP also has revenue positions. These agents enforce trade and tariff laws across the country, typically collecting over $30 billion a year, the second largest revenue for the U.S. government. These employees will serve as import specialists, auditors, international trade specialists, or textile analysts.[21]

Budgets

The budgets for CBP are noted in Table 8.1. Since FY 2010, Congress has allocated between $11.5 and $12 billion to CBP each year.

Leader

R. Gil Kerlikowske was nominated to serve as the commissioner of CBP by President Obama. After being approved by the Senate, he was sworn in on March 7, 2014. In this position, Kerlikowske is responsible for protecting national security.

Table 8.1	Budget Authority for CPB (In Billions of Dollars)
FY 2010 enacted	$11.846
FY 2011 enacted	$11,545
FY 2012 enacted	$11,781
FY 2013 enacted	$11.664
FY 2014 enacted	$12.377
FY 2015 presidential budget	$13.097

Source: Department of Homeland Security, Fiscal Year 2015 Budget in Brief, available at http://www.dhs.gov/sites/default/files/publications/FY15BIB.pdf.

Kerlikowske has a strong law enforcement background both on the state and federal level. On the state level, he served as the chief of police for Seattle, Washington for nine years. Kerlikowske was also police commissioner of Buffalo, New York. Most of his law enforcement career was in the state of Florida, serving in the St. Petersburg Police Department.

On the federal level, Kerlikowske served as the deputy director for the Office of Community Oriented Policing Services in the U.S. Department of Justice. Most recently, he was the director of the White House Office of National Drug Control Policy.

Kerlikowske has earned the respect of others in law enforcement. He was chosen twice to be president of the Major Cities Chiefs, which is a group that represents law enforcement from the largest city and county law enforcement agencies in both the United States and Canada. Kerlikowske has also received numerous awards for his strong leadership, innovation, and community service. He served in the U.S. Army, where he was awarded the Presidential Service Badge. Mr. Kerlikowske holds a B.A. and an M.A. in criminal justice from the University of South Florida.

Organization

CPB was moved to the Department of Homeland Security upon its creation after 9/11. With over 58,000 employees in the U.S. and overseas, CBP is the largest law enforcement agency within the DHS. CBP also houses teams of officers in 58 foreign seaports who work alongside agents in the host country to inspect high-risk shipments before they reach the U.S. They also work with officials from the private sector in joint government–business initiatives that are designed to strengthen border security while facilitating legitimate trade.

The agency is headed by a commissioner and a deputy commissioner, as noted in Figure 8.3. Within the commissioner's office are the Office of Chief Counsel, the Office of Program Development, the Office of Strategic Integration, the Office of the Executive Secretariat, the Office of State, Local, and Tribal Liaison, the Office of Policy and Planning, the Office of Trade Relations, the Office of Privacy and Diversity, and the Joint Operations Directorate. There are many assistant commissioners who oversee particular concerns of CBP. These offices are the Office of Administration, the Office of Air and Marine, the Office of Border Patrol, the Office of Congressional Affairs, the Office of Field Operations, the Office of Human Resource Management, the Office of Information and Technology, the Office of Intelligence and Investigative Liaison, the Office of Internal Affairs, the Office of International Affairs, the Office of International Trade, the Office of Public Affairs, the Office of Technology Innovation and Acquisition, and the Office of Training and Development. A more detailed organizational chart is shown in Figure 8.3.

Figure 8.3: Organizational Chart: U.S. Customs and Border Protection

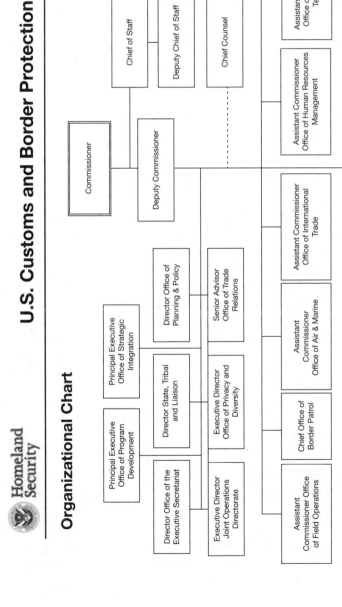

Source: U.S. Customs and Border Protection, Organizational Chart, available at http://www.cbp.gov/sites/default/files/documents/CBP%20Org%20Chart%20 Feb2014.pdf.

What They Do

Inspections at Ports and Borders

One of the primary functions of CBP is to carry out inspections of cargo and goods as they enter the U.S. to ensure the safety of the product. This is done through the Field Operations and Port Security groups. Agents conduct agricultural inspections as a way to prevent harmful pests or any organism from being introduced into the farming communities or from being used for biological warfare or terrorism.[22] CBP carries out immigration inspection programs so that those individuals who seek entry into the U.S. are inspected at ports-of-entry by CBP officers who determine their admissibility.[23]

CBP agents also examine cargo to look for radiation emanating from nuclear devices, dirty bombs, or nuclear materials.[24] They physically examine cargo when it arrives in U.S. ports but also rely on intelligence from outside sources to identify high-risk shipments.[25] They also rely on a radiation portal to detect nuclear and radiological materials in trucks and other conveyances. [26]

Border Patrol

Border Patrol is a vital component within CBP that has the goal of protecting the nation's borders and preventing terrorist (and their weapons) from entering the U.S. The Border Patrol agents are mobile, uniformed law enforcement officers who seek to deter people from entering the country illegally by enforcing U.S. immigration laws. They monitor borders and ports, responding to and attempting to prevent illicit intrusions. One objective of Border Patrol agents is to establish high probability of apprehending terrorists and their weapons if they attempt to enter the U.S. They also try to apprehend and deter human smugglers and those who try to smuggle other contraband. In the end, Border Patrol agents try to reduce crime that occurs in border communities and therefore improve the quality of life of those areas.[27]

As a way to address the unique border control issues facing the state of Arizona, the CPB created the Arizona Joint Field Command (JFC). The program integrates border security, commercial enforcement, and trade facilitation missions. The JFC oversees all CBP operations throughout Arizona.[28]

Secure Border Initiative

In 2005, the DHS established the Secure Border Initiative (SBI), a comprehensive plan to help protect America's borders. The SBI has an office within CBP that helps to manage the border security programs within the agency. The goal of the program is to achieve control of the borders through situational awareness (knowing what is going on at the borders) and having the ability to respond effectively. CBP uses a combination of three methods to achieve effective control:

personnel, tactical infrastructure, and technology. SBI supports CBP's front-line agents with technology they need to secure the border.[29]

Tactical Infrastructure/Border Fence

The Office of Border Patrol (OBP) is responsible for the long-term planning, construction, and maintenance of tactical infrastructure (roads, fencing, lights, electrical components, and drainage structures) to help the Border Patrol protect the borders. The OBP's most visible construction projects have been the pedestrian and vehicle fence projects along the southwest border of the U.S.[30] When completed, the program will have constructed approximately 670 miles of pedestrian and vehicle fence along the border.[31]

Facilitating International Trade

CBP protects legitimate international trade by enforcing U.S. trade laws that have been passed to protect the U.S. economy and the safety and health of Americans. They have created ways to keep the costs of business low while providing more consistency and predictability for trade. CPB attempts to enhance their enforcement efforts against illegal trade while at the same time tailoring enforcement needs to unique trading environments.[32]

International Training and Assistance

CBP works with international groups of all kinds in their attempts to prevent crime. The International Law Enforcement Academy (ILEA) Program was established in 1995 to help create International Law Enforcement Academies (ILEAs) throughout the world as a means to increase cooperation to more effectively combat international drug trafficking and terrorism. Today there are four ILEAs in Europe, Africa, Central and South America, and Asia. A Regional Training Center was established in Lima and an Academic ILEA was opened in Roswell, New Mexico.

The ILEAs work to combat transnational crime groups through more effective international cooperation. ILEAs help foreign agencies develop and improve their own border enforcement policies. They also focus on apprehending those who carry out transnational crimes such as drug trafficking, alien smuggling, and financial crimes. When needed, specialized training may be provided to those agencies who request it.[33]

The Bureau for International Narcotics and Law Enforcement Affairs (INL) acts as an advisor to the president, secretary of state, and others on the policies to combat international narcotics and crime. The goal of INL is to reduce the amount of illegal drugs being brought into the U.S. and to lessen the impact of international crime on the U.S. INL's counter-narcotics and anti-crime programs are part of the war on terrorism, since they promote updating operations in foreign criminal justice systems. Within INL, CBP carries out many international enforcement training programs and provides assistance to customs agencies in countries that are considered to pose a threat to the U.S. in terms of narcotics production or movement, organized crime, and terrorist activity.[34]

The Proliferation Security Initiative (PSI) is a world-wide program that aims to stop trafficking of weapons of mass destruction and related materials. It was started in 2003, and CBP became involved in 2004 when the PSI was expanded to include law enforcement cooperation. Today, 98 countries around the world have endorsed the PSI. It is a proactive approach to preventing proliferation. PSI participants use existing authorities (both national and international) to abolish weapons of mass destruction (WMD)-related trafficking. Operationally, CBP can take action to interdict WMD-related materials through its existing border search powers.

Human Trafficking

Human trafficking remains a significant world-wide problem. CBP, along with many other federal, state, and local law enforcement agencies in the U.S. government, are working to combat the problem. CPB devotes an office to the problem of human trafficking, which carries out many roles. The agents working in the Office seek to identify potential victims as they enter the U.S., and then direct them to agencies that can provide them with legal protection and assistance. They also seek to raise the awareness of the American public about this crime. Raising awareness of the crime in international groups is also a priority, especially to those who may become victims of traffickers, particularly in countries where this crime is pervasive. CBP agents work to assist the public in reporting suspected cases of human trafficking. They also identify goods that may have been produced by forced labor and stop them from being brought into the U.S.[35]

As another way to fight human trafficking, CPB created the "No Te Enganes/Don't be Fooled" program. The main objective of the program is to raise awareness among possible victims, to make them aware of the dangers of human trafficking and help them avoid becoming victimized. They also try to create awareness of human trafficking in neighborhoods where the crime is most likely to occur and to educate people on how to report suspicious activity.[36]

CBP Canine Program

The CBP Canine Program trains canine instructors, handlers, and dogs to assist CBP in the task of protecting the borders. The canines and their handlers help CBP agents detect illegal activity (i.e., drugs, large amounts of cash) while at the same time allowing for legitimate trade and travel.[37] The canines are taught to detect any humans who may be hiding in trucks odors of controlled substances (marijuana, cocaine, heroin, methamphetamine, hashish, and ecstasy), large quantities of currency, and firearms. Both the agents and the canines are taught proper search sequences to search private and commercial transportation, freight, luggage, and mail. The CBP Canine Program is the largest law enforcement canine program in the country.[38]

Community Involvement

CBP places a high priority on interaction with and feedback from members of the community such as local officials, landowners, and other community members. To this end, the agency manages many types of community outreach activities. They hold meetings with stakeholders, hold town hall meetings, and otherwise reach out to the public and local officials as a way to have dialogue with them.[39] This way, CPB is aware of the needs and concerns of the communities with whom they work and can respond quickly to those needs and concerns.

Office of Air and Marine

The mission of the Office of Air and Marine within CBP is "to protect the American people and the Nation's critical infrastructure through the coordinated use air of integrated air and marine forces to detect, interdict and prevent acts of terrorism and the unlawful movement of people, illegal drugs and other contraband toward or across the borders of the U.S."[40] The Office is the largest aviation and maritime law enforcement agency in the world, with over 360 agents. The agency has over 700 pilots and more than 290 aircraft, some of which are unmanned aircraft systems. To control waterways and seaports, the CPB has over 220 vessels, including a 39-foot Midnight Interceptor.[41]

Maritime Domain Awareness (MDA)

CBA constantly monitors vessels, craft, cargo, crews, and passengers in the global maritime domain to ensure their safety and the safety to others. The agents in this area monitor intelligence as a way to understand anything associated with the global maritime domain that could have an impact upon the security, safety, economy, or environment of the U.S. They work to identify, locate, and track any potential threats.[42]

Conclusion

Customs and Border Protection is a federal law enforcement agency that enforces the laws of the U.S. to protect the borders from illegal immigration, illicit drugs, and dangerous cargo coming into the country. At the same time, they must allow for travel into and out of the U.S. safely. The agency plays a vital role in protecting the homeland and keeping citizens safe.

Key Terms

Bureau of Customs

Immigration and Naturalization Service

Basic Naturalization Act of 1906

Labor Appropriations Act of 1924

Animal and Plant Health Inspection Service

Agricultural Research Service

Student Educational Employment Program

Operational and Mission Support

air and marine interdiction agents

agricultural agents

R. Gil Kerlikowski

Secure Border Initiative

Tactical Infrastructure/Border Fence

facilitating international trade

international training and assistance

Proliferation Security Initiative

International Narcotics and Law Enforcement Affairs

Canine Program

Office of Air and Marine

Maritime Domain Awareness

Review Questions

1. What is the mission of the U.S. Customs and Border Protection? How do they achieve that goal?

2. What are the core values of the agency?

3. How was the agency reorganized after the 9/11 terrorist attacks on the U.S.?

4. Review the early history of the Customs and Border Protection.

5. What qualifications must a person possess in order to be hired by the U.S. Customs and Border Protection?

6. Describe the trends in funding provided to Customs and Border Protection.

7. What kinds of activities do agents with the Customs and Border Protection perform?

8. How do agents with Customs and Border Protection attempt to halt human trafficking?

Endnotes

1. U.S. Customs and Border Protection, "Border Patrol Overview," available at www.cbp.gov/border-security/along-us-borders/overview.
2. U.S. Customs and Border Protection, "Along U.S. Borders," available at www.cbp.gov/border-security/along-us-borders.
3. U.S. Customs and Border Protection, CBP Mission Statement and Core Values, available at www.cbp.gov/xp/cgov/about/mission/guardians.xml.
4. U.S. Customs and Border Protection, "Customs Duty Information," available at www.cbp.gov/travel/international-visitors/kbyg/customs-duty-info.
5. U.S. Customs and Border Protection, CBP Mission Statement and Core Values.
6. U.S. Department of Homeland Security. (2003). *The Homeland Security Act of 2002*. Washington, D.C.: U.S. Department of Homeland Security.
7. U.S. Department of Homeland Security. Available online at www.dhs.gov.
8. Shaw-Taylor, Yoku. (2011). *Immigration, Assimilation, and Border Security*. Lanham, MD: Government Institutes.
9. Prince, Carl E. (1989). *The U.S. Customs Service: A Bicentennial History*. Washington, D.C.: U.S. Department of the Treasury.
10. U.S. Customs and Border Protection. (2012). "CPB Through the Years." *U.S. Customs and Border Protection*. Available online at www.cbp.gov/about/history.
11. Bumgarner, Jeffrey B. (2006). *Federal Agents*. Westport, CT: Praeger Publishers.
12. Saba, Anne. (2003). "U.S. Customs Service: Always There & Ready to Serve." *U.S. Customs Today*. February.
13. U.S. Customs and Border Protection. (2012). "U.S. Immigration and Naturalization Service – Populating a Nation: A History of Immigration and Naturalization." *U.S. Customs and Border Protection*. Available online at www.cbp.gov/about/history/legacy/immigration-history.
14. U.S. Customs and Border Protection. (2012). "Border Patrol History." *U.S. Customs and Border Protection*. Available online at www.cbp.gov/border-security/along-us-borders/history.
15. Hernandez, Kelly Lytle. (2010). *Migra!: A History of the U.S. Border Patrol*. Berkeley, CA: University of California Press.
16. Haddal, Chad C. (2010). "Border Security: Key Agencies and Their Missions." *Congressional Research Service*. Washington, D.C.: Congressional Research Service.
17. Shaw-Taylor, *Immigration, Assimilation, and Border Security*.
18. Haddal, "Border Security."
19. U.S. Customs and Border Protection, "Border Patrol Agent," available at www.cbp.gov/careers/join-cbp/which-cbp-career/border-patrol-agent.
20. U.S. Customs and Border Protection, "Border Patrol Agent."
21. U.S. Customs and Border Protection, "Customs Duty Information."
22. U.S. Customs and Border Protection, "Protecting Agriculture," available at www.cbp.gov/border-security/protecting-agriculture.
23. U.S. Customs and Border Protection, "Field Operations/Port Security," available at www.cbp.gov/border-security/ports-entry.
24. U.S. Customs and Border Protection, "CBP Cargo Examinations," available at www.cbp.gov/xp/cgov/border_security/port_activities/cargo_exam/.
25. U.S. Customs and Border Protection, "CBP Cargo Examinations.
26. U.S. Customs and Border Protection, "Radiation Portal Monitors Safeguard America from Nuclear Devices and Radiological Materials," available at www.cbp.gov/border-security/port-entry/cargo-security/cargo-exam/rad-portal1.
27. U.S. Customs and Border Protection, "2012-2016 U.S. Border Patrol Strategic Plan," available at www.cbp.gov/border-security/along-us-borders/strategic-plan.
28. U.S. Customs and Border Protection, "CBP's Arizona Joint Field Command and Federal Partners Target Drug Traffickers," available at www.cbp.gov/newsroom/local-media-release/2013-05-07-040000/cbps-arizona-joint-field-command-and-federal-partners.

29. U.S. Customs and Border Protection, "Technology Innovation and Acquisition," available at www.cbp.gov/border-security/along-us-borders/technology-innovation-acquisition.

30. U.S. Customs and Border Protection, "Border Construction and Support Facilities," available at www.cbp.gov/border-security/along-us-borders/border-construction.

31. U.S. Customs and Border Protection, "Background, History, and Purpose," available at www.cbp.gov/border-security/along-us-borders/border-construction/background-history-and-purpose.

32. U.S. Customs and Border Protection, "U.S. Customs and Border Protection Announces Two New Centers of Excellence and Expertise," available at www.cbp.gov/xp/cgov/newsroom/news_releases/national/05102012.xml.

33. U.S. Customs and Border Protection, "International Law Enforcement Academy (ILEA) Program Overview," available at www.cbp.gov/border-security/international-initiatives/international-training-assistance/law-enforce.

34. U.S. Customs and Border Protection, "International Narcotics and Law Enforcement Affairs (INL) Program Overview," available at www.cbp.gov/border-security/international-initiatives/international-training-assistance/inl.

35. U.S. Customs and Border Protection, "Blue Campaign," available at www.cbp.gov/border-security/human-trafficking.

36. U.S. Customs and Border Protection, "No Te Enganes," available at www.cbp.gov/border-security/human-trafficking/no-te-enganes.

37. U.S. Customs and Border Protection, "WHTI Program Background," available at www.cbp.gov/travel/us-citizens/whti-program-background.

38. U.S. Customs and Border Protection, "CBP Canine Disciplines," available at www.cbp.gov/border-security/along-us-borders/canine-program/disciplines-2.

39. U.S. Customs and Border Protection, "Community Involvement," available at www.cbp.gov/border-security/along-us-borders/border-construction/background-history-and-purpose/community-involvement.

40. U.S. Customs and Border Protection, "From the Air and Sea," available at www.cbp.gov/border-security/air-sea; U.S. Customs and Border Protection, "Air and Marine Agents," available at www.cbp.gov/careers/join-cbp/which-cbp-career/air-and-marine.

41. U.S. Customs and Border Protection, "Air and Marine Agents."

42. U.S. Customs and Border Protection, "Air and Marine Provides Critical Air Domain Awareness as Part of Operation Safe Return," available at http://www.cbp.gov/newsroom/spotlights/2010-01-27-050000/air-and-marine-provides-critical-air-domain-awareness-part.

9

U.S. Immigration and Customs Enforcement

As the investigative arm of the U.S. Department of Homeland Security, the U.S. Immigration and Customs Enforcement office, or ICE, is the second largest investigative agency in the federal government. It was created in 2003 to protect the national security and public safety of the nation through enforcement of immigration and customs laws. They are given the responsibility to investigate possible violations of over 400 federal statutes in their efforts to protect the nation's borders. ICE is responsible for identifying, investigating, and dismantling vulnerabilities regarding the nation's border, economic, transportation, and infrastructure security. ICE frequently works with other federal, state, and local agencies in investigating possible offenses. They also work with officials in other countries, maintaining attachés at major U.S. embassies overseas.[1]

The statutory authority of ICE and the responsibilities of the officers are found in 22 Code of Federal Regulations 127.4. This portion of the code ties ICE officers with those of Border Protection officers, as shown in Figure 9.1. The statutory authority for their power to conduct searches and investigate people and cargo is found in 32 Code of Federal Regulations, 700.860, as shown in Figure 9.2.

Figure 9.1: Authority of Immigration and Customs Enforcement

Authority of U.S. Immigration and Customs Enforcement and U.S. Customs and Border Protection officers.

(a) U.S. Immigration and Customs Enforcement and U.S. Customs and Border Protection officers may take appropriate action to ensure observance of this subchapter as to the export or the attempted export or the temporary import of any defense article or technical data, including the inspection of loading or unloading of any vessel, vehicle, or aircraft. This applies whether the export is authorized by license or by written approval issued under this subchapter or by exemption.

(b) U.S. Immigration and Customs Enforcement and U.S. Customs and Border Protection officers have the authority to investigate, detain or seize any export or attempted export of defense articles or technical data contrary to this subchapter.

(c) Upon the presentation to a U.S. Customs and Border Protection Officer of a license or written approval, or claim of an exemption, authorizing the export of any defense article, the customs officer may require the production of other relevant documents and information relating to the final export. This includes an invoice, order, packing list, shipping document, correspondence, instructions, and the documents otherwise required by the U.S. Customs and Border Protection or U.S. Immigration and Customs Enforcement.

(d) If an exemption under this subchapter is used or claimed to export, transfer, reexport or retransfer, furnish, or obtain a defense article, technical data, or defense service, law enforcement officers may rely upon the authorities noted, additional authority identified in the language of the exemption, and any other lawful means or authorities to investigate such a matter.

Figure 9.2: Authority for Immigration and Customs Inspections

(a) The commanding officer or aircraft commander shall facilitate any proper examination which it may be the duty of a customs officer or immigration officer of the United States to make on board the ship or aircraft. The commanding officer or air craft commander shall not permit a foreign customs officer or an immigration officer to make any examination whatsoever, except as hereinafter provided, on board the ship, aircraft or boats under his or her command.

(b) When a ship or aircraft of the Navy or a public vessel manned by naval personnel and operating under the direction of the Department of the Navy is carrying cargo for private commercial account, such cargo shall be subject to the local customs regulations of the port, domestic or foreign, in which the ship or aircraft may be, and in all matters relating to such cargo, the procedure prescribed for private merchant vessels and aircraft shall be followed. Government-owned stores or cargo in such ship or aircraft not landed nor intended to be landed nor in any manner trafficked in, are, by the established precedent of international courtesy, exempt from customs duties, but a declaration of such stores or cargo, when required by local customs regulations, shall be made. Commanding officers shall prevent, as far as possible, disputes with the local authorities in such cases, but shall protect the ship or aircraft and the Government-owned stores and cargo from any search or seizure.

(c) Upon arrival from a foreign country, at the first port of entry in United States territory, the commanding officer, or the senior officer of ships or aircraft in company, shall notify the collector of the port. Each individual aboard shall, in accordance with customs regulations, submit a list of articles purchased or otherwise acquired by him abroad. Dutiable articles shall not be landed until the customs officer has completed his inspection.

(d) Commanding officers of naval vessels and aircraft transporting United States civilian and foreign military and civilian passengers shall satisfy themselves that the passenger clearance requirements of the Immigration and Naturalization Service are complied with upon arrival at points within the jurisdiction of the United States. Clearance for such passengers by an immigration officer is necessary upon arrival from foreign ports and at the completion of movements between any of the following: Continental United States (including Alaska and Hawaii), the Canal Zone, Puerto Rico, Virgin Islands, Guam, American Samoa, or other outlying places subject to United States jurisdiction. Commanding officers, prior to arriving, shall advise the cognizant naval or civilian port authority of the aforementioned passengers aboard and shall detain them for clearance as required by the Immigration and Naturalization Service.

(e) The provisions of this section shall not be construed to require delaying the movements of any ship or aircraft of the Navy in the performance of her assigned duty.

History

The history of U.S. Immigration and Customs Enforcement (ICE) is strikingly similar to that of U.S. Customs and Border Protection (CBP) (see Chapter 8). The components of various agencies that CBP did not obtain with the creation of the U.S. Department of Homeland Security were formed into ICE.[2] Components of U.S. Customs and the Immigration and Naturalization Service are the two key agencies of concern when tracing the historical lineage of ICE. In addition, at least for a period of time, ICE inherited other agencies in whole or part, including the Federal Air Marshals, the Federal Protective Service, and the Transportation Security Administration. It is a complex historical lineage, but one that is important to understand how and why ICE exists as it does today.

When the U.S. Department of Homeland Security formed in the wake of the September 11 terrorist attacks, it created a series of directorates, one of these being the Directorate of Border and Transportation Security. As this directorate began absorbing and reorganizing agencies, the concept was to divide these pre-existing agencies into three different functions. The first was to create the U.S. Citizenship and Immigration Services (USCIS), which would be responsible for the administrative aspects of accepting immigrants into the United States and naturalizing citizens. The second was CBP, which was responsible for movement between and in ports of entry. They essentially served as the law enforcement element of the directorate. Finally, ICE, was responsible for the investigative duties related to immigration and customs. ICE became the largest investigative arm of the U.S. Department of Homeland Security.

The majority of U.S. Immigration and Customs Enforcement personnel came from the Immigration and Naturalization Service (INS). Originally created in 1891 with the passage of the Immigration Act, it was known as the Office of Immigration and was placed under the U.S. Department of the Treasury (see Chapter 8). As the federal role in immigration matters grew at the turn of the century, the office became the Bureau of Immigration and Naturalization and was transferred to the Department of Commerce and Labor. When that department split in 1913, so too did the Bureau of Immigration and Naturalization into its two parts, the Bureau of Immigration and the Bureau of Naturalization. In 1933, as a cost savings measure, the two were merged back together, becoming the Immigration and Naturalization Service (INS), which was soon transferred to the U.S. Department of Justice. It remained there for 70 years, until the creation of the U.S. Department of Homeland Security in 2003. At that point, the majority of INS officers involved in criminal investigations and detention were moved to ICE, while most of the remaining employees became part of CBP.

The other primary agency from which ICE derived its personnel was the U.S. Customs Service. Created in 1789 by President George Washington, U.S. Customs was largely a revenue collecting agency under the U.S. Department of the Treasury (see Chapter 8). By the late 1800s, the agency began to shift its focus away from revenue collecting to law enforcement, and by the mid-twentieth century, the investigations and intelligence section of the service dealt primarily with law enforcement. It was those employees that would come to make up the second largest transfer of agents to ICE.

In 2002, the Bush Administration determined that one part of the Homeland Security plan would be to federalize the security screeners at the nation's airports. Up to that point in time, airport management was responsible for hiring airport security screeners who usually came from large private security firms. It was determined that by federalizing these baggage and traveler screeners, America's airline transportation system would be more secure. The initial debate by members of Congress was where to place the newly created organization—under the U.S. Department of Transportation or under the U.S. Department of Justice (in 2002 the U.S. Department of Homeland Security did not yet exist). The difference between the two was a reflection of their fundamental missions. The U.S. Department of Transportation was more concerned with the movement of people and goods throughout the United States. The U.S. Department of Justice was more concerned with safety and security. Whichever department became the parent agency would fundamentally impact the focus of the new federal screeners. After numerous congressional hearings and debates, it was decided to place the Transportation Security Administration (TSA) under the U.S. Department of Transportation.

The following year, however, saw the creation of the U.S. Department of Homeland Security. The concept of transportation security appeared to be a better fit with this newly created agency, so the Homeland Security Act of 2002 moved the TSA into the new department. Within the U.S. Department of Homeland Security, it made sense to place TSA under the Directorate of Border and Transportation Security. Rather than leaving it as its own agency to report to the Directorate, however, it was decided to place the agency as part of ICE. This was done in part because CBP was already too large of an organization, and because it would allow for greater ease for ICE to conduct investigations based on evidence secured by employees of the TSA.

Another agency that would become part of the TSA in 2002 was the Federal Air Marshal Service. On November 2, 2003, the service, which had grown dramatically in the aftermath of September 11, hiring nearly 4,000 new marshals, was moved with the TSA to become part of ICE.

Yet another agency that was absorbed in its entirety into ICE was the Federal Protective Service. Originally created in 1971 to serve as a police force for the General Services Administration (GSA), the agency policed all of the federal buildings (an estimated 9,000 structures) spread out across the United States (see Chapter 10). When the U.S. Department of Homeland Security was created, it was decided to place the Federal Protective Service under the supervision of ICE.

As ICE began performing its functions in 2003, issues immediately arose between ICE and CBP.[3] As CBP's apprehension capabilities grew during its first few years, ICE's detention and removal capabilities did not. It has been noted that this "imbalance has placed an increasing strain on the Office of Detention and Removal (DRO) resources, as well as impacted CBP's alien apprehensions."[4] There is no organization requirement for CBP to notify ICE of its apprehension initiatives, nor is there any obligation for ICE to notify CBP of its initiatives. Yet, both CBP and ICE are dependent upon the same resources provided by DRO for holding and deporting illegal aliens. It is this type of issue that has plagued ICE from its creation. In many ways, the analogy is to a police department that has patrol officers and investigators. Even though they have different functions, they both work for the same agency, toward the same goal. In the case of ICE and CBP, ICE serves as the investigators and CBP as the patrol officers, but they are two separate and distinct agencies that are under no obligation to work with each other. In recent years, the Office of Inspector General conducted a study to determine whether ICE and CBP should be merged together. The conclusion was that they should not.[5]

After the creation of the U.S. Department of Homeland Security and the Directorate of Border and Transportation Security, CBP remained a fairly stable organization. ICE, on the other hand, saw numerous organizational changes. Initially, the newly created TSA was placed within the Directorate of Border and Transportation Security, which in turn placed it under the operational management of ICE. In 2005, in a reorganizational plan, it was decided that TSA would roll out from under ICE and become its own agency reporting directly to the Border and Transportation Directorate. It was also decided that the Federal Air

Marshals would be removed from ICE and placed under the supervision of TSA, which became effective October 16, 2005 (see Chapter 11). Finally, the last major organizational transfer occurred on October 28, 2009, when the Federal Protective Service was transferred from ICE and placed under a different directorate—the National Protection and Programs Directorate.

While ICE has seen a number of its early assets removed from its management function, there have been a number of internal changes as well. The primary change was the renaming and refocusing of the ICE Office of Investigation (OI).[6] In June of 2010, ICE announced it was changing the name of its Office of Investigation to Homeland Security Investigations (HSI). The primary reason for the change was to emphasize that the Office of Investigations was not solely for the investigation of immigration issues, but that they could, rather, investigate any violations related to homeland security, ranging from U.S. customs laws to drugs, and money and finance investigations to national defense statutes. It was also done to help emphasize the fact that HIS is the second largest federal law enforcement and criminal investigative agency in the United States, second only to the Federal Bureau of Investigation.

ICE has been involved in a number of investigations since it came into existence. In fact, one major investigation effort actually preceded the agency. At the turn of the century, the Immigration and Naturalization Service had created Operation Predator to target child sex abusers. When ICE began operations, it continued Operation Predator, making it one of its key organizational operations. As an extension, ICE also created the Cyber Crimes Center (C3) Child Exploitation Section (CES), which focuses on child sex abuse in the online world. Still further, ICE has also become involved in human trafficking operations, much of it aimed at the trafficking of children, as well as adults, for sex and the involuntary servitude and labor of immigrants brought into the United States.

In 2005, under the auspices of the national gang enforcement initiative Operation Community Shield (OCS), ICE established itself as the lead federal agency in the investigation of transnational criminal street gangs such as Mara Salvatrucha (MS-13). Since the launch of OCS, ICE and its partners have arrested more than 23,900 gang members and associates, representing more than 2,200 different gangs and cliques. These apprehensions include more than 12,100 criminal arrests and nearly 11,700 administrative immigration arrests. Of these, more than 270 arrests were of gang leaders and more than 8,900 of the arrested suspects had violent criminal histories. Through this initiative, ICE has also seized more than 2,400 firearms.[7]

On February 25, 2011, U.S. Immigration and Customs Enforcement, Homeland Security Investigations Special Agent Jaime Zapata was killed in an ambush by drug cartel gunmen on a highway in San Luis Potosi, Mexico. Zapata, on a temporary assignment to Mexico, was traveling in a U.S. government vehicle from Monterrey to Mexico City with another special agent, Victor Avila, while on duty. Special Agent Zapata became the first HSI special agent killed in the line of duty and was at the center of an explosive controversy surrounding the Bureau of Alcohol, Tobacco, Firearms, and Explosives (ATF). One of the guns found at the scene of the ambush was also a gun that had been "walked" over the border.

In gun-walking programs, ATF was allowing guns to be illegally purchased in the U.S., in this case in Texas, and then "walked" across the border into Mexico in order to track them to the various drug cartels. The whereabouts of the gun was unknown until it showed up at the crime scene.

Who Gets Hired

ICE employs over 20,000 employees who are assigned to positions in all 50 states and in 47 foreign countries. Some of those employees are deportation officers, who are responsible for carrying out legal research concerning decisions in cases of possible deportation and, when necessary, assisting attorneys who represent the government in court actions. These officers sometimes work alongside other federal law enforcement officers in identifying, locating, and arresting illegal aliens and are responsible for the physical removal of illegal aliens from the U.S. These officers may be required to conduct surveillance work or assist in seizing property as needed.[8] They also often recommend new procedures on detention and removal operations. Additional responsibilities may include developing budgets or assisting with investigations.[9]

Special agents, also called criminal investigators, carry out both criminal and civil investigations that revolve around national security threats, terrorism, drug smuggling, child exploitation, human trafficking, illegal arms export, financial crimes, or fraud.[10] Immigration enforcement agents are the uniformed agents within ICE. They investigate, identify, arrest, prosecute, and deport aliens to their country of citizenship.[11]

The Intelligence Division of ICE is a major portion of the organization, and there are many career opportunities within this unit. Intelligence Officers are responsible for analyzing information and preparing products, often with other intelligence agencies. Intelligence research assistants provide technical and administrative assistance for intelligence operations. Intelligence research specialists evaluate and prepare intelligence products. Management and program analyst and mission support specialists are responsible for administrative services that are needed for the effective operations of an office.[12]

There are also some support positions that are needed to help ICE function effectively as an organization. They include an auditor, a criminal research specialist, investigative assistants, mission support specialists, and technical enforcement officers.[13]

For students interested in a career at ICE, there are internship opportunities available. There are both paid and unpaid opportunities for those who are enrolled, or accepted for enrollment, at a college or university. These students must be taking at least a half-time course load.

The Student Career Experience Program is a way that ICE can provide work experience for a student that is directly related to his or her career goals. Students in this program receive payment based on education and experience. ICE also has a Student Temporary Employment Program that offers students experience that may not be related to their academic or career goals. Students in this program work for ICE for up to one year but may remain longer if they remain enrolled in school on at least a half-time basis. Students may also be part of the Student Volunteer Program at ICE, which offers unpaid training opportunities.[14]

Budgets

The 2010 budget provided to ICE from Congress was over $5.8 billion dollars, as it was in 2011 and requested in 2012, as noted in Table 9.1. The budget figures for 2013 and 2014 indicate that the budgets for ICE have declined slightly.

Organization

ICE is located within the Department of Homeland Security (DHS). It is led by a director, who is appointed by the president and confirmed by the Senate, as noted above. The director reports directly to the secretary of Homeland Security. ICE is organized into four law enforcement divisions and many support divisions, each of which is headed by a director. Found within the Director's Office is the Office of Public Affairs (OPA), Office of Congressional Relations (OCR), Office of the Principal Legal Advisor (OPLA), Office of Professional Responsibility (OPR), Office of Detention Policy and Planning (ODPP), and the Office of State, Local, and Tribal Coordination (OSLTC).[15]

The Office of Public Affairs is the unit that has the most contact with the public. They inform the public about ICE as a way to create a better under-standing of the agency.[16] The Office of Congressional Relations handles contacts between ICE and the U.S. Congress.[17] The Office of the Principal Legal Advisor provides legal advice, training, and services to ICE.[18] The Office of Professional Responsibility ensures DHS standards of integrity and professionalism by

Table 9.1	Budget Authority for ICE (In Billions of Dollars)
2010 enacted	$5.822
2011 enacted	$5.748
2012 enacted	$5.983
2013 enacted	$5.622
2014 enacted	$5.611
FY 2015 presidential budget	$5.359

Source: Department of Homeland Security, "FY 2012 Budget in Brief," available at http://www.dhs.gov/xlibrary/assets/budget-bib-fy2012.pdf; also Department of Homeland Security, "Budget in Brief: Fiscal Year 2015," available at http://www.dhs.gov/sites/default/files/publications/FY15BIB.pdf.

investigating allegations of misconduct by ICE employees.[19] ICE's efforts to revise the immigration detention system is the responsibility of the Office of Detention Policy and Planning. The Office of State, Local, and Tribal Coordination fosters partnerships with other law enforcement agencies in an effort to promote the country's security.[20]

Leader

John Morton was unanimously confirmed as the director of Immigration and Customs Enforcement by the U.S. Senate on May 12, 2009. Prior to his appointment by the president, Mr. Morton spent 15 years at the Department of Justice. At the Department, Mr. Morton served in several positions including assistant United States attorney, counsel to the deputy attorney general, and acting deputy assistant attorney general of the Criminal Division.

During his tenure at ICE, Mr. Morton has strengthened ICE's investigative efforts, with a particular emphasis on border crimes, export controls, intellectual property enforcement, and child exploitation. Mr. Morton has also sought to prioritize ICE's immigration enforcement efforts around the removal of criminal offenders, recent border violators, and those who ignore orders of removal or obtain immigration status by fraud.

What They Do

The activities of ICE are divided into four units. These are Intelligence, Investigations, National Security, and Enforcement/Removal. These are each described below.

Intelligence

The objective of the Intelligence Division of ICE is to collect, analyze, and share strategic information for DHS and ICE. It also shares their information with federal, state, local, tribal, and international law enforcement agencies. Their analysis of information plays a key role in supporting the investigations carried out by ICE investigators.[21] Some of the agencies within the Intelligence Division that assist in intelligence collection and analysis are:

- **National Intellectual Property Rights (IPR) Coordination Center:** the government's clearinghouse for investigations about counterfeiting and piracy.[22]
- **Freedom of Information Act (FOIA) Office:** receives, tracks, and processes all requests for information about ICE and what they do.[23]
- **Office of Acquisition Management (OAQ):** offers a strategic approach to procurement.[24]

- **Office of the Chief Financial Officer:** oversees all financial resources within ICE.[25]
- **Office of the Chief Information Officer (OCIO):** provides information technology (IT) services to ICE by seeking to modernize its systems and provide IT solutions to problems.[26]
- **Office of Diversity and Human Rights:** helps ensure that both applicants and existing employees are treated in a nondiscriminatory manner.[27]
- **Office of Human Capital (HC):** responsible for hiring and maintaining a qualified and diverse workforce in ICE.[28]
- **Office of Training and Development (OTD):** establishes and maintains standards for training programs carried out by ICE and oversees the accreditation of ICE training programs both in the U.S. and overseas.[29]
- **Privacy Office:** seeks to guarantee privacy protections to employees of ICE.[30]
- **National Firearms and Tactical Training Unit (NFTTU):** ensures that ICE personnel have adequate firearms and protective equipment to carry out their jobs.
- **Office of Policy (OP):** works to identify and develop policies within ICE, focusing on the areas of risk and strategic management, operations and international affairs, and management policy.[31]

Investigations

ICE agents have the responsibility to investigate criminal organizations whose crimes threaten national security or pose a threat in some way. This may include attempts to harm legitimate trade, travel, or even the financial system of the U.S.[32] Agents can seize the profits of these criminal groups to prevent them from carrying out further offenses.

One type of investigation is carried out through the SEARCH (Seizing Earnings and Assets from Retail Crime Heists) Initiative. Through this, ICE agents attempt to address organized retail crime carried out by transnational crime groups. They also investigate and work to prevent illegal trafficking in weapons, narcotics, human smuggling, money laundering, and other financial crimes, fraudulent trade, child pornography, and child sex tourism.

National Bulk Cash Smuggling Center

It has become more common for criminal organizations to smuggle large quantities of cash both into and out of the U.S. as a way to hide criminal behavior. The National Bulk Smuggling Center investigates and works to disrupt bulk cash smuggling activities. By doing this, agents attempt to stop the money available to criminal groups that they then use for offenses. The Center provides intelligence, support, and expertise for those who are involved with investigations into those criminal groups that transport and smuggle large quantities of cash. They assist law enforcement officers in following the money trail and seizing criminal proceeds.

Cultural Property, Art, and Antiquities Investigations

It has become common to loot valuable items of cultural history or art and sell them on the underground market. ICE agents use federal laws to investigate crimes revolving around the theft of cultural property and art. ICE agents can seize cultural artifacts brought into the U.S. illegally and return them to their home countries. They sometimes work with federal, state, local, and foreign agents in carrying out the investigations.[33]

Cyber Crimes Center

The main focus of agents at the Cyber Crimes Center (C3) is to carry out investigations against those who use the Internet to carry out illegal immigration. This can include using the computer for document fraud, money laundering, or financial fraud.[34] One unit found within C3 is a Child Exploitation Section that focuses on crimes of child sexual exploitation, including the use of the Internet to produce or distribute child pornography.[35] There is also a Computer Forensics Section that investigates the illegal use of computers and other digital devices. Agents are trained in computer forensics and can examine seized digital storage devices, including computer hard drives or flash drives. Agents are located in field offices worldwide and often provide expert testimony in criminal trials.[36]

Identity and Benefit Fraud

Because identity and benefit fraud is such a serious threat to public safety and national security, this section of ICE investigations is vital. Such fraud can play a role in human smuggling and human trafficking crimes, possible attacks on critical infrastructure, identity theft, or benefit fraud.[37]

Document and Benefit Fraud Task Forces

The Document and Benefit Fraud Task Forces were created in 2006 as a way to detect and disrupt document and benefit fraud. The task forces include investigators from numerous agencies, each with expertise in a different aspect of fraud. The task forces can include representatives from the U.S. Attorneys' Offices, the Department of Labor, the Social Security Administration, the Postal Inspection Service, Citizenship and Immigration Services, the Department of State, and state and local law enforcement agencies.[38]

Drug Enforcement Task Forces

ICE agents take part in task forces with federal, state, and local law enforcement agencies to fight drug trafficking. One task force is the High Intensity Drug Trafficking Area (HIDTA) Task Force that focuses on drug trafficking in parts of the country that have an unusually large amount of drug distribution or smuggling. The HIDTA task forces are administered by the Office of National Drug Control Policy. Another task force is the Organized Crime Drug Enforcement Task Force that attacks crime organizations that deal with major drug trafficking and money laundering activities.[39]

Narcotics Enforcement

ICE agents investigate organizations that smuggle and transport narcotics and contraband. Since the illegal drug market in the U.S. is largely based on narcotics grown in foreign countries, ICE agents watch different smuggling vehicles such as high-speed vessels, cargo containers, aircraft, commercial trucking, commercial vessels, and human carriers. Agents attempt to disrupt the economic basis of the smugglers.[40]

Firearms/Explosives Smuggling

Because smuggling of weapons between the U.S. and Mexico is a threat to the safety and security of both countries, ICE agents conduct investigations into the illegal export of weapons and smuggling of firearms across the borders. Weapons taken into Mexico from the U.S. can often turn up in drug cartels where they are used against both citizens and law enforcement, leading to more violence along the border. ICE continually increases its efforts to combat illegal trafficking in firearms to Mexico by conducting joint investigations and sharing information with Mexican authorities. The key components are stakeholder training, intelligence analysis, the vetted arms trafficking group, and the ICE Border Liaison Program.[41]

Foreign Corruption Investigations

ICE agents investigate corrupt foreign officials who steal from government funds for their own personal gain and then attempt to place those funds in the U.S. financial system. ICE agents in the Foreign Corrupt Investigations Group investigate corrupt officials. If left unstopped, political corruption in unstable governments can allow criminal and terrorist organizations to flourish.[42]

Forensic Document Lab

The Forensic Document Lab was created in 1978 and has become one of the federal government's top methods to combat document fraud. The lab provides both forensic and investigative services, such as comparative handwriting analyses and printing samples, document analysis, restoration of altered or damaged documents, and fingerprint analysis. The lab also holds the world's largest collection of foreign travel and identity documents and other reference materials. Agents who work in the lab develop training programs for law enforcement agencies, both domestic and international, to help them to detect fraudulent documents and provide assistance in identifying fraudulent documents.[43]

Human Smuggling

ICE is responsible for preventing human smuggling. They investigate large-scale smuggling organizations, particularly if they pose a risk to national security or if they are violent or abusive. ICE often works with CBP to ensure the investigation is completed.[44]

Human Trafficking

ICE has developed multiple approaches to deter human trafficking. One way provides support for victims of human trafficking offenses. Through their Victim Assistance Program, ICE agents coordinate services including counseling and emotional support. Through Project STAMP (Smuggler and Trafficker Assets, Monies, and Proceeds), ICE agents attack those organizations who traffic humans by following the money trail. By seizing profits, it is thought that these organizations will be stopped.[45] ICE often works with other agencies such as CBP and U.S. Citizenship and Immigration services (USCIS) to attack human trafficking.[46]

ICE ACCESS

The ICE Agreements of Cooperation in Communities to Enhance Safety and Security (ACCESS) Initiative was developed to promote cooperation between ICE and law enforcement agencies on the state, local, and tribal levels. Through this program, ICE agents work with other law enforcement agencies to identify the local community's concerns, and together ICE and the local agencies develop action plans. ICE ACCESS support and programs include asset forfeiture plans, the Border Enforcement Security Task Force (BEST), the Criminal Alien Program (CAP), the Customs Officer Cross-Designation Program, the Document and Benefit Fraud Task Forces, Immigration Officer Cross-Designation, the Intellectual Property Rights (IPR) Center, the Law Enforcement Support Center (LESC), and others.[47]

IMAGE

ICE initiated the Mutual Agreement between Government and Employees (IMAGE) Program as a way to help employers in the private sector identify undocumented workers who use false documents to obtain employment. ICE has agreed to waive fines if there are violations on less than half of the required forms. When more than half of the forms contain violations, ICE will issue minimum fines. Through IMAGE, ICE trains employers to identify fraudulent documents. Employers who voluntarily participate in IMAGE have reduced the number of fraudulent identity documents and have achieved a lawful workforce.[48]

International Affairs

The ICE Office on International Affairs carries out investigations on transnational criminal organizations as a means to prevent terrorist attacks. The agents coordinate the investigations with law enforcement agents in foreign countries and provide them with case support and intelligence related to international criminal activities and will help with removal operations as needed. They are responsible for investigating violations of immigration and customs laws and managing the Visa Security Program and the International Visitor's Program. They also provide training to foreign law enforcement agencies.[49]

Law Enforcement Information Sharing Service

The Law Enforcement Information Sharing Service (LEIS) is a Web-based program designed to allow law enforcement agencies to exchange information on criminal activities and national security quickly. The secure, online LEIS program offers a way for agencies to request and share investigative information so police can identify patterns more easily, allowing them to connect criminal activities.[50]

Money Laundering

ICE has developed complex money laundering and financial crime sections to prevent terrorist attacks. One of those, called Cornerstone, is ICE's attempt to detect potential weaknesses in the U.S. financial, trade, and transportation sectors that could be used by criminal organizations. Another, the El Dorado Task Force, is comprised of over 260 law enforcement agents from the federal government, New York, and New Jersey. The task force investigates financial crime at all levels. Moreover, agents on the task force work to educate the private sector so they can identify potential vulnerable areas. When needed, prosecutors attack offenders and work to seize the proceeds of their crimes.[51]

Operation Community Shield/Transnational Gangs

ICE identified violent transnational criminal street gangs as being a threat to public safety in neighborhoods and communities. In 2005, ICE became the foremost federal agency in investigating such street gangs. In Operation Community Shield (OCS), ICE works with federal, state, and local law enforcement agencies in the U.S. and globally as a way to create a comprehensive approach to criminal investigations. Through the investigations, law enforcement has been able to identify violent street gangs and their members and activities. They attempt to disrupt gangs by seizing the cash, weapons, and assets derived from their criminal activities. They also seek to prosecute gang members and remove them from the U.S., if possible. [52]

Child Exploitation/Operation Predator

ICE created Operation Predator as a way to protect children by identifying and arresting child predators and sexual offenders. Operation Predator uses multiple resources to target child sex abusers, including the National Child Victim Identification System. ICE works with the National Center for Missing and Exploited Children, the FBI, the Postal Inspection Service, the Secret Service, the Department of Justice, and the Internet Crimes Against Children Task Force. They also work with foreign officials, including Interpol, to investigate these crimes over the Internet.[53]

Worksite Enforcement

ICE investigates illegal immigration through a comprehensive worksite enforcement program that is geared toward protecting national security and critical infrastructure. The program focuses on those employers that violate federal employment laws. ICE also investigates charges of mistreatment, trafficking, smuggling, or harboring of immigrants. They also look into charges of visa fraud, document fraud, and money laundering. If sufficient evidence exists, ICE officials will work with U.S. attorneys to prosecute the employer.

National Security

The National Security Division of ICE is responsible for protecting the security of the country, protecting it from terrorism and threats of terrorist acts. To do this, ICE has established many agencies, such as those described in the following sections.

Border Enforcement Security Task Force (BEST)

The Border Enforcement Security Task Force (BEST) is one way that ICE helps to combat criminal smuggling as well as fight the increase in crime and violence along the country's southern border that is the result of Mexican drug cartels. ICE works with federal, state, local, and foreign law enforcement groups to identify and dismantle criminal organizations whose activities pose threats to the country's border security.[54] In some places, task forces have been formed at seaports to address security issues at ports. The groups are designed to enhance the sharing of intelligence and cooperation between the agencies involved.[55] Many international law enforcement agencies are also part of BEST. At this time, there are 22 BESTs located throughout the U.S. and Mexico.[56]

Joint Terrorism Task Force

The Joint Terrorism Task Force investigates and detects terrorist groups and then prosecutes and removes them from the country. At the same time, they attempt to dismantle the organizations that support terrorist activities. ICE is involved in practically all investigations related to terrorism and to cross-border crime.[57]

Counterterrorism and Criminal Exploitation Unit

The Counterterrorism and Criminal Exploitation Unit within ICE seeks to prevent terrorists and criminals from exploiting the country's immigration system and the student visitor program. They are also responsible for tracking the immigration status of known and suspected terrorists. The unit has three sections, the first being the National Security Threat Task Force (NSTTF). This group identifies and prosecutes people who appear in the Terrorist Identities Datamart Environment, a database of people who have obtained U.S. immigration benefits illegally. The task force helps ICE to identify these individuals and then helps in the litigation and removal process. The second section is the SEVIS Exploitation Section (SES), which helps to analyze leads about those who seek to defraud the immigration system. The unit also seeks to educate school officials about immigration fraud.

The third section is the Terrorist Tracking Pursuit Group (TTPG), which leads the Targeted Enforcement Program that tracks how long certain individuals who have been identified as security risks are permitted to stay in the U.S.[58]

Counter-Proliferation Investigations Unit

The Counter-Proliferation Investigations Unit of ICE coordinates investigations related to violations of federal export laws. This could include exports involving military items or products being sent to sanctioned or embargoed countries. In doing so, ICE seeks to prevent terrorist groups from obtaining U.S. military products and other sensitive technology, including weapons of mass destruction; chemical, biological, radiological, and nuclear material; or firearms and ammunition. [59]

Within this unit is Project Shield America, an initiative geared toward protecting the nation's technological and military advantages. ICE agents work with those who manufacture or export strategic goods that could be targeted by terrorist groups and educate them about export laws, export licensing issues, and other related information.[60] Also within this unit is the Export Enforcement Coordination Center, created in 2009 by President Obama. This is an interagency task force designed to assess the state of the U.S. system to control exports. The task force recommended the creation of the Export Enforcement Coordination Center, to be managed by ICE, to oversee export controls. The mission of the Center is to enhance the ability of the United States to combat illicit trade and to serve as a clearinghouse for the exchange of information on exports.[61]

Human Rights Violators and War Crimes Center

The Human Rights Violators and War Crimes Center works to prevents foreign war crimes suspects and human rights abusers admission into the U.S. It also works to identify and remove offenders who may already be in the U.S.

Immigration Enforcement

ICE policies to enforce immigration laws are enforced in a way that protects the safety of the public and border security. ICE requires that resources are used to identify and remove those that have broken criminal laws, recently crossed the border, repeatedly violated immigration laws, or are fugitives from immigration court.[62]

Secure Communities

ICE identifies and removes illegal aliens who have criminal convictions, illegal immigrants, repeat violators, those who fail to appear at immigration hearings, and fugitives who have previously been ordered to be removed by an immigration judge. The Congress provides ICE with appropriations to remove individuals who are in the U.S. and lack lawful status or who have a criminal conviction.[63]

Enforcement and Removal

The Enforcement and Removal Division of ICE oversees the deportation of individuals who are living in the United States illegally. The specific offices that hold these roles are described below.

Criminal Alien Program

ICE combats illegal immigration, including illegal aliens who have criminal records as identified through their Criminal Alien Program (CAP). ICE identifies and removes criminal aliens who are incarcerated in federal, state, and local prisons and jails throughout the U.S. in order to prevent illegal immigrants from being released into the general public. The program has five components:

- **Jails and prisons:** CAP agents in federal, state, and local prisons and jails place detainers on inmates identified as criminal aliens and then process them for removal prior to being released into the general public.
- **Violent Criminal Alien Section (VCAS):** VCAS identifies repeat criminal aliens encountered through CAP, the National Fugitive Operations Program, and the Law Enforcement Agency Response Unit. The VCAS works with the U.S. Attorneys' Office to pursue criminal prosecution of these offenders for illegal entry after deportation.
- **Joint Criminal Alien Removal Taskforces (JCART):** JCART locates and arrests criminal aliens with convictions for serious offenses such as drug trafficking, crimes of violence, or sex offenses who have been released from federal, state, or local custody and who may be in the community. JCART works with other agencies such as probation and parole offices, the U.S. Marshals Service, U.S. Customs and Border Protection, Bureau of Prisons, and local law enforcement agencies.
- **Enforcement and Removal Operations (ERO):** ERO helps to process inmates who are not U.S. citizens. ERO officers interview federal inmates nationwide and identify those who are not citizens. Those inmates are then taken into ERO custody when their criminal sentences are complete.
- **Rapid Removal of Eligible Parolees Accepted for Transfer:** This is a joint program with state correctional and parole agencies. It assists ICE identify and remove criminal aliens from the U.S. In some cases, nonviolent aliens can be granted a conditional, early release with the agreement that they will be removed from the U.S.[64]

ICE Health Service Corps

The Health Service Corps provides a wide range of medical care procedures to detainees in the custody of ICE, housed in federal facilities around the country. If needed, the Health Service Corps will authorize and pay for any off-site specialty or emergency care that may be necessary.[65]

Detention Management

ICE ERO agents oversee the nation's civil immigration detention system. The inmates housed by ERO are from many countries, are of both genders, and have different medical conditions. Non-U.S. citizens who are apprehended are placed in detention facilities. ERO monitors all cases as they move through immigration court proceedings and then carries out the judge's order. ERO's Detention Standards Compliance Unit ensures that all detainees who are in custody are kept in conditions that are safe, secure, and humane. [66]

Fugitive Operations

ICE created the National Fugitive Operations Program to remove criminal aliens from the U.S. The program seeks to reduce the number of criminal aliens who remain in the U.S. They identify, locate, and arrest fugitive aliens, those who have been removed from the U.S. previously, those who have been convicted of a crime, and those who have entered the country illegally.[67]

Law Enforcement Support Center

The Law Enforcement Support Center provides law enforcement agencies with information on the immigration status and identity of suspected criminal aliens. They also support the National Crime Information Center, Communications Center, and Special Response Tasks.[68]

Rapid REPAT

The ICE Rapid REPAT (Removal of Eligible Parolees Accepted for Transfer) program is a way for ICE to remove illegal aliens from the U.S. In this program, certain criminal aliens who are incarcerated in U.S. prisons and jails are offered an early release from the institution in exchange for voluntarily returning to their home country.[69]

Removal Management

ICE works to remove illegal aliens from the U.S. once they have been determined to be deportable through proceedings in an immigration court. ICE EROs coordinate the processing of illegal aliens through the immigration court system as well as their removal from the U.S. [70]

Conclusion

Immigration and Customs Enforcement is a relatively new federal law enforcement agency that enforces federal immigration laws. The agents help to ensure that those who enter the U.S. do so legally and that they are not in the U.S. with the intention of harming citizens. They do that by overseeing the nation's borders and working with international law enforcement groups to prevent many types of crimes.

Key Terms

Operation Predator

Operation Community Shield

Jaime Zapata

deportation officers

special agents

immigration enforcement agents

intelligence officers

Student Career Experience Program

Office of Public Affairs

Office of Congressional Relations

Office of Principal Legal Advisor

Office of Professional Responsibility

Office of State, Local, and Tribal Coordination

John Morton

Cyber Crimes Center

identity and benefit fraud

Document and Benefit Fraud Task Forces

Drug Enforcement Task Force

narcotics enforcement

firearms/explosives smuggling

foreign corruption investigations

Forensics Document Lab

human smuggling

human trafficking

ICE ACCESS

IMAGE

international affairs

Law Enforcement Information Sharing Service

money laundering

Border Security Task Force

Joint Terrorism Task Force

Human Rights Violators and War Crimes Center

Review Questions

1. Describe the general history of ICE.

2. What are the requirements for those people who would like to be hired as an agency in ICE?

3. How much money does Congress allocate to ICE?

4. What is the organizational structure of ICE?

5. Describe the basic responsibilities of an ICE agent.

Endnotes

1. Immigration and Customs Enforcement, "Customs Cross Designation," available at http://www.ice.gov/customs-cross-designation.
2. U.S. Immigration and Customs Enforcement. (2012). U.S. Immigration and Customs Enforcement. Available online at http://www.ice.gov/.
3. Siskin, Alison, et al. (2006). "Immigration Enforcement Within the United States." *Congressional Research Service.* Washington, D.C.: Congressional Research Service.
4. Siskin, "Immigration Enforcement Within the United States."
5. Department of Homeland Security, Office of Inspector General. (2005). *An Assessment of the Proposal to Merge Customs and Border Protection with Immigration and Customs Enforcement.* Available online at http://www.oig.dhs.gov/assets/Mgmt/OIG_06-04_Nov05.pdf.
6. Shaw-Taylor, Yoku. (2011). *Immigration, Assimilation, and Border Security.* Lanham, MD: Government Institutes.
7. U.S. Immigration and Customs Enforcement.
8. Immigration and Customs Enforcement, "Office of Public Affairs," available at http://www.ice.gov/about/offices/leadership/opa.
9. Immigration and Customs Enforcement, "Office of Public Affairs."
10. Immigration and Customs Enforcement, "Office of Public Affairs."
11. Immigration and Customs Enforcement, "Office of Public Affairs."
12. Immigration and Customs Enforcement, "Office of Public Affairs."
13. Immigration, and Customs Enforcement, "Office of Public Affairs."
14. Immigration and Customs Enforcement, "Internships," available at http://www.ice.gov/careers/internships/.
15. Immigration and Customs Enforcement, "ICE Leadership Offices," available at http://www.ice.gov/about/offices/leadership.
16. Immigration and Customs Enforcement, "Office of Public Affairs."
17. Immigration and Customs Enforcement, "Office of Congressional Relations," available at http://www.ice.gov/about/offices/leadership/ocr.
18. Immigration and Customs Enforcement, "Office of the Principal Legal Advisor," available at http://www.ice.gov/about/offices/leadership/opla.
19. Immigration and Customs Enforcement, "Office of Professional Responsibility," available at http://www.ice.gov/about/offices/leadership/opr.
20. Immigration and Customs Enforcement, "Office of State, Local and Tribal Coordination (OSLTC)," available at http://www.ice.gov/about/offices/leadership/osltc.
21. Immigration and Customs Enforcement, "Intelligence," available at http://www.ice.gov/about/offices/homeland-security-investigations/intel/.
22. Immigration and Customs Enforcement, "National IPR Coordination Center Referral," available at http://www.iprcenter.gov/referral/.
23. Immigration and Customs Enforcement, "Freedom of Information Act (FOIA) Office," available at http://www.ice.gov/about/offices/management-administration/foia/.
24. Immigration and Customs Enforcement, "Office of Acquisition Management (OAQ)," available at http://www.ice.gov/about/offices/management-administration/oaq.
25. Immigration and Customs Enforcement, "Office of the Chief Financial Officer (OFCO)," available at http://www.ice.gov/about/offices/management-administration/cfo.
26. Immigration and Customs Enforcement, "Office of the Chief Information Officer (OFCO)."
27. Immigration and Customs Enforcement, "Office of Diversity and Civil Rights," available at http://www.ice.gov/about/offices/management-administration/dcr/.
28. Immigration and Customs Enforcement, "Office of Human Capital (OHC)," available at http://www.ice.gov/about/offices/management-administration/hc/.
29. Immigration and Customs Enforcement, "Office of Training and Development (OTD)," available at http://www.ice.gov/about/offices/management-administration/otd/; Immigration and Customs Enforcement, "Office of Public Affairs."

30. Immigration and Customs Enforcement, "Privacy and Records Office," available at http://www.ice.gov/about/offices/management-administration/privacy/.

31. Immigration and Customs Enforcement, "Office of Policy," available at http://www.ice.gov/about/offices/management-administration/policy/.

32. Immigration and Customs Enforcement, "Homeland Security Investigations," available at http://www.ice.gov/about/offices/homeland-security-investigations.

33. Immigration and Customs Enforcement, "Cultural Property, Art and Antiquities Investigations" available at http://www.ice.gov/cultural-heritage-investigations/; Immigration and Customs Enforcement, "Cultural Property, Art and Antiquities Investigations Fact Sheets," available at http://www.ice.gov/cultural-heritage-investigations/factsheets.htm.

34. Immigration and Customs Enforcement, "Cyber Crimes Center," available at http://www.ice.gov/cyber-crimes/.

35. Immigration and Customs Enforcement, "Cyber Crimes Center."

36. Immigration and Customs Enforcement, "Cyber Crimes Center."

37. Immigration and Customs Enforcement, "Identity and Benefit Fraud," available at http://www.ice.gov/identity-benefit-fraud/.

38. Immigration and Customs Enforcement, "Document and Benefit Fraud Task Force (DBFTF)," available at http://www.ice.gov/document-benefit-fraud.

39. Immigration and Customs Enforcement, "Drug Enforcement Task Forces," available at http://www.ice.gov/drug-task-force/.

40. Immigration and Customs Enforcement, "Narcotics Enforcement," available at http://www.ice.gov/narcotics.

41. Immigration and Customs Enforcement, "Firearms, Ammunition and Explosives Smuggling Investigations," available at http://www.ice.gov/firearms-explosives-smuggling.

42. Immigration and Customs Enforcement, "Foreign Corruption Investigations," available at http://www.ice.gov/foreign-corruption/.

43. Immigration and Customs Enforcement, "Homeland Security Investigations Forensic Laboratory," available at https://www.ice.gov/hsi-fl/.

44. Immigration and Customs Enforcement, "Human Smuggling," available at http://www.ice.gov/human-smuggling/.

45. Immigration and Customs Enforcement, "Human Trafficking," available at http://www.ice.gov/human-trafficking/.

46. Immigration and Customs Enforcement, "Human Trafficking."

47. Immigration and Customs Enforcement, "Fact Sheets," available at http://www.ice.gov/fact-sheets.

48. Immigration and Customs Enforcement, "IMAGE Frequently Asked Questions," available at http://www.ice.gov/image/faqs.htm; Immigration and Customs Enforcement, "IMAGE," available at http://www.ice.gov/image/.

49. Immigration and Customs Enforcement, "International Operations," available at http://www.ice.gov/about/offices/homeland-security-investigations/oia/.

50. Immigration and Customs Enforcement, "Law Enforcement Information Sharing Service," available at http://www.ice.gov/le-information-sharing/.

51. Immigration and Customs Enforcement, "Money Laundering," available at http://www.ice.gov/money-laundering/.

52. Immigration and Customs Enforcement, "Operation Community Shield/Transnational Gangs," available at http://www.ice.gov/community-shield/.

53. Immigration and Customs Enforcement, "Child Exploitation/Operation Predator," available at http://www.ice.gov/predator/.

54. Immigration and Customs Enforcement, "Border Enforcement Security Task Force (BEST)," available at http://www.ice.gov/best.

55. Immigration and Customs Enforcement, "Fact Sheet: Border Enforcement Security Task Force (BEST).

56. Immigration and Customs Enforcement, "Border Enforcement Security Task Force."

57. Immigration and Customs Enforcement, "Joint Terrorism Task Force," available at http://www.ice.gov/jttf.

58. Immigration and Customs Enforcement, "Counterterrorism and Criminal Exploitation Unit," available at http://www.ice.gov/counterterrorism-criminal-exploitation/.

59. Immigration and Customs Enforcement, "Counter-Proliferation Investigations Program," available at http://www.ice.gov/counter-proliferation-investigations/; Immigration and Customs Enforcement, "Identity and Benefit Fraud," available at http://www.ice.gov/identity-benefit-fraud/.

60. Immigration and Customs Enforcement, "Identity and Benefit Fraud"; Immigration and Customs Enforcement, "Project Shield America," available at http://www.ice.gov/project-shield/.

61. Immigration and Customs Enforcement, "Counter-Proliferation Investigations Program," available at http://www.ice.gov/counter-proliferation-investigations/.

62. Immigration and Customs Enforcement, "FY 2013 ICE Immigration Removals," available at http://www.ice.gov/immigration-enforcement/.

63. Immigration and Customs Enforcement, "Secure Communities," available at http://www.ice.gov/secure_communities.

64. Immigration and Customs Enforcement, "Criminal Alien Program," available at http://www.ice.gov/criminal-alien-program/.

65. Immigration and Customs Enforcement, "ICE Health Service Corps," available at http://www.ice.gov/about/offices/enforcement-removal-operations/ihs/.

66. Immigration and Customs Enforcement, "Detention Management," available at http://www.ice.gov/detention-management/.

67. Immigration and Customs Enforcement, "Fugitive Operations," available at http://www.ice.gov/fugitive-operations/.

68. Immigration and Customs Enforcement, "Law Enforcement Support Center," available at http://www.ice.gov/lesc/.

69. Immigration and Customs Enforcement, "Rapid REPAT," available at http://www.ice.gov/rapid-repat/.

70. Immigration and Customs Enforcement, "FY 2013 ICE Immigration Removals," available at http://www.ice.gov/removal-statistics/.

10

Federal Protective Service (GSA Police)

The Federal Protective Service (FPS), also known as the GSA Police, is the federal law enforcement agency that is charged with protecting facilities owned or leased by the General Services Administration (GSA) nationwide.[1] In other words, they provide security and law enforcement services to federally owned and leased buildings, facilities, properties, and other assets, keeping them safe and secure for employees, officials, and visitors. They also investigate any threats made against federal facilities. The FPS is the police force of the Secretary of Homeland Security. As such, they are responsible for policing, securing, and ensuring a safe environment in which federal agencies can conduct their business. Protecting federal properties in the United States is necessary for our nation's security, public health and safety, economic vitality, and way of life.[2] The GSA Police work to prevent terrorist attacks within the United States and minimize any potential damage from possible attacks on government property.

The statutory authority of the FPS is found in 40 U.S.C §1315, particularly b(2), as shown in Figure 10.1.

Figure 10.1: Statutory Authority of FPS

> **(a) In General.**—To the extent provided for by transfers made pursuant to the Homeland Security Act of 2002, the Secretary of Homeland Security (in this section referred to as the "Secretary") shall protect the buildings, grounds, and property that are owned, occupied, or secured by the Federal Government (including any agency, instrumentality, or wholly owned or mixed-ownership corporation thereof) and the persons on the property.
>
> **(b) Officers and Agents.**—
>
> **(1) Designation.**—The Secretary may designate employees of the Department of Homeland Security, including employees transferred to the Department from the Office of the Federal Protective Service of the General Services Administration pursuant to the Homeland Security Act of 2002, as officers and agents for duty in connection with the protection of property owned or occupied by the Federal Government and persons on the property, including duty in areas outside the property to the extent necessary to protect the property and persons on the property.
>
> **(2) Powers.**—While engaged in the performance of official duties, an officer or agent designated under this subsection may—
>
> **(A)** enforce Federal laws and regulations for the protection of persons and property;
>
> **(B)** carry firearms;
>
> **(C)** make arrests without a warrant for any offense against the United States committed in the presence of the officer or agent or for any felony cognizable under the laws of the United States if the officer or agent has reasonable grounds to believe that the person to be arrested has committed or is committing a felony;
>
> **(D)** serve warrants and subpoenas issued under the authority of the United States;
>
> **(E)** conduct investigations, on and off the property in question, of offenses that may have been committed against property owned or occupied by the Federal Government or persons on the property; and
>
> **(F)** carry out such other activities for the promotion of homeland security as the Secretary may prescribe.
>
> **(c) Regulations.**—
>
> **(1) In general.**—The Secretary, in consultation with the Administrator of General Services, may prescribe regulations necessary for the protection and administration of property owned or occupied by the Federal Government and persons on the property. The regulations may include reasonable penalties, within the limits prescribed in paragraph (2), for violations of the regulations. The regulations shall be posted and remain posted in a conspicuous place on the property.
>
> **(2) Penalties.**—A person violating a regulation prescribed under this subsection shall be fined under title 18, United States Code, imprisoned for not more than 30 days, or both.
>
> **(d) Details.**—
>
> **(1) Requests of agencies.**—On the request of the head of a Federal agency having charge or control of property owned or occupied by the Federal

Government, the Secretary may detail officers and agents designated under this section for the protection of the property and persons on the property.

(2) Applicability of regulations.—The Secretary may—

(A) extend to property referred to in paragraph (1) the applicability of regulations prescribed under this section and enforce the regulations as provided in this section; or

(B) utilize the authority and regulations of the requesting agency if agreed to in writing by the agencies.

(3) Facilities and services of other agencies.—When the Secretary determines it to be economical and in the public interest, the Secretary may utilize the facilities and services of Federal, State, and local law enforcement agencies, with the consent of the agencies.

(e) Authority Outside Federal Property.—For the protection of property owned or occupied by the Federal Government and persons on the property, the Secretary may enter into agreements with Federal agencies and with State and local governments to obtain authority for officers and agents designated under this section to enforce Federal laws and State and local laws concurrently with other Federal law enforcement officers and with State and local law enforcement officers.

(f) Secretary and Attorney General Approval.—The powers granted to officers and agents designated under this section shall be exercised in accordance with guidelines approved by the Secretary and the Attorney General.

(g) Limitation on Statutory Construction.—Nothing in this section shall be construed to—

(1) preclude or limit the authority of any Federal law enforcement agency; or

(2) restrict the authority of the Administrator of General Services to promulgate regulations affecting property under the Administrator's custody and control.

History

The FPS, ostensibly, like the United States Park Police, can trace its roots back to the legislative authorization under President George Washington for the appointment of three commissioners to establish the federal territory that would become Washington, D.C. (see Chapter 4). The commissioners hired six night watchmen to patrol the city grounds and to protect the federal buildings that were being built in the nation's new capital. Hence, the fact that these night watchmen protected federal buildings creates the link between these men in 1790 and today's current members of the FPS, who are charged with the mission of protecting all of the federal buildings located throughout the United States.

The official date to which the FPS traces its lineage is to June of 1948 when the responsibility to protect federal buildings was established in the Federal Works Agency.[3] This agency was an independent agency, created in 1939, by the

Franklin D. Roosevelt administration, to administer the construction of a number of federal buildings, pursuant to the Reorganization Act of 1939. Specifically, Congress authorized the Federal Works administrator to appoint uniformed guards as special policemen with the responsibility of "the policing of public buildings and other areas under the jurisdiction of the Federal Works Agency."[4] The special policemen were given the same responsibility as sheriffs and constables on federal property to enforce the laws enacted for the protection of property and to "prevent breaches of peace, suppress affrays or unlawful assemblies."[5]

On June 30, 1949, the Federal Works Agency was abolished, and all of its functions, including the protection of federal buildings, were transferred to the General Services Administration (GSA), effective the following day. The GSA was established by President Harry Truman on July 1, 1949, to streamline the administrative work of the federal government.[6] GSA consolidated the National Archives Establishment, the Federal Works Agency, and the Public Buildings Administration; the Bureau of Federal Supply and the Office of Contract Settlement; and the War Assets Administration into one federal agency tasked with administering supplies and providing workplaces for federal employees. Interestingly, GSA's original mission was to dispose of war surplus goods, manage and store government records, handle emergency preparedness, and stockpile strategic supplies for wartime. GSA also regulated the sale of various office supplies to federal agencies and managed some unusual operations, such as hemp plantations in South America.

In September 1961, Congress authorized the GSA administrator to appoint nonuniformed special policemen to conduct investigations in order to protect property under the control of GSA. In addition, they were to enforce federal law to protect persons and property and to make arrests without a warrant for any offense committed upon a federal property if a policeman had reason to believe the offense was a felony and the person to be arrested was guilty of the felony. Thus was established the more law enforcement-oriented organization, a GSA police force that would become the Federal Protective Service.

The GSA formally established the FPS in January of 1971, through GSA Administrative Order Number 5440.46.[7] The FPS was to be an official GSA agency that would continue to protect federal property and buildings with both uniformed and nonuniformed police. In a sense, it became a police department for all of the federal government buildings located throughout the United States, and the agency head reported to the GSA administrator. In fact, the Civil Service Commission authorized a special classification for the FPS officers, who became known as federal protective officers.

The FPS played an important role in the Mariel Boatlift during the Cuban Refugee Crisis of 1980. In the late 1970s, the Cuban economy plummeted and U.S. and Cuban relations were strained. As refugees began coming into the U.S., President Carter took an open-arms policy toward them and began granting them refugee status. Cuba's dictator, Fidel Castro, experiencing his own issues internally in Cuba, claimed that he was opening up the port of Mariel to allow anyone wishing to leave Cuba to do so. The U.S. took it as an opportunity to welcome refugees from Cuba. In the end, what Castro did was to release his inmates and patients from his jails and mental institutions and to place them on boats and flotation devices and send these individuals north to Key West. When it was discovered what he was effectively doing and to deal with the thousands of refugees pouring into the United States, Carter ordered the military to pick up the refugees and to transport them to various military installations, including Fort Chaffee, Arkansas; Fort McCoy, Wisconsin; and Fort Indiantown Gap, Pennsylvania for temporary detention. Because the Immigration and Naturalization Service (INS) and Border Patrol were already understaffed, the FPS was mobilized to provide security for these makeshift refugee camps. FPS officers were also some of the primary responding law enforcement officers when the Cuban refugees rioted in Fort Chaffee.

In 2000, the FPS moved to a nationwide system for electronic monitoring of the federal buildings. Under the old system, alarms were typically monitored locally or by a linkage among federal buildings located in a dense geographical area. The level of consistency was uneven and depended entirely on the group or outsourced company responsible for monitoring the system. In addition, if the system failed, there was typically no alternative means for ensuring the security of the federal building. The FPS moved to four regional centers, known as MegaCenters. These centers (located in Battle Creek, Michigan; Denver, Colorado; Philadelphia, Pennsylvania; and Suitland, Maryland) use electronic equipment to monitor the alarm systems for all federal buildings in their region. Further, the system is entirely redundant, so that if one of the MegaCenters is disabled, the other three can pick up the monitoring of the disabled region. These operation centers operate around the clock and have the capability of accessing video monitoring to further secure the facilities and to direct local FPS officers, contractors, and police to specific locations. The system also allows for continual communications of all FPS personnel across the country.

In the wake of the September 11, 2001 terrorist attacks on the United States, there was quick discussion of creating a new department of homeland security and a strong possibility that the FPS would be moved from under the GSA and placed in this new department. In 2003, that discussion became a reality when the Federal Protective Service was transferred to the U.S. Department of Homeland Security (DHS) and placed within the U.S. Immigration and Customs Enforcement (ICE), by way of the Homeland Security Act of 2002. The act required the DHS secretary to "protect the buildings, grounds, and property that are owned, occupied, or secured by the Federal Government (including any agency, instrumentality, or wholly owned or mixed ownership corporation thereof) and persons on the property."[8]

At the time of the transfer, the FPS employed over 1,000 federal law enforcement officers, yet they were required to cover thousands of federal buildings spread out across the United States. The means by which they did this was to hire contract security guards. In fiscal year 2006, for example, there were 950 FPS law enforcement officers, while there were 15,000 contract security guards. These contract security guards came from a wide array of private security firms, both large and small, that obtain contracts through the FPS to assign guards to specific federal buildings. FPS contract security guard responsibilities include federal building access control, employee and visitor identification checks, security equipment monitoring, and roving patrols of the interior and exterior of federal property. The guards will be armed or unarmed depending upon the assignment. Typically, interior assignments are unarmed while exterior and perimeter assignments are armed. As a result of such a high number of contract guards, the FPS in many ways is the supervising authority over contract security guards.

In fiscal year 2007, the FPS realigned its workforce and reduced the number of FPS law enforcement officers and investigators. The idea was to rely more on security contract guards and less on full-time FPS officers. The full-time law enforcement officers would serve primarily as supervisors of the contract security guards. A Government Accountability Office (GAO) report was issued in June of 2008, which found that the FPS officers had been reduced approximately 20 percent over the previous year.[9] The GAO report also concluded that this reduction in FPS's staff resulted in the reduction of security at federal facilities and increased the risk of crime or terrorist attacks. The failure, according to the report, had to do with the transfer of the FPS from GSA to DHS; it was this transfer to ICE that had caused the diminishing number of staff. In particular, it cited the reduction in staff as a result of the FPS allowing for voluntary early retirement and giving FPS law enforcement officers the option (and ease) of transferring to other ICE assignments. Because ICE was over FPS, and the mission of FPS was not the primary mission of ICE, management was more concerned with maintaining the level of ICE agents than FPS law enforcement officers. Thus, under ICE (and DHS), the FPS as an agency was diminished in not only number, but in their capability for carrying out their mission.

This diminishing ability became very evident the following year when the Senate Committee on Homeland Security and Governmental Affairs began to hold congressional hearings related to the FPS. What the congressional oversight committee found was primarily poor performance on the part of the contract guards. These private security guards, hired through FPS contracts, were often poorly trained, did not conduct themselves well in the performance of their duties, and were not properly monitored by the full-time FPS law enforcement officers. The findings were often shocking and, if not so serious, they would have bordered on the comical.

In one city, tenant representatives in a major federal building stated that many of the building employees complained about the quality of the contract guard services saying they did not have enough guidance from FPS inspectors and, as a result, there had been several security breaches, such as stolen property. According to the Federal Bureau of Investigation (FBI) and GSA officials in one of the regions, contract guards failed to report the theft of an FBI surveillance trailer worth over $500,000, even though security cameras captured the trailer being stolen while guards were on duty. The FBI did not realize it was missing until three days later. Only after the FBI started making inquiries did the guards report the theft to the FPS and the FBI. During another incident, FPS officials reported contract guards—who were armed—taking no action as a shirtless suspect wearing handcuffs on one wrist ran through the lobby of a major federal building while being chased by an FPS inspector. In addition, one officer reported that during an off-hours alarm call to a federal building, the official arrived to find the front guard post empty, while the guard's loaded firearm was left unattended in the unlocked post. Inspectors also reported they witnessed an incident where an individual was attempting to enter a secure facility with illegal weapons, and the contract security guards did not confiscate the weapons but waived the individual on through.[10]

In other cases, guards were found sleeping on duty, both during the night and the day. One guard was found sleeping on his post and when questioned why, he explained he was taking the drug Percocet for pain. He was armed. Another guard was caught using government computers, while he was supposed to be standing post, to further his private for-profit adult pornography Web site. On another occasion, a guard had attached a motion sensor to a pole at the entrance to a federal facility garage in order to alert him when someone was approaching his post so that he could sleep or watch television and not get caught. His device was discovered and it was reported to the FPS. Another guard, located on duty during the day at a federal building accidentally fired his service weapon in the men's bathroom. He was practicing his quick draw in front of the mirror. And in another case, a box being carried into a federal building was scanned through the x-ray machines and was allowed to enter the building. The box contained multiple firearms and ammunition.[11]

As a result of the problems identified by the Senate Committee on Homeland Security and Governmental Affairs and the diminishing emphasis of the FPS under ICE, Department of Homeland Security Secretary Janet Napolitano, under the 2010 DHS appropriations proposal, requested Congress fund the movement of the FPS to the National Protection and Programs Directorate within the Department of Homeland Security. Congress approved the transfer and on October 29, 2009, FPS moved to the new directorate. Under the National Protection and Programs Directorate, the FPS joined the Office of Cybersecurity and Communications (CS&C), the Office of Infrastructure Protection (IP), the Office of Risk Management and Analysis (RMA), and U.S.-VISIT, a biometrics-based technology solution that includes digital fingerprinting and photography for tracking foreign visitors into the United States.

Under the new Directorate, the FPS continues its primary mission of securing federal buildings throughout the United States. In addition to the primary federal buildings, there are also judicial buildings. In this case, because court security is primarily a function of the U.S. Marshals Service (USMS), the USMS maintains security inside the buildings and, until 2009, worked with the FPS in regard to perimeter and outside security. In the appropriations of fiscal year 2009, it was decided that USMS would maintain all interior and perimeter security and that FPS would only be responsible for outside security.

Despite the changes in organizational structure and the U.S. Governmental Accountability Office reports highlighting many of the problems of the FPS, Congressional hearings by the House Homeland Security Subcommittee on

Cybersecurity, Infrastructure Protection, and Security Technologies, in July of 2011, continued to find problems with the FPS's contract security guards. As the chair of the subcommittee, Representative Bennie Thompson (D-Miss.) pointed out that every year the FPS provides documentation about the improvements of the FPS and their contract security guards, yet every year something happens to make him realize that these private security guards have not improved. In 2011, Rep. Thompson discovered that a private security contract guard in Detroit, Michigan found a bag outside of the McNamara Federal Building. He picked up the bag, brought it inside, and placed it in the lost and found. Three weeks later, someone came across the bag in the lost and found and discovered it had a bomb inside. Fortunately, the bomb failed to detonate and did not explode, "no thanks to the guard whose job it is to protect the building."[12] The current chair of the subcommittee noted the agency's "fundamental ineptitude at managing contracts" and that the bomb case is the perfect example of "how not to respond to suspicious packages."[13]

As of 2012, there were 900 FPS officers managing 13,000 private security guards from 130 different private security contact companies in order to protect over 9,000 federal buildings. The FPS Director, Leonard E. Patterson, noted at the July 2011 hearing that the agency's problem was "our ability to ensure the training is being delivered in an acceptable manner" due to the high number of contract companies and security guards. Essentially, he argued that with the 130 different private security companies providing training to the 13,000 guards, the FPS could not ensure a certain level of standard in the training. David Wright, an FPS officer and president of the American Federal of Government Employees Local 918, in a written statement, summed it up this way: "The sole Federal agency charged with the critical mission of protecting thousands of federal buildings and millions of people from these terrorist and criminal attacks is faced with potential failure that if not immediately remedied by the Congress, will likely result in tragic loss of life."[14]

Who Gets Hired

The FPS currently employs 1,225 federal staff (which includes 900 law enforcement security officers, criminal investigators, police officers, and support personnel) and 15,000 contract guard staff that work to secure over 9,000 buildings and their occupants.[15] They also employ 1,279 staff personnel.[16]

New FPS agents must attend training at the FPS Academy at the Federal Law Enforcement Training Center in Glynco, Georgia. Following graduation from this program, new FPS agents must attend additional training before becoming sworn FPS agents. Once this happens, the new agents are then assigned to an FPS office in one of eleven regions throughout the country. FPS law enforcement officers also undergo additional training depending on their assignment to special units within the service.

Successful candidates for the FPS will be a U.S. citizen, at least 21 years of age, possess a valid driver's license, be able to qualify for a service revolver on an annual basis, pass a physical test, and pass the training program. Earning a bachelor's or master's degree increases the chance of being hired by FPS.[17]

The recruits who are assigned to be physical security specialist/ law enforcement security officers (LESO) are considered to be the backbone of the FPS workforce. These are sworn law enforcement officers and trained security experts who provide security assessments, inspections, and oversight for contract guards and who respond to crimes in progress. Those hired to be criminal investigators will receive training to provide investigative follow-up response to criminal activity that occurs at federal facilities.

Budgets

The FY 2011 budget for the FPS was $1.115 billion, which was increased in FY 2012 and again in the request for 2014. This is outlined in Table 10.1.

Leader

L. Eric Patterson was appointed director of the FPS, a subcomponent of the National Protection and Programs Directorate in September 2010. He previously served as the deputy director of the Defense Counterintelligence (CI) and HUMINT Center (DCHC) at the Defense Intelligence Agency (DIA), where he directed and conducted CI and HUMINT activities worldwide to meet Department of Defense requirements.

Prior to joining DIA, Mr. Patterson served as a principal with Booz Allen Hamilton, where he supported two of the Defense Technical Information Center analysis centers, one focused on information assurance and the other on the survivability and vulnerability of defense systems.

Mr. Patterson is a retired United States Air Force brigadier general with 30 years of service. He started his Air Force career as a missile launch officer at Little

Table 10.1   **Budget Authority for FPS (In Billions of Dollars)**

FY 2011 enacted	$1.115
FY 2012 enacted	$1.286
FY 2013 enacted	$1.335
FY 2014 enacted	$1.470
FY 2015 presidential budget	$1.515

Source: Department of Homeland Security, "FY 2015 Budget in Brief," available at http://www.dhs.gov/sites/default/files/publications/FY15BIB.pdf.

Rock, Arkansas and transitioned to the Air Force Office of Special Investigations (AFOSI) after four years. He has served in a variety of assignments from overseeing all CI investigations and operations in Turkey and Honduras to serving as the director of security programs and policy in the Office of the Secretary of the Air Force. His final assignment on active duty was as the commander of the AFOSI, where he directed all criminal, fraud, and counterintelligence investigations for the U.S. Air Force. His awards and decorations include the Distinguished Service Medal, Legion of Merit, Meritorious Service Medals, Air Force Commendation Medals, and other campaign and service medals.

Mr. Patterson was born in Washington, D.C., and possesses a bachelor of science degree in business administration from Howard University; master of arts degree in business and public administration from Webster University in St. Louis, Missouri, and is an alumnus of the Air War College in Montgomery, Alabama. He resides in Maryland with his wife and daughter and has two sons who serve in the U.S. Air Force and U.S. Navy.

Organization

The FPS was transferred to the Department of Homeland Security (DHS) when DHS was created. Within DHS, the FPS became part of the National Protection and Programs Directorate. This directorate is the agency that oversees the department's goal of reducing the risk to the nation's physical and cyber infrastructure from terrorist attacks and natural disasters. In 2009, there were 164 field offices of the FPS spread throughout 11 regions around the country.

FPS coordinates their responses to incidents through four MegaCenters that are equipped with state-of-the-art communication systems. They are able to monitor multiple types of alarm systems from different facilities. They also oversee other types of security measures including closed circuit television and wireless dispatch communications within federal facilities that are located across the nation. This is done 24-hours a day, seven days a week. The FPS MegaCenters are found in Michigan, Colorado, Pennsylvania, and Maryland.[18]

What They Do

FPS agents provide security and law enforcement services to over 9,000 federal facilities and their occupants. They also provide risk assessment of those facilities to determine, recommend, and install measures to reduce the possibility of attack and harm. The FPS oversees up to 15,000 armed contracted protective security officers and conducts criminal investigations when needed. They provide security awareness training to personnel and provide support to major events.[19]

In 2011, the FPS responded to 53,000 incidents, carried out 1,975 arrests, and confiscated over 680,000 weapons and other prohibited items during routine checks at federal facilities. FPS agents also investigated over 1,300 threats and assaults made toward facilities and employees.[20]

Over the years, the FPS has established a successful security program to provide and ensure protection to federal facilities and personnel. This includes installation of alarm systems, x-rays, magnetometers, and entry control systems, with monitoring 24-hours a day, 7 days a week. There are also uniformed police and investigative follow-ups to any incidents.[21] Moreover, the FPS conducts facility security assessments, designs countermeasures for tenant agencies, maintains armed contract security guards, and performs background suitability checks for contract employees. When needed, the FPS conducts criminal investigations and shares any relevant intelligence among local, state, and federal law enforcement agencies. They work to protect the safety of those attending special events, work with FEMA to respond to natural disasters such as earthquakes and hurricanes, offer special operations including K-9 explosive detection, and train federal tenants in crime prevention and occupant emergency planning.

In recent years, the FPS created a new program, the Risk Assessment and Management Program (RAMP), which provides FPS agents with a centralized source of information for each of the federal facilities they are assigned to protect. RAMP collects information on threats, including historical information, documentation, and other related assessments. This data can be used by FPS officers in their tasks of managing security at these facilities. RAMP helps agents collect, analyze, and share risk data concerning security of federal sites. Officials can then use the data to analyze any potential risks that threaten federal facilities, from terrorist threats to natural hazards. They can recommend and track the implementation of countermeasures. They carry out analyses of the risks posed to federal facilities and the means of reducing them. They can track financial information for countermeasures and provide occupancy emergency plan information.

Conclusion

Agents working for the Federal Protective Service help to ensure the federal buildings and people in them are safe from harm. They are just one of the federal law enforcement bureaucracies that plays a role in crime control efforts across the nation.

Key Terms

GSA Administrative Order Number 5440.46

Mariel Boatlift

MegaCenters

National Protection and Programs Directorate

Leonard E. Patterson

Risk Assessment and Management Program

Review Questions

1. What is the function of the FPS?

2. Describe the history of the GSA Police.

3. How did the terrorist attacks of 9/11 affect the FPS?

4. What are some characteristics of the typical person hired by the FPS?

5. What are the trends in budgetary allocations for the FPS?

6. Provide an overview of the FPS organizational structure.

Endnotes

1. Department of Homeland Security, "The Federal Protective Service," available at http://www.dhs.gov/federal-protective-service-0.
2. Department of Homeland Security, "The Federal Protective Service."
3. Reese, Shawn. (2009). The Federal Protective Service and Contract Security Guards: A Statutory History and Current Status. Congressional Research Service. Washington, D.C.
4. Reese, The Federal Protective Service and Contract Security Guards.
5. Reese, The Federal Protective Service and Contract Security Guards, p. 1.
6. General Services Administration. (2012). "A Brief History of GSA." *U.S. General Services Administration.* Available online at http://www.gsa.gov/portal/content/103369.
7. Bumgarner, Jeffrey B. (2006). *Federal Agents: The Growth of Federal Law Enforcement in America.* Westport, CT: Praeger.
8. Homeland Security Act (2002). Public law 107-296. Available online at http://www.dhs.gov/xlibrary/assets/hr_5005_enr.pdf.
9. U.S. Government Accountability Office. (2008). *Homeland Security: The Federal Protective Service Faces Several Challenges That Hamper Its Ability to Protect Federal Facilities.* Available online at http://www.gao.gov/new.items/d08683.pdf.
10. U.S. Government Accountability Office, *Homeland Security.*
11. U.S. Government Accountability Office. (2009). *Preliminary Results Show Federal Protective Service's Ability to Protect Federal Facilities Is Hampered By Weaknesses in Its Contract Security Guard Program.* Available online at http://www.gao.gov/new.items/d09859t.pdf.
12. Davidson, Joe. (2011). "A Look at the Sorry State of the Federal Protective Service." *The Washington Post.* July 13.
13. Davidson, "A Look at the Sorry State of the Federal Protective Service."
14. Davidson, "A Look at the Sorry State of the Federal Protective Service."
15. Department of Homeland Security, "The Federal Protective Service."
16. Department of Homeland Security, "FY 2013 Budget in Brief," available at http://www.dhs.gov/xlibrary/assets/mgmt/dhs-budget-in-brief-fy2013.pdf.
17. U.S. Police, "Federal Protective Service," available at http://uspolice.com/federal-protective-service.
18. Department of Homeland Security, "Statement for the Record of Federal Protective Service Director Leonard E. Patterson, National Protection and Programs Directorate, before the House Committee on Homeland Security, Subcommittee on Cybersecurity, Infrastructure Protection, and Security Technologies, 'Securing Federal Facilities: Challenges of the Federal Protective Service and the Need for Reform'" available at http://www.dhs.gov/ynews/testimony/20110713-patterson-nppd-securing-federal-facilities.shtm.
19. Department of Homeland Security, "FY 2013 Budget in Brief."
20. Department of Homeland Security, "FY 2013 Budget in Brief."
21. Department of Homeland Security, "The Federal Protective Service."

11

Federal Air Marshal Service

The Federal Air Marshal Service (FAMS) seeks to detect and deter terrorist acts against U.S. air carriers, airports, passengers, and crew. They also work to promote confidence in the nation's civil aviation system. Their role is to enhance aviation security and provide a security presence during flights inside commercial passenger aircraft. Air marshals fly undercover on commercial aircraft to observe and protect the passengers. A federal air marshal is an undercover law enforcement officer who is trained to respond to potential terrorist threats or other criminal activity on board U.S. domestic and foreign flights. The marshals are on call 24-hours a day and can be deployed anywhere in the world with less than an hour's notice. They are trained to detect and deal with hostile situations in U.S. airports or aircraft that may harm passengers and crew. Air marshals are often required to operate without backup.

Air marshals protect airline passengers by blending in with those flying and relying on their training, including investigative techniques, criminal terrorist behavior recognition, firearms proficiency, aircraft specific tactics, and close quarters self-defense measures to detect terrorists and stop them from bringing harm.

The statutory authority for the Air Marshals is found in both the Code of Federal Regulations and the U.S. Code. Shown in Figure 11.1 is 49 CFR 1544.223, which describes the specific duties of the air marshals on board an aircraft. Figure 11.2 contains 49 U.S.C §44917, which describes the deployment of air marshals.

Figure 11.1: Transportation of Federal Air Marshals

(a) A Federal Air Marshal on duty status may have a weapon accessible while aboard an aircraft for which screening is required.

(b) Each aircraft operator must carry Federal Air Marshals, in the number and manner specified by TSA, on each scheduled passenger operation, and public charter passenger operation designated by TSA.

(c) Each Federal Air Marshal must be carried on a first priority basis and without charge while on duty, including positioning and repositioning flights. When a Federal Air Marshal is assigned to a scheduled flight that is canceled for any reason, the aircraft operator must carry that Federal Air Marshal without charge on another flight as designated by TSA.

(d) Each aircraft operator must assign the specific seat requested by a Federal Air Marshal who is on duty status. If another LEO is assigned to that seat or requests that seat, the aircraft operator must inform the Federal Air Marshal. The Federal Air Marshal will coordinate seat assignments with the other LEO.

(e) The Federal Air Marshal identifies himself or herself to the aircraft operator by presenting credentials that include a clear, full-face picture, the signature of the Federal Air Marshal, and the signature of the FAA Administrator. A badge, shield, or similar device may not be used or accepted as the sole means of identification.

(f) The requirements of § 1544.219(a) do not apply for a Federal Air Marshal on duty status.

(g) Each aircraft operator must restrict any information concerning the presence, seating, names, and purpose of Federal Air Marshals at any station or on any flight to those persons with an operational need to know.

(h) Law enforcement officers authorized to carry a weapon during a flight will be contacted directly by a Federal Air Marshal who is on that same flight.

Figure 11.2: Deployment of Federal Air Marshals

(a) **In General.**—The Under Secretary of Transportation for Security under the authority provided by section 44903 (d)—

(1) may provide for deployment of Federal air marshals on every passenger flight of air carriers in air transportation or intrastate air transportation;

(2) shall provide for deployment of Federal air marshals on every such flight determined by the Secretary to present high security risks;

(3) shall provide for appropriate training, supervision, and equipment of Federal air marshals;

(4) shall require air carriers providing flights described in paragraph (1) to provide seating for a Federal air marshal on any such flight without regard to the availability of seats on the flight and at no cost to the United States Government or the marshal;

(5) may require air carriers to provide, on a space-available basis, to an off-duty Federal air marshal a seat on a flight to the airport nearest the marshal's home at no cost to the marshal or the United States Government if the marshal is traveling to that airport after completing his or her security duties;

(6) may enter into agreements with Federal, State, and local agencies under which appropriately-trained law enforcement personnel from such agencies, when traveling on a flight of an air carrier, will carry a firearm and be prepared to assist Federal air marshals;

(7) shall establish procedures to ensure that Federal air marshals are made aware of any armed or unarmed law enforcement personnel on board an aircraft; and

(8) may appoint—

(A) an individual who is a retired law enforcement officer;

(B) an individual who is a retired member of the Armed Forces; and

(C) an individual who has been furloughed from an air carrier crew position in the 1-year period beginning on September 11, 2001,

as a Federal air marshal, regardless of age, if the individual otherwise meets the background and fitness qualifications required for Federal air marshals.

(b) Long Distance Flights.—In making the determination under subsection (a)(2), nonstop, long distance flights, such as those targeted on September 11, 2001, should be a priority.

(c) Interim Measures.—Until the Under Secretary completes implementation of subsection (a), the Under Secretary may use, after consultation with and concurrence of the heads of other Federal agencies and departments, personnel from those agencies and departments, on a nonreimbursable basis, to provide air marshal service.

(d) Training for Foreign Law Enforcement Personnel.—

(1) In general.—The Assistant Secretary for Immigration and Customs Enforcement of the Department of Homeland Security, after consultation with the Secretary of State, may direct the Federal Air Marshal Service to provide appropriate air marshal training to law enforcement personnel of foreign countries.

(2) Watchlist screening.—The Federal Air Marshal Service may only provide appropriate air marshal training to law enforcement personnel of foreign countries after comparing the identifying information and records of law enforcement personnel of foreign countries against all appropriate records in the consolidated and integrated terrorist watchlists maintained by the Federal Government.

(3) Fees.—The Assistant Secretary shall establish reasonable fees and charges to pay expenses incurred in carrying out this subsection. Funds collected under this subsection shall be credited to the account in the Treasury from which the expenses were incurred and shall be available to the Assistant Secretary for purposes for which amounts in such account are available.

History

On December 17, 1903, Wilbur and Orville Wright were the first humans to fly in an airplane. The first commercial airplane flight occurred just a little over ten years later on January 1, 1914, when a flight carrying passengers flew from St. Petersburg to Tampa, Florida. By the 1920s, commercial flights were becoming very common. So, it is not all too surprising that by 1930, the first hijacking of a plane would occur.

In May of 1930, Peruvian revolutionaries successfully seized a Pan American mail plane with the aim of dropping propaganda leaflets over Lima.[1] Less than one year later, on February 21, 1931, the first recorded hijacking would take place in Arequipa, Peru. Byron Rickards, flying a Ford Tri-Motor, was approached on the ground by armed revolutionaries. He refused to fly them anywhere and after a 10-day standoff, Rickards was informed that the revolution was successful and he could go free in return for taking one group member to Lima. The next hijacking did not take place until July 25, 1947, but it was the first fatal hijacking, when Romanian terrorists killed an aircrew member on board a Romanian Airlines flight.

This Romanian terrorist hijacking became the catalyst for a series of hijackings. From the years 1947 to 1958, there were a recorded 23 hijackings of airplanes, most occurring in Eastern Europe and most for purposes of people seeking political asylum.[2] One, however, was clearly an act of criminal violence. On November 1, 1955, Jack Graham placed a bomb in his mother's luggage in the hopes of killing her and collecting her life insurance policy. The bomb detonated, killing all 44 people on board the Denver flight. Graham confessed to the crime, recanted, and then tried to kill himself in prison. He was found guilty and was executed in the Colorado State Penitentiary gas chamber on January 11, 1957.

While hijackings between 1947 and 1958 averaged a little over two a year, between 1958 and 1967 they increased to approximately five hijackings each year. At first it was believed that the increased number of hijackings was a result of individuals attempting to escape Cuba after Castro came to power in 1959. For instance, on April 15, 1959, a United States federal agent received information that a Cuban airliner was about to land at the Miami airport after four individuals had forced the pilots at gunpoint to change course minutes after takeoff from Havana. When the aircraft landed, officers from U.S. Immigration, U.S. Customs, and the U.S. Border Patrol, as well as local police, met, escorted, and interviewed passengers after the four terrorists surrendered their weapons. Additional aircraft were hijacked in Cuba and diverted to the United States over the next several years. On May 1, 1961, however, a National Airlines flight from Marathon, Florida, was hijacked by a man carrying a gun and knife who demanded that the flight be diverted to Havana, Cuba.[3] Additional hijacking attempts took place through the year, forcing the United States federal government to place armed guards on commercial planes. In 1961, President John F. Kennedy took office with commercial aviation security as a focal point of his administration.[4]

The issue was raised in the fall of 1961, and at a press conference, President Kennedy explained: "Now, let me say that we are—have ordered today (August 10, 1961) on a number of our planes a Border Patrol man who will ride on a number of our flights. We are also going to insist that every airplane lock its door, and that the door be strong enough to prevent entrance by force, and that possession of the key be held by those inside the cabin so that pressure cannot be put on the members of the crew outside to have the door opened."[5] This then prompted legislation in Congress, creating a hijacking bill that made air piracy a crime punishable by death or imprisonment for at least 20 years. On September 5, 1961, President Kennedy signed the bill into law. Shortly after the bill was signed, a special force of Federal Aviation safety inspectors volunteered to carry out sky marshal duties. In March of 1962, 18 sky marshals were trained at the U.S. Border Patrol Academy in Port Isabel, Texas. They were sworn in and appointed as "special deputy U.S. Marshals," but they were dubbed "Sky Marshals."[6] Agents flew on board commercial flights armed with revolvers, teargas guns disguised as fountain pens, and a blackjack.

Whether as a result of the Sky Marshals Program or other factors, the total number of hijackings dropped in the year 1968, but they grew exponentially in 1969.[7] In that year, in January alone, there were eight airliners hijacked to Cuba. The annual average between 1968 and 1977 had increased to 41 hijackings each year. Although deputy U.S. marshals continued to perform duties as sky marshals until 1973, and their number eventually reached 230 deputies, it was quickly becoming clear that more needed to be done to stem the rising tide of hijackings.

In January of 1969, the Federal Aviation Administration created the Task Force on the Deterrence of Air Piracy. They developed a profile to be used by the security screeners in concert with the deployment of metal detectors. In addition, the U.S. Customs Service became involved in assisting the U.S. Marshals Service by dedicating some of their agents to the Sky Marshal Program. Although these deputies came from both the U.S. Marshals Service and U.S. Customs, the Federal Aviation Administration's director of Civil Aviation Security oversaw the sky marshals and their program.

In September of 1970, the Popular Front for the Liberation of Palestine (PFLP) attempted to hijack three aircraft. One of the flights had Israeli sky marshals on board and they were able to thwart the hijacking. This motivated President Nixon to increase the program, so, through an Executive Order, additional agents from the Federal Bureau of Investigation, the U.S. Secret Service, and the U.S. Marshals were ordered into the Sky Marshals Program. At the same time, the inspection of all luggage and screening of every passenger in every airport in the United States was implemented. September 2, 1974 witnessed the last flight of a sky marshal; the implementation of the screening system was believed to be so successful that the sky marshals were no longer necessary. Inside of two years, that decision was deemed a mistake.

In early 1976, the Federal Aviation Administration once again implemented the Sky Marshals Program. Although a total of 69 aircraft were hijacked between 1974 and 1985, and 975 died, the new Sky Marshals Program limped along, wholly understaffed.[8] In 1980, like the Federal Protection Service (see Chapter 10), the Sky Marshals were called on to assist in the Mariel Boatlift, only their numbers were so low, they were unable to contribute much to the effort. They continued in this manner until June of 1985.

On June 14, 1985, TWA Flight 847 was hijacked en route from Athens, Greece to Rome, Italy and forced to land in Beirut, Lebanon.[9] Hijackers held the plane for 17 days. When their demands for the release of more than 700 Shiite Muslim prisoners was not met, hostage and U.S. Navy Diver Robert Dean Stethem was tortured and shot and his body was dumped out onto the airport tarmac. The entire world was watching. So, too, was President Ronald Reagan.

On June 22, President Reagan directed the secretary of transportation, in coordination with the secretary of state and the attorney general, to immediately expand the Federal Aviation Administration's Federal Air Marshal Program aboard international flights of U.S. carriers.[10] Then, on August 8, 1985, Reagan signed into law the International Security and Development Cooperation Act, which established the explicit statutory bases for the Federal Air Marshal Program, and the Air Marshals became a permanent part of the FAA. Unfortunately, as the decade wound to an end, the number of skyjackings decreased, and the number of Air Marshals decreased along with them. The Federal Air Marshals were only hovering around a little over 300 agents by the beginning of the last decade of the twentieth century. And then, things got worse again.

In 1992, the Federal Aviation Administration decided to reduce the number of Federal Air Marshals from 300 to 50.[11] Over the decade, as air marshals retired, no additional air marshals were hired. By 1999, the agency was down to 33 air marshals, working out of a small office in Atlantic City, New Jersey. They flew on a limited number of flights and most of these were international flights coming into the United States. Then came the terrorist attacks on September 11, 2001. It was decided within weeks that the FAMS needed to be greatly expanded. Congress passed a mandate for this through the USA PATRIOT Act, and President George W. Bush demanded that the expansion happen quickly.[12]

On October 10, 2001, the first Federal Air Marshal class post 9/11 graduated. Their training had lasted only three weeks. They were the augmentees for the expanded service. The following month, that agency was given more authority and standing. On November 19, 2001, the Aviation and Transportation Security Act was passed by Congress and signed into law by President George W. Bush. The Transportation Security Administration (TSA) was created and all aviation security duties were transferred from the Federal Aviation Administration to the new TSA. In addition, the FAMS was given new statutory authority, including the right to carry firearms, the right to fly on flights required by the U.S. government, and the authority to seek and execute arrest and search warrants.[13]

In what was probably the first major incident involving the newly expanded FAMS, a man flying from Pittsburgh to Washington, D.C. was subdued, on November 12, 2001. As the plane prepared for landing, all passengers were told to return to their seats. The man, however, decided to use the restroom and refused to take his seat. Federal air marshals subdued the man and held him until the plane landed.[14]

The decision to expand the FAMS was deemed a good one after the December 22, 2001 attempt to destroy a commercial aircraft coming from Paris, France to Miami, Florida. Richard Colvin Reid attempted to ignite a bomb hidden in his shoes. The fuse failed because it was too damp. Reid became known as the "shoe-bomber," but it highlighted the need for more federal air marshals.

In January of 2002, Thomas D. Quinn, a former Secret Service administrator, became the director of the FAMS under the Transportation Security Administration. As the plans for creating a Department of Homeland Security were developed in 2002, it was determined that the FAMS would become part of the new federal bureaucracy. The following year, as the Department of Homeland Security came into existence, it was determined that the FAMS would fall under the newly created U.S. Immigration and Customs Enforcement (ICE). Quinn moved the agency over to Homeland Security, effective November 2, 2003, and led the FAMS until March of 2006.

In the summer of 2002, the first controversy surrounding the Federal Air Marshals began to surface. The FAMS administration issued a dress code to the Air Marshals. They were required to fly on the airplanes in business attire. The Air Marshals argued that by wearing the traditional federal business suit they would be blowing their cover as ordinary passengers, especially if they flew in coach. The fight would continue for nearly four years before the House Judiciary Committee stepped in, held hearings, and issued a report that prompted the administration to ease the dress code requirements.[15]

As part of the Homeland Security Act of 2002, a new program was created through Title 14, the Arming Pilots Against Terrorism Act. This program directed the TSA to deputize pilots as federal law enforcement officers as long as they underwent some form of training. TSA assigned this task to the Federal Air Marshal Service. The program established by FAMS is known as the Federal Flight Deck Officers (FFDO) program. Any U.S. citizen flight crew member working on a passenger plane, private charter, or cargo air carrier is eligible for the program. These crewmen must apply to the FFDO program, pass a physical and psychological test, and complete training in the handling of firearms, use of force, and defensive tactics. While those successfully completing the FFDO program are recognized as federal law enforcement officers, they do not have the power to make arrests and have no authority outside of an airplane's flight deck. On April 19, 2003, the FAMS deputized its first group of federal flight deck officers.

In 2003, the Federal Air Marshals' new training facility located in Atlantic City, New Jersey was completed. The facility had an indoor and outdoor firing range, classrooms, and lodging for the students. By the end of 2003, FAMS had reached their mass hiring goal that had been mandated by Congress (which was classified so that terrorists and criminals would not be able to figure out the odds of a federal air marshal being on any given flight).

In March of 2004, a series of train bombings occurred in Madrid, Spain. This terrorist attack caused the TSA to consider how best to prevent similar types of bombings. They developed what has become known as Visible Intermodal Prevention and Response (VIPR) teams, which can provide security nationwide for all types of transportation—buses, trains, airplanes, etc. These teams are comprised of TSA personnel and include federal air marshals, who operate in teams to enhance security by creating a deterrent presence and through the use of bomb detection capabilities. Air marshals rotate through these ground-based assignments.[16]

In 2005, secretary of the Department of Homeland Security Michael Chertoff ordered a review of the organizational structure of the department. It was determined that the transfer of the FAMS from the TSA had been a mistake and not in the best interest of the organization's mission. Therefore, effective October 16, 2005, the FAMS was ordered to move back under TSA. At this point, Director Quinn stepped down as director of the FAMS and Dana A. Brown, another Secret Service administrator, was appointed as the new director of the FAMS. He was then responsible for moving the agency back under the TSA.

The FAMS saw itself taking on a number of unique rolls during this time period. In August of 2005, in the wake of Hurricane Katrina, the Federal Air Marshals were called upon to assist with the evacuation of New Orleans. Then, in July of 2006, the Air Marshals were called upon to assist in the evacuation of American citizens from Lebanon as the threat level rose because of hostilities between Hezbollah militants and Israel. The FAMS moved 15,000 citizens out of Lebanon. And, in August of 2006, when a transatlantic aircraft plot was discovered that was intended to detonate liquid explosives on at least 10 airliners, the FAMS deployed en masse, and ultimately the plot was foiled.

On December 7, 2005, Federal Air Marshals had their first deadly force encounter post 9/11. A mentally ill passenger, Rigoberto Alpizar, a United States citizen born in Costa Rica, ran off a flight in Miami, carrying a backpack. He was supposed to be flying to Orlando, Florida with his wife. He said he had a bomb in his backpack. Federal air marshals ordered him to put the backpack down and move away. When he did not comply with the air marshals and reached into the backpack, they shot and killed him on the tarmac.[17]

In 2008, Robert Bray stepped into the position of director of the FAMS, making him the first director to have initially served as a federal air marshal. Despite that fact, Bray inherited a workforce that did not have a high morale. A workforce survey had found the morale of the federal air marshals very low, so measures were put in place to attempt to boost their morale, open up lines of communication between management and the air marshals, and allow them to have input into changes in the organization. Some of the initiatives included field office focus groups, visits to the field by the FAMS director, listening sessions, dinners with the director once a week for air marshals transiting through Washington, D.C., establishing a dedicated email to communicate issues to the director, and an anonymous Web site for feedback.[18] A follow up in July of 2009 found that air marshals were responding favorably to changes.[19]

On Christmas day of 2009, another individual attempted to detonate a bomb, this time hidden in his underwear, and the media dubbed him the "underwear bomber." The reaction from Congress was to increase the number of federal air marshals, and once again a mass hiring was conducted to increase the number of marshals.

One controversy that arose during the Obama Administration regarding the Federal Flight Deck Officers program had to do with the TSA and the FAMS covering the cost of training and equipment. The administration argued that the program was too expensive and wanted to cut the budget for the program, while those running the program argued that the participants are required to cover the majority of expenses related to the training. In fact, the executive vice president of the Federal Flight Deck Officers Association has estimated that the "average pilot who volunteers for their program may spend somewhere in the range of $10,000 of his own money attending training and other activities, such as biannual firearms requalification."[20] In fact, the most glaring dispute is over the costs of the FFDO versus a federal air marshal. It is estimated that the cost of a FFDO on a flight is about $15. The cost of a federal air marshal on any given flight is about $3,300.[21] It is highly likely that with the budget being a major issue in the 2012 election, the budget of the FAMS may come under scrutiny in the very near future.

In 2012 the Federal Air Marshals celebrated their 50th anniversary. Tracing their history directly to the creation of the Sky Marshals by the Kennedy Administration, the FAMS has been in existence for over 50 years.[22]

Who Gets Hired

In addition to hiring air marshals, the FAMS also hires people with superior analytical skills to serve as curriculum specialists, logistics management specialists, program analysts, information technology specialists, and medical records technicians. There are also administrative officers, support staff, security assistants, and secretaries who help with planning, development, and the monitoring of administrative functions.[23]

Newly hired agents are highly trained to perform their jobs and must pass an intense training program that is comprised of two parts. The first stage of training consists of a seven-week basic law enforcement course at the Federal Law Enforcement Training Center in Artesia, New Mexico. Air marshals then receive follow-up training at the William J. Hughes Technical Center in New Jersey. The training the new marshals receive is specific to their jobs. Their training includes the study of constitutional law, marksmanship, physical fitness, behavioral observation, defensive tactics, and emergency medical assistance.

Candidates who successfully complete the training will be assigned to one of 21 field offices where they will begin their careers. Throughout their careers, air marshals may be deployed on an hour's notice to high-risk locations.

Budgets

The 2010 annual budget for the Federal Air Marshals was $860 million dollars. The budget allocations have decreased since 2012, with a budget of $819 million in 2014. This is outlined in Table 11.1.

Organization

The Federal Air Marshals serve as the primary law enforcement agency within the TSA. They are housed in the TSA of the U.S. Department of Homeland Security. There are 21 field offices across the U.S. that provide a "home away from home" for agents. An organization chart is presented in Figure 11.3.

Leader

Robert Bray was named assistant administrator for law enforcement and director of the FAMS in June 2008. He also served as TSA's acting deputy administrator from April to June 2010.

Bray began his career with the FAMS on May 5, 2003 as the assistant special agent in charge of the Mission Operations Center at the FAA Technical Center in Atlantic City, New Jersey. In November 2003, he was appointed as the deputy assistant director for the Office of Training and Development and subsequently selected as the assistant director, Office of Security Services and Assessments in March 2006. During his 20-year career with the United States Secret Service, Bray was assigned to offices in Denver, Colorado; Palm Springs, California; Tulsa, Oklahoma; and Washington, D.C. He served as a supervisor on the Vice Presidential Protective Division, under Vice President Gore, and as a supervisor on the Presidential Protective Division under President Clinton and President Bush. Bray, as the special agent in charge of the Office of Administration, United

Table 11.1	Budget Authority for Federal Air Marshals (In Millions of Dollars)
FY 2010 enacted	$860
FY 2012 enacted	$966
FY 2013 enacted	$874
FY 2014 enacted	$819

Source: U.S. Department of Homeland Security, "Budget in Brief, Fiscal Year 2014," available at http://www.dhs.gov/sites/default/files/publications/MGMT/FY%20 2014%20BIB%20-%20FINAL%20-508%20Formatted%20%20%284%29.pdf; U.S. Department of Homeland Security, "Budget in Brief, Fiscal Year 2015," available at http://www.dhs.gov/sites/default/files/publications/FY15BIB.pdf.

Figure 11.3. Organizational Chart: Transportation Security Administration

Senior Leadership
Organization Chart

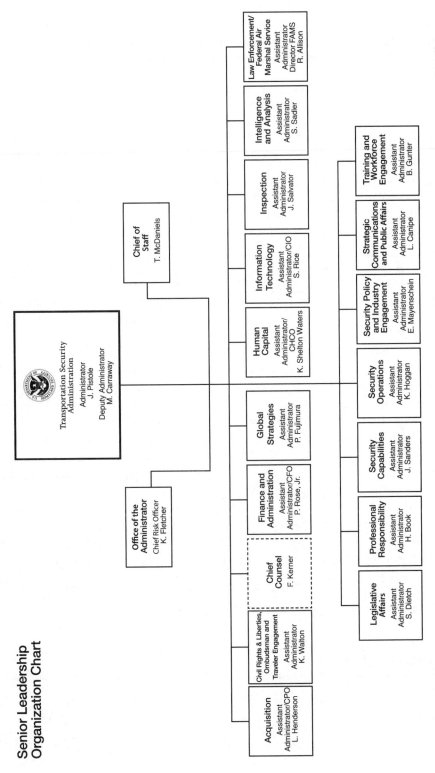

Source: Transportation Security Administration, "Organizational Chart," available at http://www.tsa.gov/sites/default/files/assets/pdf/tsa_orgchart.pdf.

States Secret Service, supervised the development and implementation of the annual budget for the Secret Service.

Bray began his law enforcement career as a police officer for the Metro Dade Police Department in Miami, Florida. Bray then worked as a police agent for the Lakewood, Colorado Police Department prior to his appointment to the United States Secret Service. He holds a bachelor of science degree in criminology from Florida State University.

What They Do

On the day that terrorists attacked four domestic flights in 2001, there were only 50 federal air marshals, and they were restricted by law to travelling on international flights. After the attacks, several thousand new air marshals were hired. Air marshals board airplanes every day for both domestic and international flights to protect the passengers on board airplanes and make travel safe for the public. They are armed federal law enforcement officers who are deployed on passenger flights worldwide. The air marshals are trained to recognize behaviors that may indicate criminal behavior. They are also trained in using handguns in case they would be needed. Marshals are trained to be experts in explosives response. Each field office has explosives-trained personnel as well as a nationally coordinated explosives team.[24]

The FAMS also gathers intelligence and evaluates that information concerning aviation threats to other agencies in the U.S. as well as internationally. They have an increasing role in homeland security and therefore work closely with other law enforcement agencies to accomplish their missions. They hold several positions at different organizations such as the National Counterterrorism Center and the National Targeting Center and they are part of the FBI's Joint Terrorism Task Forces.[25] Employees of the FAMS assist in protecting the nation's critical infrastructure, including transportation systems and other elements of the infrastructure that keep the economy strong.

The FAMS oversees the Law Enforcement Officers Flying Armed program that allows officers to take flights with weapons. In order for an officer to participate in the program, he must be a federal law enforcement officer or a full-time municipal, county, or state officer; be sworn and commissioned to enforce criminal statutes or immigration statutes; be authorized by his agency to have a weapon in connection with his duties; and have completed a training program. The weapon must be accessible to the officer during the flight.[26]

Conclusion

The Federal Air Marshals have evolved since they were first established in 1962. They now fly regularly on commercial air flights to protect the public from terrorist threats and other crimes. As a federal law enforcement agency, the Air Marshals play a key role in keeping America safe.

Key Terms

Sky Marshals

Task Force on Deterrence of Air Piracy

International Security and Development Cooperation Act

Aviation and Transportation Security Act

Transportation Security Administration

Thomas D. Quinn

Arming Pilots Against Terrorism Act

Robert S. Bray

Review Questions

1. What is the primary role of the Federal Air Marshals?

2. How did the terrorist attacks of 9/11 impact the Air Marshals?

3. What is the history of the Air Marshals?

4. What kind of skills must a person have to become a federal air marshal?

5. Provide an overview of the budgets for this agency.

6. How are the Federal Air Marshals organized?

Endnotes

1. Federal Air Marshal Service. (2012). *Federal Air Marshal Service Celebrates 50 Years!* Available online at http://blog.tsa.gov/2012/03/federal-air-marshal-service-celebrates.html.
2. Federal Air Marshal Service, *Federal Air Marshal Service Celebrates 50 Years!*
3. Grabell, Michael. (2008). "History of the Federal Air Marshal Service." *ProPublica.* Available online at http://www.propublica.org/article/history-of-the-federal-air-marshal-service.
4. Federal Air Marshal Service, *Federal Air Marshal Service Celebrates 50 Years!*
5. Grabell, Michael. (2008). "History of the Federal Air Marshal Service." *ProPublica.*Available online at http://www.propublica.org/article/history-of-the-federal-air-marshal-service
6. Federal Air Marshal Service, *Federal Air Marshal Service Celebrates 50 Years!*
7. Taillon, J. Paul de B. (2002). *Hijacking and Hostages: Government Response to Terrorism.* Westport, CT: Praeger Publishers.
8. Federal Air Marshal Service, *Federal Air Marshal Service Celebrates 50 Years!*
9. Taillon, *Hijacking and Hostages.*
10. Federal Air Marshal Service, *Federal Air Marshal Service Celebrates 50 Years!*
11. Federal Air Marshal Service, *Federal Air Marshal Service Celebrates 50 Years!*
12. Federal Air Marshal Service. (2012). *History.* Available online at www.tsa.gov/about-tsa/history.
13. U.S. Government Accountability Office. (2009). Aviation Security: Federal Air Marshal Service Has Taken Actions to Fulfill Its Core Mission and Address Workforce Issues, but Additional Actions Are Needed to Improve Workforce Survey. Washington, D.C.: U.S. Government Accountability Office.
14. Grabell, "History of the Federal Air Marshal Service."
15. Grabell, "History of the Federal Air Marshal Service."
16. Lord, Steve. (2009). Federal Air Marshal Service: Actions Taken to Fulfill Core Mission and Address Workforce Issues. Washington, D.C.: U.S. Government Accountability Office.
17. Grabell, "History of the Federal Air Marshal Service."
18. U.S. Government Accountability Office, Aviation Security.
19. Lord, Federal Air Marshal Service.
20. Zuckerman, Jessica. (2012). Federal Flight Deck Officer Program: First Line of Deterrence, Last Line of Defense. *The Heritage Foundation.* Available online at http://www.heritage.org/research/reports/2012/03/impact-of-cutting-the-budget-of-the-federal-flight-deck-officer-program.
21. Zuckerman, Federal Flight Deck Officer Program.
22. Federal Air Marshal Service, *Federal Air Marshal Service Celebrates 50 Years!*
23. Transportation Security Administration, "OLE/FAMS Positions," available at www.tsa.gov/careers/olefams-positions; Transportation Security Administration, "Law Enforcement & Federal Air Marshal Service Careers," available at www.tsa.gov/careers/law-enforcement-federal-air-marshal-service-careers.
24. Transportation Security Administration, "Our People," available at www.tsa.gov/stakeholders/our-people.
25. Transportation Security Administration "Federal Air Marshals," available at www.tsa.gov/about-tsa/federal-air-marshals.
26. Transportation Security Administration, "Law Enforcement Officers Flying Armed," available at www.tsa.gov/stakeholders/law-enforcement-officers-flying-armed.

12

Other Federal Law Enforcement Agencies

Introduction

There are many smaller federal law enforcement agencies, each with a different jurisdiction and role in deterring criminal acts. For example, the U.S. Mint Police protect the U.S. Treasury and Mint, its assets, employees, and property[1] while the Pentagon Force Protection Agency oversees the employees, visitors, and infrastructure of the Pentagon complex. The agencies vary in their age, size, and mission. This chapter highlights some of the more well-known smaller federal agencies.

Supreme Court Police

The Supreme Court Police was established in 1935 and tasked with providing protection for the Supreme Court building. The Court had previously resided in the U.S. Capitol building, and the original force of 33 officers was selected from the ranks of the U.S. Capitol Police.

The mission of the Supreme Court Police is to protect the Supreme Court by protecting the Supreme Court building, the justices, employees, guests, and visitors. They are responsible for protecting the chief justice, associate justices, building occupants, and the Court's historic building and grounds. Additional responsibilities include courtroom security, dignitary protection, emergency response, and providing assistance to Court guests.

The duties of the Supreme Court Police are found in 40 U.S.C. §6121, as shown in Figure 12.1.

Figure 12.1: Authority of Supreme Court Police

(a) Authority of Marshal of the Supreme Court and Supreme Court Police.—In accordance with regulations prescribed by the Marshal of the Supreme Court and approved by the Chief Justice of the United States, the Marshal and the Supreme Court Police shall have authority—

(1) to police the Supreme Court Building and grounds and adjacent streets to protect individuals and property;

(2) in any State, to protect—

(A) the Chief Justice, any Associate Justice of the Supreme Court, and any official guest of the Supreme Court; and

(B) any officer or employee of the Supreme Court while that officer or employee is performing official duties;

(3) while performing duties necessary to carry out paragraph (1) or (2), to make arrests for any violation of federal or state law and any regulation under federal or state law; and

(4) to carry firearms as may be required while performing duties under section 6102 of this title, this subchapter, and subchapter IV.

(b) Additional Requirements Related to Subsection (a)(2).—

(1) Authorization to carry firearms.—Duties under subsection (a)(2)(A) with respect to an official guest of the Supreme Court in any State (other than the District of Columbia, Maryland, and Virginia) shall be authorized in writing by the Chief Justice or an Associate Justice, if those duties require the carrying of firearms under subsection (a)(4).

(2) Termination of authority.—The authority provided under subsection (a)(2) expires on December 29, 2019.

Headquartered in Washington, D.C., the Supreme Court Police are comprised of Uniformed Services, Protective Services, a Threat Assessment Unit, a Background Investigation Unit, an Honor Guard, a Key Response Squad, a HazMat/Bomb Response Team, and a Canine Unit. Future Supreme Court officers are provided with training at the Federal Law Enforcement Training Center in Glynco, Georgia.

The Supreme Court of the United States has within its organizational structure a marshal of the United States Supreme Court.[2] This individual, similar to a bailiff for the court, is also in charge of overseeing the Supreme Court Police. In 1935, a security force, consisting of 33 officers from the U.S. Capitol Police, was created to protect the Supreme Court building. In 1949, a police force was created that was given statutory authority to patrol the Supreme Court and surrounding buildings. In 1982, Chief Justice Warren E. Burger made the request to expand the powers of the Supreme Court Police, allowing for them to have greater authority, beyond the confines of the buildings. The Supreme Court Police were given the additional responsibilities of courtroom security, dignitary protection, and providing protection to the United States Supreme Court justice, as deemed necessary.

U.S. Capitol Police

The mission of the U.S. Capitol Police (USCP) is to protect the U.S. Congress and its visitors,[3] as well as members of Congress, officers of Congress, and their families.[4] They have jurisdiction within a 47-square-block radius around the U.S. Capitol, as well as federal police authority throughout the United States and its territories. These agents have the power to protect life and property by preventing, detecting, and investigating criminal acts. They also have the power to enforce traffic regulations throughout the complex of congressional buildings, parks, and thoroughfares. Their statutory authority is found in 13.2 U.S.C. §1961, shown in Figure 12.2.

Figure 12.2: 13.2 U.S.C. §1961 — Policing of Capitol Buildings and Grounds

(a) The Capitol Police shall police the United States Capitol Buildings and Grounds under the direction of the Capitol Police Board, consisting of the Sergeant at Arms of the United States Senate, the Sergeant at Arms of the House of Representatives, and the Architect of the Capitol, and shall have the power to enforce the provisions of this section, sections 1922, 1966, 1967, and 1969 of this title (and regulations promulgated under section 1969 of this title), and chapter 51 of title 40, and to make arrests within the United States Capitol Buildings and Grounds for any violations of any law of the United States, of the District of Columbia, or of any State, or any regulation promulgated pursuant thereto: Provided, That for the fiscal year for which appropriations are made by this Act the Capitol Police shall have the additional authority to make arrests within the District of Columbia for crimes of violence, as defined in section 16 of title 18, committed within the Capitol Buildings and Grounds and shall have the additional authority to make arrests, without a warrant, for crimes of violence, as defined in section 16 of title 18, committed in the presence of any member of the Capitol Police performing official duties: Provided further, That the Metropolitan Police force of the District of Columbia are authorized to make arrests within the United States Capitol Buildings and Grounds for any violation of any such laws or regulations, but such authority shall not be construed as authorizing the Metropolitan Police force, except with the consent or upon the request of the Capitol Police Board, to enter such buildings to make arrests in response to complaints or to serve warrants or to patrol the United States Capitol Buildings and Grounds. For the purpose of this section, the word "grounds" shall include the House Office Buildings parking areas and that part or parts of property which have been or hereafter are acquired in the District of Columbia by the Architect of the Capitol, or by an officer of the Senate or the House, by lease, purchase, intergovernment transfer, or otherwise, for the use of the Senate, the House, or the Architect of the Capitol.

(b) For purposes of this section, "the United States Capitol Buildings and Grounds" shall include any building or facility acquired by the Sergeant at Arms of the Senate for the use of the Senate for which the Sergeant at Arms of the Senate has entered into an agreement with the United States Capitol Police for the policing of the building or facility.

(c) For purposes of this section, "the United States Capitol Buildings and Grounds" shall include any building or facility acquired by the Chief Administrative Officer of the House of Representatives for the use of the House of Representatives for which the Chief Administrative Officer has entered into an agreement with the United States Capitol Police for the policing of the building or facility.

(d) For purposes of this section, "United States Capitol Buildings and Grounds" shall include the Library of Congress buildings and grounds described under section 167j of this title, except that in a case of buildings or grounds not located in the District of Columbia, the authority granted to the Metropolitan Police Force of the District of Columbia shall be granted to any police force within whose jurisdiction the buildings or grounds are located.

The origins of the USCP date back to 1800 when Congress moved from Philadelphia to Washington, D.C., and a lone watchman, John Golding, was paid $371.75 per year to protect the Capitol Building.[5] The USCP traditionally commemorates May 2, 1828 as the founding of the force. On that date, Congress passed an act which expanded the police regulations of the City of Washington to include the Capitol and Capitol Square. With the passage of this act, Congress brought the responsibility of policing the Capitol under the direction of the presiding officers of the House and Senate and empowered the Capitol watchmen with full law enforcement authority. This act sparked the evolution of the USCP from a watch force to a recognized police department. The new force consisted of a captain and three men who worked 15-hour shifts when Congress was in session and 10-hour shifts at all other times and were not required to wear uniforms. Their area of authority was limited to the Capitol building and the neighboring walks and streets. By 1854, the police were wearing uniforms and were armed with heavy hickory canes, but it was not until 1861 that USCP officers were authorized to wear badges.

In 1867, responsibility for the USCP was transferred from the commissioner of the Public Buildings Service to the sergeant at arms of the Senate and House of Representatives. In 1873, the Capitol Police Board was established, and the architect of the Capitol was added to the board.

By 1935, the Capitol grounds had been expanded to 126 acres and the head of the force requested additional men to augment the 132-man force. At this time, the force consisted of men ranging in age from 19 to 75 years old. The captain of the USCP asked for the adoption of the same standards held by the Metropolitan Washington Police Department, and Congress agreed to allow the USCP Board to establish specific qualifications.

As a result of a 1954 incident, when terrorists fired shots from the House of Representatives gallery, security was tightened and visitors were first required to check all packages before entering the galleries. After a bombing in the Senate wing in 1971, several new security measures were put into place. In addition, a hazardous devices unit and K-9 explosives detection team were established to respond to threats. In September 1974, the first female USCP officers were hired.

In 1981, the jurisdiction of the USCP was expanded from the Capitol building and grounds to the entire nation. Statutory authority was received to protect members and officers of Congress when those members and their families traveled away from Capitol Hill. Since that time, the department has continued to expand through recruiting and hiring and the development of many other specialty units.

In 2003, as part of a larger federal law enforcement reorganization, Congress decided to abolish a police force that had existed since at least the early 1970s—the Library of Congress Police—and absorb it into the USCP. On February 20, 2003, the Library of Congress Police began their transfer of authority to the USCP, and on September 30, 2009, the merger was completed. Effective October 1, 2009, the Library of Congress Police ceased operations.

Candidates for positions at the USCP must be at least 21 years old but less than 37 at the time of appointment. They must be a high school graduate or possess a GED certificate. They must be a U.S. citizen, possess a valid United States' driver's license, be in excellent physical health, and their weight must be proportionate to their height. The candidate's vision must be no worse than 20/100 uncorrected, correctable to 20/20 in each eye. The candidate must have no record of felony convictions and must not be involved in pending criminal litigation.[6]

New officer candidates are given one week of orientation training at the USCP training facility in the Washington, D.C. area. When that is completed, new agents receive 12 weeks of intensive law enforcement training at the Federal Law Enforcement Training Center (FLETC) in Glynco, Georgia or Artesia, New Mexico. The new officers receive training in areas including police procedures, psychology, criminal law, laws of interest, search and seizure, physical defense techniques, and physical fitness. After graduation from FLETC, candidates attend the Capitol Police Training Academy for 13 weeks of additional training specific to the USCP functions. When this is completed, new officers are assigned to a field training officer for on-the-job training.[7]

There are many different units that comprise the USCP. One of those units is the Office of Inspector General. These agents supervise any audits, inspections, and investigations that involve USCP programs. The Office is also responsible for maintaining efficiency in their programs and for preventing fraud, waste, and abuse in USCP programs.[8] They report directly to the USCP Board.

The chief of police for the USCP is Kim C. Dine, an officer who had 37 years of experience in law enforcement before joining the USCP force. Before taking the helm at the Capitol Police, Dine served as the chief of the Frederick Police Department in Maryland for ten years. Dine's career began in the Washington, D.C. Metropolitan Police Department, where he held a variety of positions in his 27 years on the force. These included the commander of the First District and the assistant police chief. As assistant police chief, Dine was responsible for internal affairs, disciplinary reviews, and related internal matters. He was also the assistant chief for the Office of Professional Responsibility.

The USCP agents who work in the Office of Professional Responsibility (OPR) help to oversee any investigations that have to do with personnel within the agency to ensure the integrity of the agency. The OPR investigates allegations of misconduct by USCP employees.[9] The Ceremonial Unit provides law enforcement services for ceremonial events such as funerals in the U.S. Capitol or congressional functions. This group of officers is sometimes called the "honor guard experts of law enforcement." The Ceremonial Unit also receives visiting heads of state and world leaders and also participates in drills and competitions.

The Patrol/Mobile Response Division of the USCP provides law enforcement services on the grounds of the Capitol and other areas by use of motorized, bicycle, and foot patrols, as well as with canines. They can be used for prisoner processing and transportation, drug and alcohol enforcement, crime scene search, and by the Containment and Emergency Response Team (CERT).

The Canine (K-9) Section of the USCP is primarily responsible for detecting explosives. The officers in the K-9 section are specially trained (handlers) who work with a specific canine (or "bomb dog") who is trained to detect explosives. In 2011, the Department had 50 canine teams that were trained to detect explosives. These canines help officers conduct explosive detection sweeps of buildings and vehicles and areas where the public may assemble. Other K-9 teams (the Street Service Teams and the Urban Search and Rescue (USAR) Teams) have been trained to locate victims who are trapped in the rubble of a collapsed building.

Six crime-scene search officers make up the Crime Scene Search Unit of the USCP. Each officer has been trained to investigate and process a crime scene and identify, preserve, and conduct tests on physical evidence. Other officers are part of the CERT and provide specialized law enforcement services for special events that require heightened measures, such as those that involve visiting heads of state or other dignitaries. Related to this is the Dignitary Protection Division that provides protective coverage for official congressional events.

Some agents in the USCP are recognized by their jurisdiction. For example, the House Division provides police services within the geographic boundaries of the House office buildings. This is the largest division. Similarly, the Senate Division provides police services for the Senate office buildings. Finally, the Capitol Division provides law enforcement services to the Capitol building and Capitol Square. Finally, there is a unit that provides protection for the Library of Congress.

Amtrak Police

The Amtrak Police is a national police force that protects the passengers, employers, and patrons of Amtrak. They patrol the stations and trains every day. They work closely with the Transportation Security Administration and other federal, state, and local law enforcement and counterterrorism agencies across the country. They also collaborate with agencies worldwide. Figure 12.3 shows the statutory authorization and responsibilities of the Amtrak Police as stated in 49 U.S.C. §24305.

Figure 12.3: General Authority of Amtrak Police

(a) Acquisition and Operation of Equipment and Facilities.—

(1) Amtrak may acquire, operate, maintain, and make contracts for the operation and maintenance of equipment and facilities necessary for intercity and commuter rail passenger transportation, the transportation of mail and express, and auto-ferry transportation.

(2) Amtrak shall operate and control directly, to the extent practicable, all aspects of the rail passenger transportation it provides.

(3)

(A) Except as provided in subsection (d)(2), Amtrak may enter into a contract with a motor carrier of passengers for the intercity transportation of passengers by motor carrier over regular routes only—

(i) if the motor carrier is not a public recipient of governmental assistance, as such term is defined in section 13902 (b)(8)(A) of this title, other than a recipient of funds under section 5311 of this title;

(ii) for passengers who have had prior movement by rail or will have subsequent movement by rail; and

(iii) if the buses, when used in the provision of such transportation, are used exclusively for the transportation of passengers described in clause (ii).

(B) Subparagraph (A) shall not apply to transportation funded predominantly by a State or local government, or to ticket selling agreements.

(b) Maintenance and Rehabilitation.—Amtrak may maintain and rehabilitate rail passenger equipment and shall maintain a regional maintenance plan that includes—

(1) a review panel at the principal office of Amtrak consisting of members the President of Amtrak designates;

(2) a systemwide inventory of spare equipment parts in each operational region;

(3) enough maintenance employees for cars and locomotives in each region;

(4) a systematic preventive maintenance program;

(5) periodic evaluations of maintenance costs, time lags, and parts shortages and corrective actions; and

(6) other elements or activities Amtrak considers appropriate.

(c) Miscellaneous Authority.—Amtrak may—

(1) make and carry out appropriate agreements;

(2) transport mail and express and shall use all feasible methods to obtain the bulk mail business of the United States Postal Service;

(3) improve its reservation system and advertising;

(4) provide food and beverage services on its trains only if revenues from the services each year at least equal the cost of providing the services;

(5) conduct research, development, and demonstration programs related to the mission of Amtrak; and

(6) buy or lease rail rolling stock and develop and demonstrate improved rolling stock.

(d) Through Routes and Joint Fares.—

(1) Establishing through routes and joint fares between Amtrak and other intercity rail passenger carriers and motor carriers of passengers is consistent with the public interest and the transportation policy of the United States. Congress encourages establishing those routes and fares.

(2) Amtrak may establish through routes and joint fares with any domestic or international motor carrier, air carrier, or water carrier.

(3) Congress encourages Amtrak and motor common carriers of passengers to use the authority conferred in sections 11322 and 14302 of this title for the purpose of providing improved service to the public and economy of operation.

(e) Rail Police.—Amtrak may employ rail police to provide security for rail passengers and property of Amtrak. Rail police employed by Amtrak who have complied with a State law establishing requirements applicable to rail police or individuals employed in a similar position may be employed without regard to the law of another State containing those requirements.

(f) Domestic Buying Preferences.—

(1) In this subsection, "United States" means the States, territories, and possessions of the United States and the District of Columbia.

(2) Amtrak shall buy only—

(A) unmanufactured articles, material, and supplies mined or produced in the United States; or

(B) manufactured articles, material, and supplies manufactured in the United States substantially from articles, material, and supplies mined, produced, or manufactured in the United States.

(3) Paragraph (2) of this subsection applies only when the cost of those articles, material, or supplies bought is at least $1,000,000.

(4) On application of Amtrak, the Secretary of Transportation may exempt Amtrak from this subsection if the Secretary decides that—

(A) for particular articles, material, or supplies—

(i) the requirements of paragraph (2) of this subsection are inconsistent with the public interest;

(ii) the cost of imposing those requirements is unreasonable; or

(iii) the articles, material, or supplies, or the articles, material, or supplies from which they are manufactured, are not mined, produced, or manufactured in the United States in sufficient and reasonably available commercial quantities and are not of a satisfactory quality; or

(B) rolling stock or power train equipment cannot be bought and delivered in the United States within a reasonable time.

The mission of the Amtrak Police is to protect America's railroad.[10] They are the front line in protecting the trains, the employees, and passengers against all hazards. They have created partnerships with other law enforcement agencies as a way to extend their protection beyond the stations and the trains to the surrounding areas.[11]

To be hired as an officer with Amtrak Police, an applicant must be 21 years of age, a U.S. citizen (or have the right to work in the U.S.), have earned a high school diploma or GED, have completed a basic training program at a state-authorized police training academy or have experience as a police officer, and preferably have an associate's degree or 60 hours/credits from an accredited college or university. A candidate must possess a valid driver's license and be able to obtain a police commission. They must be able to pass a medical examination, psychological exam, and a background investigation.[12]

For those who seek to be a communications officer, they must be at least 18 years old, be a U.S. citizen, have a high school diploma, have an accurate typing speed of 35 words per minute, and be able to pass a medical examination, psychological exam, and background investigation.[13] For those who seek to be a security officer, a candidate must be at least 18 years old, a U.S. citizen, have a high school diploma or GED, be eligible for a driver's license or possess a valid driver's license, and be able to pass a medical examination, psychological exam, and background investigation.[14]

There are three divisions within the Amtrak Police. The first is the Patrol Division, which makes up the majority of the force. Amtrak patrol officers are the backbone of the department and are largely responsible for protecting Amtrak facilities, passengers, and employees. They also help people who need assistance. They must also work closely with local, state, and federal agencies to provide a safe environment.[15]

The second division is the Special Operations Division, which is comprised of Intelligence, K-9, Station Action Team (SAT) coordinators, and the Special Operations Unit. The Intelligence Unit gathers information on offenses and trends and shares that information with federal, state, and local enforcement agencies in their attempts to detect threats and defend against them.[16]

The K-9 units are deployed in stations to provide both a psychological and physical deterrent to potential criminal activities. The dogs are trained in explosives detection. The Amtrak Police currently has the most K-9 units in the railroad industry.[17] The SAT coordinators oversee communications, physical security, cyber-security, continuity of operations, and emergency response plans to defend against either an attack or a natural disaster.[18] The Special Operations Unit conducts screening and sweeps, surveillance, and other counter-terror activities that deter and defend against attack, and they respond if attack occurs. Some officers are visible and wear tactical equipment and carry guns and conduct security sweeps aboard trains. Others are undercover and rarely recognized.[19] Finally, the Corporate Security Division of Amtrak identifies and implements counterterrorism strategies in the form of policies, programs, and standards to ensure the protection of Amtrak's employees, passengers, assets, and critical infrastructure.[20]

Currently, the vice president and chief of police for the Amtrak Police is Polly Hanson. She began her career in law enforcement in the United States Park Police, serving as a dispatcher. In 1981, Hanson joined the Washington Metropolitan Area Transit Authority Police Department where she worked for 27 years. During that time, she served as the chief of police from 2002-2007 and also as the assistant general manager for Safety, Security, and Emergency Management. Upon leaving this agency, Hanson began employment at the Metropolitan Police Department (MPDC) as executive director, Strategic Services Bureau. Here, her responsibilities included development of policies and procedures, tactical crime analysis, strategic planning, performance management, and government relations. Not long after, she moved to serve as the director of the Office of Law Enforcement and Security at the U.S Department of Interior. She was commissioned as a federal special agent to provide policy guidance and oversight of law enforcement, security, and intelligence programs. It was after this that she joined the Amtrak Police as the chief.[21]

National Oceanic and Atmospheric Administration Office for Law Enforcement

The National Oceanic and Atmospheric Administration Office for Law Enforcement (NOAAOLE) enforces federal laws that are intended to conserve and protect the nation's living marine resources and their natural habitats so that they will be available for people to enjoy them for recreation, such as recreational fishing, or for business, such as commercial fishing.[22] They also make sure the environment is protected to ensure the quality of seafood for those who consume it. The officers ensure that the resources will be viable for many future generations by protecting the fish stocks from depletion and the marine mammals from extinction.[23] Agents in the NOAA watch over Marine Protected Areas (MPAs), including national marine sanctuaries, fishery management zones, national seashores, national parks, national monuments, critical habitats, and national wildlife refuges, among others.

The NOAAOLE's mission statement is as follows:

"We are dedicated to excellent service through partnerships that build trust, protect resources, create a safe environment, reduce crime, and enhance the overall quality of life for all Americans. We adhere to the highest moral and ethical standards. We are honest and sincere in dealing with each other and the public. We have the courage to uphold these principles and are proud that they guide us in all we do. We recognize the value of our unique cultural diversity in America and treat all people with kindness, tolerance and dignity. We cherish and protect the rights, liberties and freedoms of all as granted under the Constitution and by the laws of the U.S. We are consistent in our treatment of all persons. Objective, impartial decisions and policies are the foundation of our interactions. Our actions are tempered with reason and equality."[24]

The NOAAOLE has developed enforcement agreements with 27 coastal states and also works with other federal agencies to enforce laws, including the U.S.

Coast Guard, the Bureau of Immigration and Customs Enforcement, the Bureau of Customs and Border Protection, the U.S. Fish and Wildlife Service, the FBI, the DEA, the Department of Justice, the EPA, and the FDA. They also have international partners as the Office for Law Enforcement (OLE) enforces international laws, treaties, and agreements. All instances of violations are referred to NOAA's Office of General Counsel, the Department of Justice, or the U.S. Attorneys' Office for their review and possible prosecution.[25]

In addition to enforcing laws, the OLE works to teach the American public about the need to protect and conserve ocean resources. Special agents from the OLE, along with enforcement officers and support personnel, make presentations to schools and other civic groups to help in this regard.[26] They also take part in symposiums, conferences, and trade shows that allow officers to interact with the general public, answer any questions they may have, and educate the public about the laws and regulations that the OLE enforces.[27]

The NOAAOLE has primary geographic jurisdiction over the waters within the U.S. Exclusive Economic Zone, which includes ocean waters between 3 and 200 miles off shore and adjacent to all U.S. states and territories. They also have jurisdiction over protected marine species and national marine sanctuaries.[28]

The OLE enforcement officers provide the uniformed patrol/inspection for NOAA. They have many key activities, such as monitoring vessel offloads, inspecting plants and records, and actively patrolling to deter and detect violations. Criminal investigators look into both civil and criminal violations; perform undercover work as needed, and collect evidence that builds cases against those who commit crimes. Often, the OLE relies on community oriented policing and problem solving and other partnerships to promote compliance.[29]

Those who are hired to work in the OLE must meet strict qualifications and physical standards. All candidates must complete basic law enforcement training followed by agency specific basic training, advanced training, and on-the-job training. OLE special agents must complete FLETC's Criminal Investigator Training Program (CITP). OLE enforcement officers are required to complete FLETC's Land Management Police Training Program. Both agents and officers often attend specialized courses and are required to attend refresher training and perform recurring qualifications to maintain proficiency in performing law enforcement-related functions.[30]

The NOAAOLE provides a basic training program for its agents and officers. Special emphasis is placed upon laws and regulations enforced as well as agency specific policies and procedures.[31] The primary source of basic training for criminal investigators in the federal government is the 12-week Criminal Investigator Training Program. The program includes basic law enforcement concepts and teaches prospective agents the specific knowledge and skills necessary so they are able to perform the job.[32]

For those federal agents who have been hired to perform law-enforcement duties related to natural resources and land management in rural or isolated areas, the government offers a Land Management Training Program.[33] The Marine Law Enforcement Training Program provides basic marine law enforcement training for NOAA employees that focus on marine law enforcement. The focus of this training program is on the safe and proper operation of patrol vessels and the implementation of law enforcement operations in the maritime environment.[34]

NOAAOLE special agents and enforcement officers enforce laws related to protecting and conserving our nation's living marine resources. Agents and enforcement officers conduct criminal and civil investigations, board vessels fishing at sea, inspect fish processing plants, review sales of wildlife products on the Internet and conduct patrols on land, in the air, and at sea. They rely on their seamanship skills, emerging technologies, and close partnerships with various local, state, tribal, federal, and international law enforcement partners to protect over 3.36 million square miles of water and enforce international treaties on the high seas.[35]

The NOAA has a component of community oriented policing as part of their agency. There are six components of this tactic, the first of which is community outreach, which teams the OLE with stakeholders in partnerships that seek to identify, define, and solve enforcement problems. The "Fix-It Notice" Program provides first-time offenders with the opportunity to "fix" minor technical violations within a short time frame without threat of a penalty. The ProACTION plan is a way to use education as a way to promote a deeper understanding of the mission of the NOAA.

The fourth component of the Community Policing Program is the Fisheries Enforcement Hotline. This provides a live operator 24-hours a day, 7 days a week, for those who would like to report a federal fisheries violation. The program of the NOAA entitled Recognition and Rewards provides recognition for those marine resource stakeholders who have given special contributions towards conserving the nation's marine resources. Finally, the Community Relations Team (CRT) develops and coordinates the OLE's community relations functions and programs.[36]

The NOAAOLE is housed within the Department of Commerce's National Oceanic and Atmospheric Administration National Marine Fisheries Service (NOAA Fisheries). The OLE is the lead agency responsible for the ecosystem protection and conservation of most of the U.S. living marine resources. NOAA is divided by program of interest, which includes highly migratory species, protected resources, training, computer support, fiscal management, and vessel monitoring systems. One component of the OLE is a CRT that consists of a National Media and Constituent Affairs Office.[37] The 2015 presidential budget request for the NOAA is $5.5 billion. This is an increase of $174 million over the 2014 enacted budget.[38]

The NOAAOLE has jurisdiction over 3 million square miles of ocean and over 85,000 miles of coastline. They also oversee the country's 13 National Marine Sanctuaries and its Marine National Monuments. They enforce U.S. treaties and international law related to the high seas and international trade.[39]

The OLE has responsibility for enforcing more than 35 federal statutes, one of which is the Magnuson-Stevens Fishery Conservation and Management Act. This law created regulations concerning domestic commercial and recreational fishing. It is estimated that about half of the agency's enforcement actions are carried out as a way to ensure compliance with this act.

Two other important laws that must be enforced by the OLE are the Marine Mammal Protection Act of 1972 and the Endangered Species Act of 1973. These laws were passed by Congress to ensure the protection of all marine mammals and endangered species, including salmon, sea turtles, and whales.

The Lacey Act Amendments of 1981 are the third key set of laws that determine the activities of the OLE. These amendments deal with the harvest, processing, and trafficking of marine resources, both domestically and internationally. Specifically, they prohibit violations of the laws of other countries, including the introduction of products resulting from those violations into the U.S. Finally, the National Marine Sanctuaries Act provides for the conservation and management of National Marine Sanctuaries.[40] The OLE enforces many other laws, including the Agricultural Marketing Act of 1946, American Fisheries Act of 1998, Certificate of Legal Origin for Anadromous Fish Products, Antarctic Conservation Act of 1948; Antarctic Marine Living Resources Convention Act of 1984, Antarctic Protection Act of 1990, Atlantic Coastal Fisheries Cooperative Management Act, and the Atlantic Tunas Convention Act of 1975.[41]

The NOAA agents use four primary methods to enforce these laws. They use traditional approaches to law enforcement, including investigations and patrols; they create partnerships with state and federal agencies; they use technological tools, such as vessel monitoring systems; and they use different methods of outreach and education strategies that are designed to enhance voluntary compliance of the laws mentioned above.[42]

Bureau of Indian Affairs Police

The Bureau of Indian Affairs (BIA) Police is the law enforcement arm of the Bureau of Indian Affairs. Officers who are assigned to the BIA enforce laws on Indian reservations throughout the U.S. They provide police services to Indian tribes and reservations that do not have their own police force. They also oversee other tribal police organizations. In some cases, BIA police officers may also be required to enforce local, state, and federal laws as needed. Officers conduct patrol operations, undercover operations, serve on task forces, investigate allegations of crime, make arrests, and testify in court as needed.

The BIA police will receive ongoing training for their specific duties, as defined by 25 U.S.C. §2451, shown in Figure 12.4.

Figure 12.4: Bureau of Indian Affairs Law Enforcement and Judicial Training

> **(a) Training programs**
> **(1) In general**
> The Secretary of the Interior, in coordination with the Attorney General, the Administrator of the Drug Enforcement Administration, and the Director of the Federal Bureau of Investigation, shall ensure, through the establishment of a new training program or by supplementing existing training programs, that

all Bureau of Indian Affairs and tribal law enforcement and judicial personnel have access to training regarding—
        (A) the investigation and prosecution of offenses relating to illegal narcotics; and
        (B) alcohol and substance abuse prevention and treatment.
(2) Youth-related training
    Any training provided to Bureau of Indian Affairs or tribal law enforcement or judicial personnel under paragraph (1) shall include training in issues relating to youth alcohol and substance abuse prevention and treatment.
(b) Authorization
    For the purposes of providing the training required by subsection (a) of this section, there are authorized to be appropriated $2,000,000 for fiscal year 1993 and such sums as are necessary for each of fiscal years 2011 through 2015.

BIA police agents are trained in a 16-week program at the Indian Police Academy in Artesia, New Mexico, the national law enforcement training academy for federal and tribal law enforcement programs in Indian country. This training includes courses in criminal law, use of force, rules of evidence, surveillance, criminal investigation, arrest procedures, search warrant procedures, detention and arrest, use of force, police management, crime scene processing, use of firearms, vehicle operations, courtroom demeanor, child abuse investigation, community policing, and Indian country law. There is also training in photography, crime scene investigation, foot and vehicle patrol, conducting raids, interviewing suspects and witnesses, searching for evidence, and collecting evidence. Once officers complete this training, there is typically a period of field experience where new officers receive training with those who are more experienced. Those hired to be special agents in the BIA receive additional training in a 10-week program at the Federal Law Enforcement Training Center (FLETC).[43]

The Division of Operations is comprised of six regional districts that incorporate 208 Bureau and tribal law enforcement programs. Within those 208 programs, 43 are operated by the BIA. The Operations Division consists of telecommunications, uniformed police, and criminal investigations. The headquarters for the district is in Albuquerque, New Mexico, and the district offices are found in Aberdeen, South Dakota (district I); Muskogee, Oklahoma (district II); Phoenix, Arizona (district III); Albuquerque, New Mexico (district IV); Billings, Montana (district V); and Nashville, Tennessee (district IV). The Operations Division provides oversight of Bureau programs, while at the same time also providing technical assistance.[44]

BIA officers respond to calls about possible violations of federal, state, local, and tribal laws. They carry out typical law enforcement duties such as patrol, traffic control, and crowd control. They have the authority to investigate suspicious situations and possible criminal activity such as homicide, rape, sexual assault, or assault. They investigate possible violations of drug laws (i.e., possession, use, distribution, trafficking, or manufacturing of controlled substances). They serve warrants and subpoenas and testify at hearings. Moreover, BIA agents have the authority to apprehend, arrest, and detain those people who are charged with criminal offenses. To do this, agents sometimes perform surveillance or undercover operations, collect evidence, interview witnesses, and appear in front of grand juries and trials. When needed, some special agents may be assigned to work in special task forces.

U.S. Fish and Wildlife Service Office of Law Enforcement

The mission of the U.S. Fish and Wildlife Service Office of Law Enforcement is to enforce federal laws meant to protect wildlife and their habitats. Agents seek to protect endangered species, migratory birds, fisheries, and, at the same time, combat invasive species and promote global wildlife conservation.[45] They attempt to eliminate the threats to wildlife, including illegal trade, commercial exploitation, the destruction of animal habitat, and other potential environmental hazards. The officers work to educate the public as to the need to comply with laws to protect wildlife. They sometime work with federal, state, local, and tribal officials as well as international officials as they carry out their duties.

Federal wildlife law enforcement celebrated its centennial in 2000 with the 100th anniversary of the Lacey Act, the nation's first federal wildlife protection law.[46] That act's prohibitions on the importation of injurious wildlife and interstate commerce in illegally taken game species were followed by a series of measures aimed specifically at protecting migratory birds. With these laws and treaties came the age of the "duck cop." Policing waterfowl hunters and protecting waterfowl populations from commercial exploitation would long be a major focus for federal wildlife law enforcement.

During the middle decades of the century, however, increasing human pressures on populations and habitats of many different animals, from whooping cranes to American alligators, began to take their toll. Special protections for bald eagles (1940) and then golden eagles (1962) were put in place. The 1960s saw the first steps to protect a broader range of endangered species —steps that would culminate in the comprehensive 1973 Endangered Species Act and negotiation of the Convention on International Trade in Endangered Species of Wild Fauna and Flora (CITES). Laws to protect specific types of wildlife, from marine mammals and African elephants to wild birds and tigers, targeted special conservation concerns.

With these developments came new roles and responsibilities for Service law enforcement. From 1918 until the early 1970s, the word "game" consistently appeared in the job titles used for federal wildlife law enforcement officers. In 1973, however, the Service began calling its investigators "special agents," a name better suited to the expanding challenges of the job. In 1975, the Wildlife Service hired a biological technician to inspect wildlife shipments in New York, marking the beginning of a trade inspection force that would expand the following year to cover eight ports of entry. The opening of the world's first wildlife forensics laboratory in 1988 made science and technology an integral part of the Service's enforcement team.

The Wildlife Service today focuses on combating international wildlife trafficking, unlawful commercial exploitation of native species, environmental contamination, and habitat destruction. Partnerships with states, tribes, and foreign countries make Service special agents, wildlife inspectors, and forensic scientists part of a national and global network committed to protecting wildlife resources.

There are about 250 special agents in the Wildlife Service. These men and women are criminal investigators who are responsible for enforcing federal laws. To do this, they conduct investigations through surveillance and undercover work and arrest those suspected of committing offenses. Some agents are assigned to border ports to enforce laws concerning trade of domestic and foreign wildlife species.

The Wildlife Service also employs wildlife inspectors. These officers focus on the illegal wildlife trade and work to ensure that wildlife shipments comply with both U.S. and international wildlife protection laws. Inspectors work out of major international airports, ocean ports, and border crossings. They attempt to halt any illegal shipments of illegal wildlife or related products by making sure that shipments have required permits and licenses. They ensure that any living wildlife are treated humanely.[47]

To become a special agent, candidates must meet medical, physical, and psychological requirements. They must pass a drug test, psychological test, and background test. Candidates must hold a four-year degree in wildlife management, criminal justice, or related field. Successful candidates must be a U.S. citizen, be at least 21 years old but less than 37 at the time of appointment, and must be in excellent physical condition.[48]

Agents working in the Clark R. Bavin National Fish and Wildlife Forensics Laboratory conduct scientific analyses to support investigations of possible crimes against wildlife. The Wildlife Service also maintains a National Wildlife Property Repository, which supplies abandoned and forfeited wildlife items to schools, universities, museums, and other nongovernmental organizations to be used for public education. They also operate the National Eagle Repository, which seeks to address the needs of Native Americans for eagles and eagle feathers necessary for religious purposes.[49]

The Wildlife Service staffs about 261 special agents and 122 wildlife inspectors. They report through seven regional offices. The headquarters provide oversight, support, policy, and guidance for investigations and the wildlife inspection program.

One primary focus of the Wildlife Service is to combat global wildlife trafficking of animal species. The U.S. is one of the world's largest markets for wildlife and products. The Wildlife Service works to identify and close any illegal markets for animals that are prohibited under the Convention on International Trade and Endangered Species. It is necessary for agents to inspect shipments as a way to discover illegal trade in wildlife and to attempt to break up international and domestic smuggling rings that target wildlife. They are also trained to use forensic techniques as a way to analyze evidence to solve wildlife crimes. Agents sometimes distribute information about illegal trading in wildlife as a way increase the public's understanding of wildlife conservation and to promote compliance with wildlife protection laws.[50]

The Wildlife Service also helps protect wildlife resources and habitat by preventing the importation of injurious species.[51] At the same time, agents seek to facilitate legal wildlife trade. They understand the need to allow legitimate businesses and individuals to import and export wildlife that is permitted by law. That includes any wildlife that is declared to the Service by the business and then cleared by inspectors. Officers provide guidance to those who trade in wildlife to ensure they follow the laws.[52]

Pentagon Force Protection Agency

The Pentagon Force Protection Agency (PFPA) is a civilian defense agency found within the Department of Defense that is given the authority to protect the employees, visitors, and infrastructure of the Pentagon, Navy Annex, and other Pentagon facilities, including sensitive information and equipment. It prepares for and seeks to prevent terrorist attacks from chemical, biological, radiological, and nuclear offenses. The Force provides a safe work environment for the defense community.

The PFPA traces its roots directly to the General Services Administration's (GSA) United States Special Policemen (USSP) and a variety of security and security-related functions originally located throughout the Office of the Secretary of Defense.[53]

Prior to 1971 the GSA's USSP provided law enforcement, safety, and security functions at the Pentagon. The protection programs were a "guard-watchman" operation, where USSP focused primarily on the protection of property. However, as a result of a growing number of disruptive incidents throughout the country, the GSA reexamined its security program. In response to the mass demonstrations, bombings, and bomb threats of the era, the Federal Protective Service was established to provide comprehensive protection of the Pentagon and its personnel rather than the previous policy of concentration on property.

On October 1, 1987, the GSA administrator delegated the authority for protecting the Pentagon Reservation to the Department of Defense (DoD). To carry out the new mission, DoD established the Defense Protective Service (DPS) as a new element within the Washington Headquarters Service (WHS), a DoD Field Operating Activity. In addition, the scope of the mission of the DPS was expanded beyond the 280-acre "Pentagon Reservation" to numerous other DoD activities and facilities within the National Capital Region (NCR). During the early 1990's, the various security and security-related functions located within WHS were consolidated and transferred to the DPS.

On May 3, 2002, in response to the terrorist attack against the Pentagon on September 11, 2001 and the subsequent anthrax incidents, deputy secretary of defense Paul Wolfowitz established the Pentagon Force Protection Agency

(PFPA) as a DoD agency under the cognizance of the director of Administration and Management, under the Office of the Secretary of Defense. This new agency absorbed the DPS and its role of providing basic law enforcement and security for the Pentagon.

Since its creation, PFPA has expanded its mission and provides force protection against a full spectrum of potential threats. While law enforcement is still a major portion of its mission, the agency also handles operations security, building surveillance, crisis prevention, consequence management, counterintelligence, antiterrorism, HazMat and explosives, protection of high-ranking DoD officials, information technology, and administrative issues.

U.S. Pentagon police officers and special agents are sworn federal law enforcement officers. As such, they receive initial training at FLETC. Upon completion of the FLETC training, candidates must then complete an in-house, 12-week training program that provides more specific training for those who will be protecting the Pentagon.

To become a Pentagon police officer, a candidate must be a U.S. citizen; must have at least one year of police experience or a bachelor's degree in criminal justice (or a similar field) from an accredited university or college; must be able to obtain a secret security clearance; must possess a valid driver's license and good driving record; must not have been convicted of any offense involving domestic violence or a felony offense; must successfully complete an interview, medical exam, physical fitness evaluation, drug test, and a background check; must have vision of at least 20/200 in each eye, correctable to 20/20, and must pass a hearing test.

Steven E. Calvery was selected as the second director of the PFPA on May 1, 2006. This position is a senior executive service position within the Office of the Director of Administration and Management. Mr. Calvery is responsible for providing a full range of services to protect the employees at the Pentagon, as well as the facilities, infrastructure, and other resources there. Prior to holding this position, Calvery held the most senior law enforcement and security positions at the Department of Interior, as the director of Law Enforcement and Security. He was also a senior advisor for the under-secretary for enforcement in the Department of the Treasury and a special agent in the U.S. Secret Service. Mr. Calvery holds a bachelor of science in business administration from University of Maryland.[54]

The officers in the PFPA are divided into many divisions, including criminal investigative and protective services agents; threat management agents; chemical, biological, radiological, nuclear, and explosive technicians; and antiterrorism/force protection and physical security personnel. There are also motorized, bicycle, and motorcycle patrols, an Emergency Response Team, a K-9 Unit, a Protective Service Unit, a Training Branch, an Evidence and Court Liaison, and a Recruiting Branch Unit.

The mission of the agents in the Antiterrorism/Force Protection Directorate (AT/FP) is to protect the lives, facilities, information, and equipment at the Pentagon. The AT/FP Division conducts antiterrorism training for personnel; gathers, analyzes, and disseminates threat information; and develops plans related to antiterrorism and force protection.

The mission of the Criminal Investigations and Protective Directorate (CIPD) is to investigate violations of the federal law and to provide protection to High Risk Personnel (HRP) in the DoD. They also provide protection for ministers of defense and other officials who are visiting the continental United States.

Smithsonian National Zoological Park Police

The Smithsonian Institution Office of Protection Services is the "guard force" of the Smithsonian Institution. The officers protect visitors, staff, property, and grounds of the federally owned museums and research centers in Washington, D.C. and New York City and the Smithsonian Environmental Research Center in Maryland. They also provide oversight of the security operations in the Smithsonian Facility in Panama.[55]

The National Zoological Park is a Smithsonian facility, yet it maintains its own security police, the National Zoological Park Police (NZPP). This agency consists of 50 full-time and part-time officers. They have concurrent jurisdiction over the zoo with the U.S. Park Police and the Washington, D.C. Metropolitan Police. The NZPP agency is one of the oldest police forces in D.C. and is staffed 24-hours a day. The zoo also maintains a 3,200 acre research facility (Smithsonian Conservation Biology Institute) in Fort Royal, Virginia that is staffed by the National Zoological Park Police.

Smithsonian Museum Protection Officers are "special police" under the U.S. Code and as such have limited law enforcement powers. They receive 40 hours of minimal training, which covers basic firearms use, arrest and hand-cuffing procedures, and proper use of pepper spray. Officers are assigned to one of the museums or research sites. The Department also has a specialized canine unit with bomb-detection dogs that help officers to patrol museum grounds. Officers also use patrol vehicles, ATVs, and boats, depending on their assignment.

The NZPP officers are under the authority of the Smithsonian Institution Office of Protection Services, but are assigned to protect the National Zoo. All NZPP officers are trained at the Federal Law Enforcement Training Center.

Bureau of Diplomatic Security

The Bureau of Diplomatic Security is the law enforcement arm of the U.S. Department of State. It conducts international investigations, threat analysis, cyber security, counterterrorism, security technology, and protection of people, property, and information.[56] The Bureau is responsible for providing a safe environment to allow for U.S. foreign policy to be conducted safely. Officers with the Bureau protect the secretary of state and other high-ranking foreign dignitaries and officials visiting the U.S., investigate allegations of passport and visa fraud, and conduct personnel security investigations.[57]

While no single office or designated group of individuals was in charge of diplomatic security until World War I, America has always been concerned about diplomatic security.[58] From the early days of John Jay traveling to England to negotiate a treaty to Europe's entry into World War I, America had a history of ensuring that the information and intelligence diplomats' carried was protected. It was not until 1916, however, when the U.S. Department of State created the Bureau of Secret Intelligence, operating out of both Washington, D.C. and New York City, that a handful of agents would begin to formally protect and investigate the security of state secrets. The impetus was World War I and the fact that German and Austrian spies were found to be conducting operations in New York City. Agents from the U.S. Secret Service and the U.S. Postal Inspection Service were borrowed to establish the Office of the Chief Special Agent.

In 1918, the U.S. Congress passed legislation requiring that Americans travel abroad with passports and visas and that those coming into the U.S. had to do the same. The newly created Office was initially in charge of investigating passport and visa fraud. While this was a vastly large undertaking, in reality the agency focused more on the comings and goings of key diplomats traveling into the United States, especially those from designated enemy states.

During the 1930s and the buildup to World War II, it became clear that what was truly needed was not so much an agency for monitoring passports (U.S. Customs would eventually pick up this duty), but one within the State Department that would deal with the protection of state secrets, the carrying of diplomatic papers, and the protection of the diplomats themselves. The State Department thus created the Office of Security to perform these functions. Naturally, the Office of Security's functions grew throughout the war as did its number of personnel. And despite the end of the hot war, the Cold War necessitated their continued work in the field.

By the 1950s, the Office of Security had become a critical part of the intelligence community, working closely with the Central Intelligence Agency and the FBI's Counterintelligence Unit. The expansion of the Office of Security would continue steadily throughout the Cold War, lasting into the 1980s, before the wall fell and the Cold War ended.

During the Reagan Administration, Secretary of State George Shultz reorganized the Department of State, and this affected the Office of Security. On November 4, 1985, the U.S. Bureau of Diplomatic Security (DS) was officially created. While the DS continued the security of all state information, a smaller unit was created, the U.S. Diplomatic Security Service (DSS), a federal law enforcement agency within the DS that was charged with the security and law enforcement duties at U.S. missions, consulates, and embassies, as well as with protecting U.S. diplomats and high-level foreign diplomats that do not rise to the level of requiring U.S. Secret Service protection. These agents are also charged with pursuing American fugitives that have fled to other countries.

The Bureau hires special agents, security engineering officers, security technicians, diplomatic couriers, and Civil Service specialists. Special agents are sworn federal law enforcement agents who protect Foreign Service personnel, property, and sensitive information throughout the world.

Security engineering officers are responsible for managing the security of technology, information, projects, and resources in the United States and overseas from espionage and terrorism. These officers develop and maintain equipment such as perimeter controls, closed-circuit televisions, alarms, locks, and x-ray and bomb detection equipment. Those hired to be security technicians are support personnel who assist in implementing the technical security programs of the Bureau as a way to provide protection for the facilities and personnel who work there. Diplomatic couriers are officers who protect sensitive information by ensuring that important documents are transferred from one place to another safely, sometimes also across international borders.

The director of the DS has the title of principal deputy assistant secretary for diplomatic security. The position is currently held by Bill A. Miller, who was appointed to the position on April 14, 2011. Miller has been a member of the DSS since 1987. He is a career member of the Senior Foreign Service. Before working in Diplomatic Security, Miller was the deputy assistant secretary of state for high threat posts in the DS.

While overseas, Miller spent three years as the regional security officer at the U.S. Mission in Cairo, Egypt. Miller was presented with the State Department's Superior Honor Award for his leadership in during the events of the "Arab Spring" in Egypt. Miller also served in Baghdad as the regional security coordination officer for the Coalition Provisional Authority, and in Iraq as the first regional security officer for the U.S. Mission to Iraq. He has also served tours in Pakistan, Jerusalem, and the Philippines.

In addition to his international positions, Mr. Miller has had domestic assignments as well. He served as the chief of the Security and Law Enforcement Training Division at the Diplomatic Security Training Center in Dunn Loring, Virginia. He has also served as the regional director for Contingency Operations, chief of Counterintelligence Investigations for DSS, and served in the Post Graduate Intelligence Program at the Joint Military Intelligence College. Miller served almost five years on the secretary of state's Protective Detail and in the Washington Field Office.

Miller served as a U.S. Marine infantry officer and was given the honor as the 2004 Diplomatic Security Service Employee of the Year. He has also received the Department of State's Award for Valor, several Superior Honor Awards, the Department of Defense Joint Civilian Service Commendation Award, and the Marine Security Guard Battalion's award of RSO of the Year.

The DS has offices in 25 U.S. cities and 150 foreign countries.

Agents with the Bureau have many responsibilities both in the United States and overseas. They are responsible for protecting all diplomatic personnel, including the secretary of state and visiting foreign dignitaries, the U.S. ambassador to the UN, and cabinet-level foreign dignitaries who visit the United States. They investigate passport and visa fraud. Agents assist foreign embassies and consulates within the United States with security concerns by conducting personnel security investigations and issuing security clearances.

Through the Office of Investigations and Counterintelligence, the Bureau conduct counterintelligence programs that are designed to deter, detect, and neutralize the efforts of foreign intelligence services that might be targeting personnel, facilities, and diplomatic missions worldwide.

The DSS oversees numerous joint terrorism task forces around the country. The Office of Protective Intelligence and Investigations in the Threat Intelligence and Analysis Division has DSS special agents who travel all over the world investigating threats to the secretary of state and U.S. embassies and consulates. The DSS is widely represented throughout the world, so it is able to track and capture fugitives who have fled the United States as a way to avoid prosecution.

Conclusion

There are many federal law enforcement agencies within the United States, each with its own history, jurisdiction, and mission. Despite their differences, each agency exists to protect the people and facilities that help our government and society function each day. Each agency plays a role in ensuring that federal laws are followed and that those who violate the law are punished.

Key Terms

Supreme Court Police

U.S. Capitol Police

Amtrak Police

National Oceanic and Atmospheric Administration Office for Law Enforcement

Bureau of Indian Affairs Police

U.S. Fish and Wildlife Service Office of Law Enforcement

Pentagon Force Protection Agency

Smithsonian National Zoological Park Police

Bureau of Diplomatic Security

Review Questions

1. What is the role of the Supreme Court Police?

2. What is the function of the U.S. Capitol Police?

3. Describe the history of the U.S. Capitol Police.

4. What characteristics are the Capitol Police looking for in a candidate?

5. The Amtrak Police have what responsibilities?

6. The National Oceanic and Atmospheric Administration Office for Law Enforcement has different roles than other agencies. What are they?

7. The Bureau of Indian Affairs provides police services to whom? How is the agency organized?

8. Provide an analysis of the U.S. Fish and Wildlife Service Office of Law Enforcement.

9. Illustrate the role that the Pentagon Force Protection Agency has in protecting the safety of the community.

10. What are the activities of the Smithsonian National Zoological Park Police?

11. The Bureau of Diplomatic Security has different duties than other agencies. What are they?

Endnotes

1. "U.S. Mint Police," available at http://www.specwarnet.net/taclink/Federal/US_Mint_SRT.htm.
2. U.S. Supreme Court. (2012). "Supreme Court of the United States Police." Available online at http://uspolice.com/supreme-court-of-the-united-states-police.
3. "U.S. Capitol Police," available at http://www.uscapitolpolice.gov/home.php.
4. "U.S. Capitol Police," available at http://govcentral.monster.com/benefits/articles/1665-us-capitol-police?print=true.
5. United States Senate. (2012). "The Capitol Police." Available online at http://www.senate.gov/artandhistory/history/common/briefing/Capitol_Police.htm.
6. "U.S. Capitol Police," available at http://www.uscapitolpolice.gov/training.php.
7. "U.S. Capitol Police," available at http://www.uscapitolpolice.gov/training.php.
8. "U.S. Capitol Police," available at http://www.uscapitolpolice.gov/oig.php.
9. "U.S. Capitol Police," available at http://www.uscapitolpolice.gov/office_professional_responsibility.php.
10. Amtrak Police Department, "Protecting," available at http://police.amtrak.com/index.php?option=com_content&view=article&id=52&itemid=2.
11. Amtrak Police Department, "Protecting."
12. Amtrak Police Department, "Careers with the APD," available at http://police.amtrak.com/index.php?option=com_content&view=article&id=55&Itemid=37.
13. Amtrak Police Department, "Careers with the APD."
14. Amtrak Police Department, "Careers with the APD."
15. Amtrak Police Department, "Protecting: Patrol," available at http://police.amtrak.com/index.php?option=com_content&view=article&id=46&Itemid=34.
16. Amtrak Police Department, "Protecting: Intelligence Unit," available at http://police.amtrak.com/index.php?option=com_content&view=article&id=66&itemid=61.
17. Amtrak Police Department, "Protecting: K9 Unit," available at http://police.amtrak.com/index.php?option=com_content&view=article&id=49&Itemid=56.
18. Amtrak Police Department, "Protecting: Station Action Team Coordinators," available at http://police.amtrak.com/index.php?option=com_content&view=article&id=50&Itemid=57.
19. Amtrak Police Department, "Protecting: Special Operations Unit," available at http://police.amtrak.com/index.php?option=com_content&view=article&id=53&Itemid=55.
20. Amtrak Police Department, "Protecting: Corporate Security," available at http://police.amtrak.com/index.php?option=com_content&view=article&id=48&Itemid=54.
21. Amtrak Police Department, available at http://police.amtrak.com/from-the-chief.html.
22. NOAA Fisheries Web site, available at http://www.nmfs.noaa.gov/ole/index.html.
23. NOAA Fisheries Web site.
24. NOAA Fisheries, "Our Mission," available at http://www.nmfs.noaa.gov/aboutus/our_mission.html.
25. NOAA Fisheries Web site.
26. NOAA Fisheries, "NOAA Fisheries Education Program," available at http://www.nmfs.noaa.gov/stories/2012/10/noaa_fisheries_education.html.
27. NOAA, Office of Education, "Outreach," available at http://www.oesd.noaa.gov/outreach/.
28. NOAA Fisheries Web Site.
29. NOAA Fisheries, "Director's Message," available at www.fisheries.noaa.gov/ole/director/2014/training.html.
30. NOAA Fisheries, "Director's Message."
31. NOAA Fisheries, "Director's Message," available at www.fisheries.noaa.gov/ole/director/2014/training.html.
32. NOAA Fisheries, "Director's Message," available at www.fisheries.noaa.gov/ole/director/2014/training.html.
33. NOAA Fisheries, "Director's Message," available at www.fisheries.noaa.gov/ole/director/2014/training.html.

34. NOAA Fisheries, "Director's Message," available at www.fisheries.noaa.gov/ole/director/2014/training.html.
35. NOAA Fisheries, "Enforcement Programs and Operations," available at http://www.nmfs.noaa.gov/sfa/reg_svcs/Councils/Training2010/Tab%20P%20%20Enforcement%20Considerations/Tab%20P%20NOAA%20Office%20of%20Law%20Enforcement%20Presentation.pdf.
36. NOAA, Office of Law Enforcement, "Enforcement Program Update," available at www.nmfs.noaa.gov/ocs/mafac/meetings/2010_10/docs/mafac_enforcement_presentation.ppt.
37. NOAA Fisheries, "Contacts," available at www.nmfs.noaa.gov/ole/about/contacts.html.
38. "NOAA: $5.5 Billion FY 2015 Budget Request Promotes Environmental Intelligence." Available at http://www.noaanews.noaa.gov/stories2014/20140313_budget_statement.html.
39. NOAA Fisheries Web Site.
40. NOAA Fisheries Web Site.
41. NOAA Fisheries, "Laws We Enforce," available at www.nmfs.noaa.gov/ole/about/what_we_do/laws.html.
42. NOAA Fisheries Web Site.
43. Indian Affairs, "Indian Police Academy," available at http://www.bia.gov/WhoWeAre/BIA/OJS/IPA/index.htm.
44. "Indian Affairs: Division of Law Enforcement," available at http://www.nmfs.noaa.gov/sfa/reg_svcs/Councils/Training2010/Tab%20P%20%20Enforcement%20Considerations/Tab%20P%20NOAA%20Office%20of%20Law%20Enforcement%20Presentation.pdf.
45. U.S. Fish and Wildlife Service, Office of Law Enforcement, "Annual Report FY 2010," available at http://www.fws.gov/le/pdf/final-annual-report-fy-2010.pdf.
46. U.S. Fish & Wildlife Service, Office of Law Enforcement. (2012). "Law Enforcement Historical Background." Available online at www.fws.gov/le/history.html.
47. U.S. Fish and Wildlife Service, Office of Law Enforcement, "About Service Wildlife Inspectors," available at http://www.fws.gov/le/AboutLE/wildlife_inspectors.htm.
48. U.S. Fish and Wildlife Service, Office of Law Enforcement, "About Service Special Agents," available at http://www.fws.gov/le/AboutLE/special_agents.htm.
49. U.S. Fish and Wildlife Service, Office of Law Enforcement, "About Service Law Enforcement."
50. U.S. Fish and Wildlife Service, Office of Law Enforcement, "About Service Law Enforcement."
51. U.S. Fish and Wildlife Service, Office of Law Enforcement, "Annual Report FY 2010."
52. U.S. Fish and Wildlife Service, Office of Law Enforcement, "Annual Report FY 2010."
53. The Pentagon Force Protection Agency. (2012). "The History of PFPA." Available at http://www.pfpa.mil/history.html.
54. The Pentagon Force Protection Agency, "Steven E. Calvery," available at http://www.pfpa.mil/director.html.
55. Metropolitan Police Department, "Cooperative Agreements," available at http://mpdc.dc.gov/page/cooperative-agreements.
56. U.S. Department of State, "Bureau of Diplomatic Security," available at http://www.state.gov/m/ds/.
57. U.S. Department of State, "Bureau of Diplomatic Security."
58. Bureau of Diplomatic Security. (2011). History of the Bureau of Diplomatic Security of the United States Department of State. Washington, D.C.: U.S. Department of State.

Index